ONE STORY HOMES
Over 2,000 Sq. Ft. • Contemporary & Traditional Styles

HOME PLANNERS, INC.

Contents

Published by Home Planners, Inc., 3275 West Ina Road, Suite 110, Tucson, Arizona 85741. All designs and illustrative material Copyright © MCMLXXXVI by Home Planners, Inc. All rights reserved. Reproduction in any manner or form not permitted. Printed in the United States of America. International Standard Book Number (ISBN): 0-918894-51-4.

How To Read Floor Plans and Blueprints

cting the most suitable house plan for your family is a
of matching your needs, tastes, and life-style against the
lesigns we offer. When you study the floor plans in this
and the blueprints that you may subsequently order,
ber that they are simply a two-dimensional represen-
of what will eventually be a three-dimensional reality.

r plans are easy to read. Rooms are clearly labeled, with
sions given in feet and inches. Most symbols are logical
elf-explanatory: The location of bathroom fixtures,
rs, fireplaces, tile floors, cabinets and counters, sinks,
nces, closets, sloped or beamed ceilings will be obvious.

lueprint, although much more detailed, is also easy to
ll it demands is concentration. The blueprints that we
ome in many large sheets, each one of which contains a
nt kind of information. One sheet contains foundation
cavation drawings, another has a precise plot plan. An
ions sheet deals with the exterior walls of the house;
drawings show precise dimensions, fittings, doors,
ws, and roof structures. Our detailed floor plans give the
uction information needed by your contractor. And each
blueprints contains a lengthy materials list with size and
ties of all necessary components. Using this list, a
ctor and suppliers can make a start at calculating costs
u.

en you first study a floor plan or blueprint, imagine that
re walking through the house. By mentally visualizing
room in three dimensions, you can transform the
cal data and symbols into something more real.

t at the front door. It's preferable to have a foyer or
nce hall in which to receive guests. A closet here is
ble; a powder room is a plus.

k for good traffic circulation as you study the floor plan.
hould not have to pass all the way through one main
to reach another. From the entrance area you should
direct access to the three principal areas of a house—the
, work, and sleeping zones. For example, a foyer might
le separate entrances to the living room, kitchen, patio,
hallway or staircase leading to the bedrooms.

dy the layout of each zone. Most people expect the living
to be protected from cross traffic. The kitchen, on the
hand, should connect with the dining room—and
ps also the utility room, basement, garage, patio or deck,
secondary entrance. A homemaker whose workday
rs in the kitchen may have special requirements: a
ow that faces the backyard; a clear view of the family
where children play; a garage or driveway entrance that

allows for a short trip with groceries; laundry facilities close at
hand. Check for efficient placement of kitchen cabinets,
counters, and appliances. Is there enough room in the kitchen
for additional appliances, for eating in? Is there a dining nook?

Perhaps this part of the house contains a family room or a
den/bedroom/office. It's advantageous to have a bathroom or
powder room in this section.

As you study the plan, you may encounter a staircase,
indicated by a group of parallel lines, the number of lines
equaling the number of steps. Arrows labeled "up" mean that
the staircase leads to a higher level, and those pointing down
mean it leads to a lower one. Staircases in a split-level will
have both up and down arrows on one staircase because two
levels are depicted in one drawing and an extra level in
another.

Notice the location of the stairways. Is too much floor space
lost to them? Will you find yourself making too many trips?

Study the sleeping quarters. Are the bedrooms situated as
you like? You may want the master bedroom near the kids, or
you may want it as far away as possible. Is there at least one
closet per person in each bedroom or a double one for a
couple? Bathrooms should be convenient to each bedroom—if
not adjoining, then with hallway access and on the same floor.

Once you are familiar with the relative positions of the
rooms, look for such structural details as:

• Sufficient uninterrupted wall space for furniture arrangement.

• Adequate room dimensions.

• Potential heating or cooling problems—i.e., a room over a
garage or next to the laundry.

• Window and door placement for good ventilation and
natural light.

• Location of doorways—avoid having a basement staircase or
a bathroom in view of the dining room.

• Adequate auxiliary space—closets, storage, bathrooms,
countertops.

• Separation of activity areas. (Will noise from the recreation
room disturb sleeping children or a parent at work?)

As you complete your mental walk through the house, bear
in mind your family's long-range needs. A good house plan
will allow for some adjustments now and additions in the
future.

Each member of your family may find the listing of his, or
her, favorite features a most helpful exercise. Why not try it?

Index to Designs

On the Cover: Cover design can be found on page 166.

How To Choose a Contractor

A contractor is part craftsman, part businessman, and part magician. As the person who will transform your dreams and drawings into a finished house, he will be responsible for the final cost of the structure, for the quality of the workmanship, and for the solving of all problems that occur quite naturally in the course of construction. Choose him as carefully as you would a business partner, because for the next several months that will be his role in your life.

As soon as you have a building site and house plans, start looking for a contractor, even if you do not plan to break ground for several months. Finding one suitable to build your house can take time, and once you have found him, you will have to be worked into his schedule. Those who are good are in demand and, where the season is short, they are often scheduling work up to a year in advance.

There are two types of residential contractors: the construction company and the carpenter-builder, often called a general contractor. Each of these has its advantages and disadvantages.

The carpenter-builder works directly on the job as the field foreman. Because his background is that of a craftsman, his workmanship is probably good—but his paperwork may be slow or sloppy. His overhead—which you pay for—is less than that of a large construction company. However, if the job drags on for any reason, his interest may flag because your project is overlapping his next job and eroding his profits.

Construction companies handle several projects concurrently. They have an office staff to keep the paperwork moving and an army of subcontractors they know they can count on. Though you can be confident that they will meet deadlines, they may sacrifice workmanship in order to do so. Because they emphasize efficiency, they are less personal to work with than a general contractor. Many will not work with an individual unless he is represented by an architect. The company and the architect speak the same language; it requires far more time to deal directly with a homeowner.

To find a reliable contractor, start by asking friends who have built homes for recommendations. Check with local lumber yards and building supply outlets for names of possible candidates.

Once you have several names in hand, ask the Chamber of Commerce, Better Business Bureau, or local department of consumer affairs for any information they might have on each of them. Keep in mind that these watchdog organizations can give only the number of complaints filed; they cannot tell you what percent of those claims were valid. Remember, too, that a large-volume operation is logically going to have more complaints against it than will an independent contractor.

Set up an interview with each of the potential candidates. Find out what his specialty is—custom houses, development houses, remodeling, or office buildings. Ask each to take you into—not just to the site of—houses he has built. Ask to see projects that are complete as well as work in progress, emphasizing that you are interested in projects comparable to yours. A $300,000 dentist's office will give you little insight into a contractor's craftsmanship.

Ask each contractor for bank references from both his commercial bank and any other lender he has worked with. If he is in good financial standing, he should have no qualms about giving you this information. Also ask if he offers a warranty on his work. Most will give you a one-year warranty on the structure; some offer as much as a ten-year warranty.

Ask for references, even though no contractor will give you the name of a dissatisfied customer. While previous clients may be pleased with a contractor's work overall, they may, for example, have had to wait three months after they moved in before they had any closet doors. Ask about his follow-through. Did he clean up the building site, or did the owner have to dispose of the refuse? Ask about his business organization. Did the paperwork go smoothly, or was there a delay in hooking up the sewer because he forgot to apply for a permit?

Talk to each of the candidates about fees. Most work on a "cost plus" basis; that is, the basic cost of the project—materials, subcontractors' services, wages of those working directly on the project, but not office help—plus his fee. Some have a fixed fee; others work on a percentage of the basic cost. A fixed fee is usually better for you if you can get one. If a contractor works on a percentage, ask for a cost breakdown of his best estimate and keep very careful track as the work progresses. A crafty contractor can always use a cost overrun to his advantage when working on a percentage.

Do not be overly suspicious of a contractor who won't work on a fixed fee. One who is very good and in great demand may not be willing to do so. He may also refuse to submit a competitive bid.

If the top two or three candidates are willing to submit competitive bids, give each a copy of the plans and your specifications for materials. If they are not each working from the same guidelines, the competitive bids will be of little value. Give each the same deadline for turning in a bid; two or three weeks is a reasonable period of time. If you are willing to go with the lowest bid, make an appointment with all of them and open the envelopes in front of them.

If one bid is remarkably low, the contractor may have made an honest error in his estimate. Do not try to hold him to it if he wants to withdraw his bid. Forcing him to build at too low a price could be disastrous for both you and him.

Though the above method sounds very fair and orderly, it is not always the best approach, especially if you are inexperienced. You may want to review the bids with your architect, if you have one, or with your lender to discuss which to accept. They may not recommend the lowest. A low bid does not necessarily mean that you will get quality with economy.

If the bids are relatively close, the most important consideration may not be money at all. How easily you can talk with a contractor and whether or not he inspires confidence are very important considerations. Any sign of a personality conflict between you and a contractor should be weighed when making a decision.

Once you have financing, you can sign a contract with the builder. Most have their own contract forms, but it is advisable to have a lawyer draw one up or, at the very least, review the standard contract. This usually costs a small flat fee.

A good contract should include the following:

• Plans and sketches of the work to be done, subject to your approval.

• A list of materials, including quantity, brand names, style or serial numbers. (Do not permit any "or equal" clause that will allow the contractor to make substitutions.)

• The terms—who (you or the lender) pays whom and when.

• A production schedule.

• The contractor's certification of insurance for workmen's compensation, damage, and liability.

• A rider stating that all changes, whether or not they increase the cost, must be submitted and approved in writing.

Of course, this list represents the least a contract should include. Once you have signed it, your plans are on the way to becoming a home.

A frequently asked question is: "Should I become my own general contractor?" Unless you have knowledge of construction, material purchasing, and experience supervising subcontractors, we do not recommend this route.

How To Shop For Mortgage Money

Most people who are in the market for a new home spend months searching for the right house plan and building site. Ironically, these same people often invest very little time shopping for the money to finance their new home, though the majority will have to live with the terms of their mortgage for as long as they live in the house.

The fact is that all banks are not alike, nor are the loans that they offer—and banks are not the only financial institutions that lend money for housing. The amount of down payment, interest rate, and period of the mortgage are all, to some extent, negotiable.

• Lending practices vary from one city and state to another. If you are a first-time builder or are new to an area, it is wise to hire a real estate (not divorce or general practice) attorney to help you unravel the maze of your specific area's laws, ordinances, and customs.

• Before talking with lenders, write down all your questions. Take notes during the conversation so you can make accurate comparisons.

• Do not be intimidated by financial officers. Keep in mind that *you are not begging for money,* you are buying it. Do not hesitate to reveal what other institutions are offering; they may be challenged to meet or better the terms.

• Use whatever clout you have. If you or your family have been banking with the same firm for years, let them know that they could lose your business if you can get a better deal elsewhere.

• Know your credit rights. The law prohibits lenders from considering only the husband's income when determining eligibility, a practice that previously kept many people out of the housing market. If you are turned down for a loan, you have a right to see a summary of the credit report and change any errors in it.

A GUIDE TO LENDERS

Where can you turn for home financing? Here is a list of sources for you to approach:

Savings and loan associations are the best place to start because they write well over half the mortgages in the United States on dwellings that house from one to four families. They generally offer favorable interest rates, require lower down payments, and allow more time to pay off loans than do other banks.

Savings banks, sometimes called mutual savings banks, are your next best bet. Like savings and loan associations, much of their business is concentrated in home mortgages.

Commercial banks write mortgages as a sideline, and when money is tight many will not write mortgages at all. They do hold about 15 percent of the mortgages in the country, however, and when the market is right, they can be very competitive.

Mortgage banking companies use the money of private investors to write home loans. They do a brisk business in government-backed loans, which other banks are reluctant to handle because of the time and paperwork required.

Some credit unions are now allowed to grant mortgages. A few insurance companies, pension funds, unions, and fraternal organizations also offer mortgage money to their membership, often at terms more favorable than those available in the commercial marketplace.

A GUIDE TO MORTGAGES

The types of mortgages available are far more various than most potential home buyers realize.

Traditional Loans

Conventional home loans have a fixed interest rate and fixed monthly payments. About 80 percent of the mortgage money in the United States is lent in this manner. Made by private lending institutions, these fixed rate loans are available to anyone whom the bank officials consider a good credit risk. The interest rate depends on the prevailing market for money and is slightly negotiable if you are willing to put down a large down payment. Most down payments range from 15 to 33 percent.

You can borrow as much money as the lender believes you can afford to pay off over the negotiated period of time—usually 20 to 30 years. However, a 15 year mortgage can save you considerably and enable you to own your home in half the time. For example, a 30 year, $60,800 mortgage at 12% interest will have a monthly payment of $625.40 per month vs $729.72 per month for a 15 year loan at the same interest rate. At the end of 30 years you have paid $164,344 in interest vs $70,550 for the 15 year. Remember - this is only $104.32 more per month. Along with saving with a 15 year mortgage, additional savings

can be realized with a biweekly payment plan. So be sure to consult your borrowing institution for all of your options.

The FHA does not write loans; it insures them against default in order to encourage lenders to write loans for first-time buyers and people with limited incomes. The terms of these loans make them very attractive, and you may be allowed to take as long as 25 to 30 years to pay it off.

The down payment also is substantially lower with an FHA-backed loan. At present it is set at 3 percent of the first $25,000 and 5 percent of the remainder, up to the $75,300 limit. This means that a loan on a $75,300 house would require a $750 down payment on the first $25,000 plus $2,515 on the remainder, for a total down payment of $3,265. In contrast, the down payment for the same house financed with a conventional loan could run as high as $20,000.

Anyone may apply for an FHA-insured loan, but both the borrower and the house must qualify.

The VA guarantees loans for eligible veterans, and the husbands and wives of those who died while in the service or from a service-related disability. The VA guarantees up to 60 percent of the loan or $27,500, whichever is less. Like the FHA, the VA determines the appraised value of the house, though with a VA loan, you can borrow any amount up to the appraised value.

The Farmers Home Administration offers the only loans made directly by the government. Families with limited incomes in rural areas can qualify if the house is in a community of less than 10,000 people and is outside of a large metropolitan area; if their income is less than $18,000; and if they can prove that they do not qualify for a conventional loan.

For more information, write Farmers Home Administration, Department of Agriculture, Washington, D.C. 20250, or your local office.

New loan instruments

If you think that the escalating cost of housing has squeezed you out of the market, take a look at the following new types of mortgages.

The graduated payment mortgage features a monthly obligation that gradually increases over a negotiated period of time—usually five to ten years. Though the payments begin lower, they stabilize at a higher monthly rate than a standard fixed rate mortgage. Little or no equity is built in the first years, a disadvantage if you decide to sell early in the mortgage period.

These loans are aimed at young people who can anticipate income increases that will enable them to meet the escalating payments. The size of the down payment is about the same or slightly higher than for a conventional loan, but you can qualify with a lower income. As of last year, savings and loan associations can write these loans, and the FHA now insures five different types.

The flexible loan insurance program (FLIP) requires that part of the down payment, which is about the same as a conventional loan, be placed in a pledged savings account. During the first five years of the mortgage, funds are drawn from this account to supplement the lower monthly payments.

The deferred interest mortgage, another graduated program, allows you to pay a lower rate of interest during the first few years and a higher rate in the later years of the mortgage. If the house is sold, the borrower must pay back all the interest, often with a prepayment penalty. Both the FLIP and deferred interest loans are very new and not yet widely available.

The variable rate mortgage is most widely available in California, but its popularity is growing. This instrument features a fluctuating interest rate that is linked to an economic indicator—usually the lender's cost of obtaining funds for lending. To protect the consumer against a sudden and disastrous increase, regulations limit the amount that the interest rate can increase over a given period of time.

To make these loans attractive, lenders offer them without prepayment penalties and with "assumption" clauses that allow another buyer to assume your mortgage should you sell.

Flexible payment mortgages allow young people who can anticipate rising incomes to enter the housing market sooner. They pay only the interest during the first few years; then the mortgage is amortized and the payments go up. This is a valuable option only for those people who intend to keep their home for several years because no equity is built in the lower payment period.

The reverse annuity mortgage is targeted for older people who have fixed incomes. This new loan allows those who qualify to tap into the equity on their houses. The lender pays them each month and collects the loan when the house is sold or the owner dies.

ENGLISH TUDOR VERSIONS . . . *have be-*

come increasingly popular in recent years. This style has emanated from the more massive two-story with its many gabled roofs, exposed half-timber work, stucco and muntined windows. More correctly identified as Elizabethan style, the Tudor term of reference has become an accepted misnomer. Other distinguishing features include large sculptured chimneys, brick and stone exterior surfaces and panelled doors. Of interest in this section are the houses which feature complete one-story livability, including first floor bedrooms, but deliver bonus sleeping fa-cilities either upstairs or on a lower level. Truly an impressive and distinctive style.

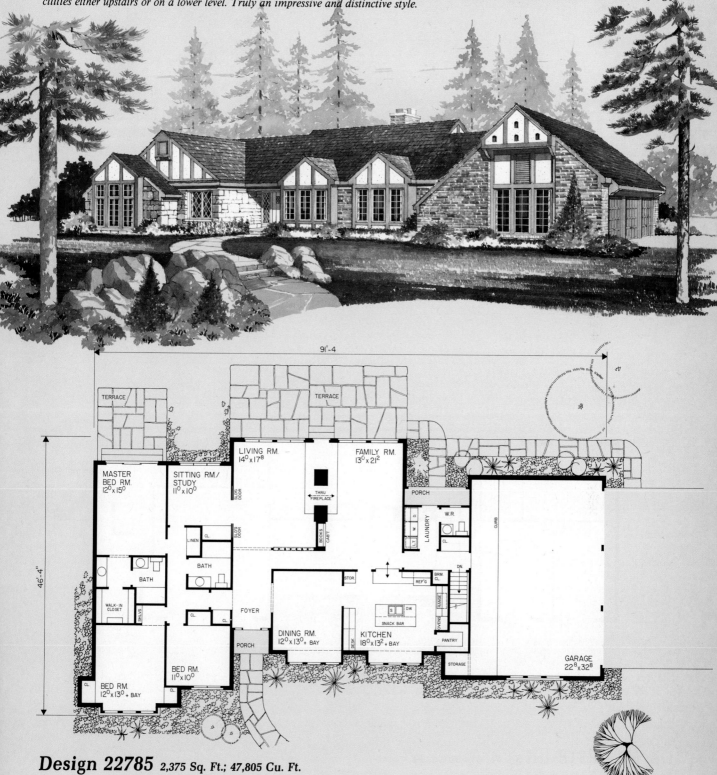

Design 22785 2,375 Sq. Ft.; 47,805 Cu. Ft.

● Exceptional Tudor design! Passers-by will take a second glance at this fine home wherever it may be located. And the interior is just as pleasing. As one enters the foyer and looks around, the plan will speak for itself in the areas of convenience and efficiency.

Cross room traffic will be avoided. There is a hall leading to each of the three bedrooms and study of the sleep-ing wing and another leading to the living room, family room, kitchen and laundry with washroom. The formal dining room can be entered from both

the foyer and the kitchen. Efficiency will be the by-word when describing the kitchen. Note the fine features: a built-in desk, pantry, island snack bar with sink and pass-thru to the family room. The fireplace will be enjoyed in the living and family rooms.

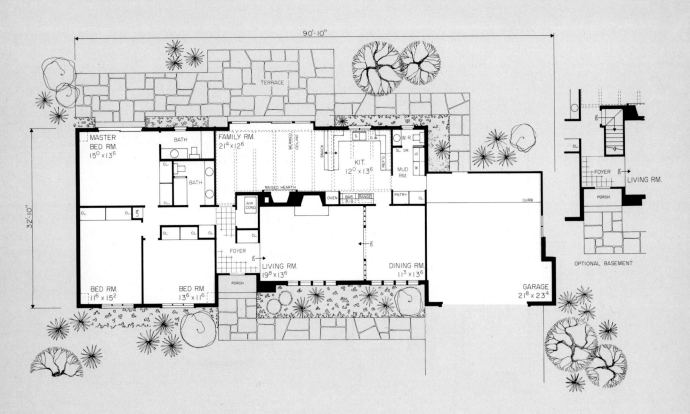

Design 22318 *2,029 Sq. Ft.; 31,021 Cu. Ft.*

● Warmth and charm are characteristics of Tudor adaptations. This modest sized home with its twin front-facing gabled roofs represents a great investment. While it will be an exciting and refreshing addition to any neighborhood, its appeal will never grow old.

The covered, front entrance opens to the center foyer. Traffic patterns flow in an orderly and efficient manner to the three main zones — the formal dining zone, the sleeping zone and the informal living zone. The sunken living room with its fireplace is separated

from the dining room by an attractive trellis divider. A second fireplace, along with beamed ceiling and sliding glass doors, highlights the family room. Note snack bar, mud room, cooking facilities, two full baths and optional basement.

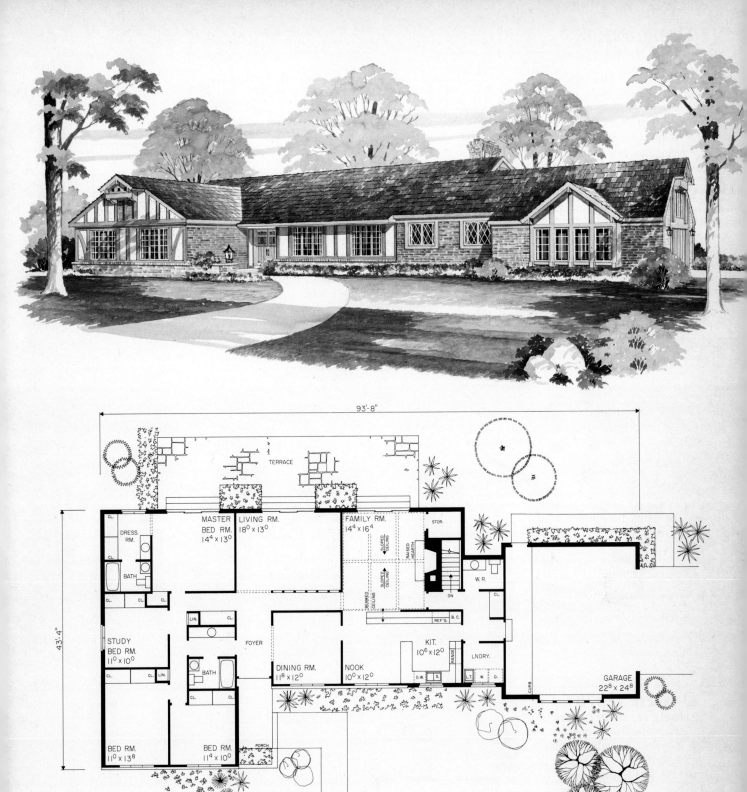

Design 22515 *2,363 Sq. Ft.; 46,676 Cu. Ft.*

● Another Tudor adaptation with all the appeal that is inherent in this design style. The brick veneer exterior is effectively complimented by the beam work, the stucco and the window treatment. The carriage lamp, perched on the planter wall, adds a delightful touch as do the dovecotes of the bedroom wing and over the garage door. The livability of the interior is just great. The kitchen, nook and dining room overlook the front yard. The laundry is around the corner from the kitchen. An extra washroom is not far away. Sloping, beamed ceiling and raised hearth fireplace are highlights of the family room. Like the living room and master bedroom, it functions with the rear terrace. Note vanity outside main bath. Wood posts separate the living room and hall.

Design 21989
2,282 Sq. Ft.; 41,831 Cu. Ft.

● High style with a plan as contemporary as today and tomorrow. There is, indeed, a feeling of coziness that emanates from the ground-hugging qualities of this picturesque home. Inside, there is livability galore. There's the sunken living room and the separate dining room to function as the family's formal living area. Then, overlooking the rear yard, there's the informal living area with its beamed ceiling family room, kitchen and adjacent breakfast room.

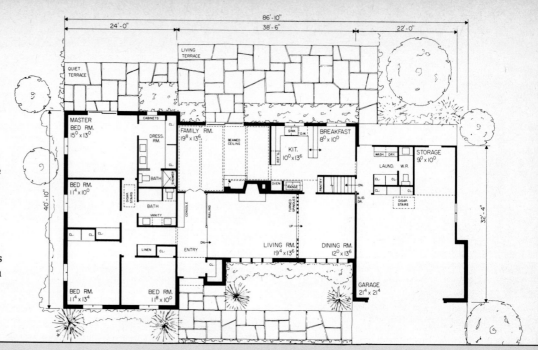

Design 22378
2,580 Sq. Ft.; 49,792 Cu. Ft.

● If yours is a preference for an exterior that exudes both warmth and formality, the styling of English Tudor may suit your fancy. A host of architectural features blend together to produce this delightfully appealing exterior. Notice the interesting use of contrasting exterior materials. Don't overlook the two stylish chimneys. The manner in which the interior functions to provide the fine living patterns is outstanding. Each of four main rooms — look out on the rear terrace.

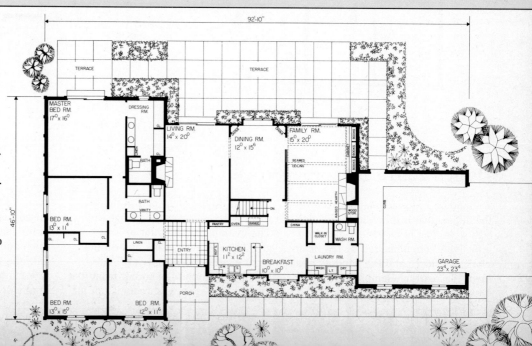

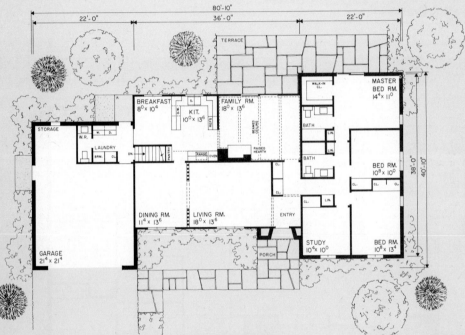

Design 22129
2,057 Sq. Ft.; 36,970 Cu. Ft.

● This four bedroom home is zoned for convenient living. The sleeping area, with its two full baths and plenty of closets, will have a lot of privacy. The formal living and dining rooms function together and may be completely by-passed when desired. The informal living areas are grouped together and overlook the rear yard. The family room with its beamed ceiling is but a step from the kitchen. The U-shaped kitchen is handy to both the breakfast and dining rooms.

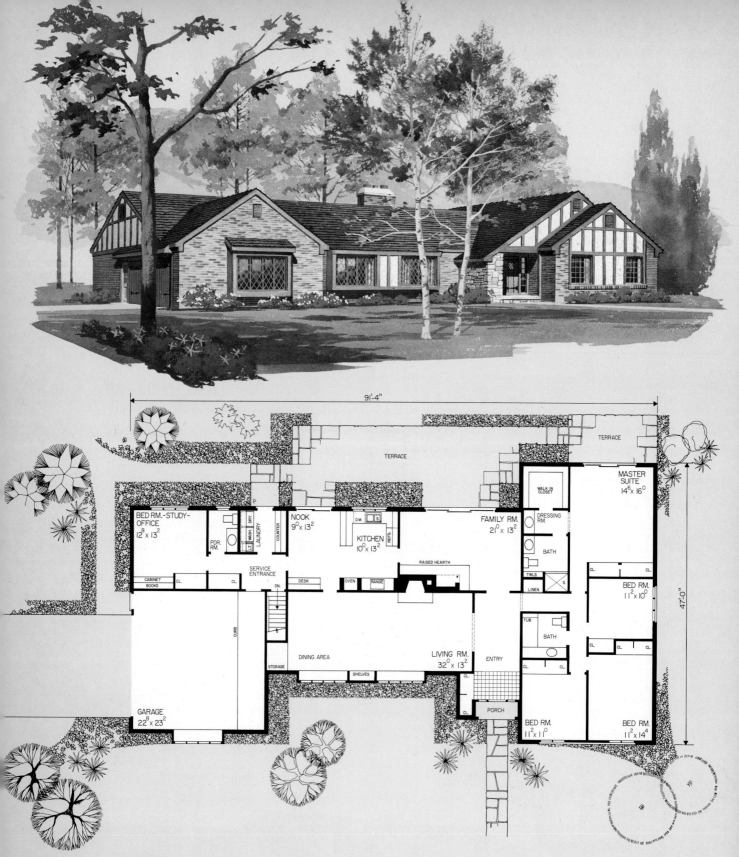

Design 22573 2,747 Sq. Ft.; 48,755 Cu. Ft.

● A Tudor ranch! Combining brick and wood for an elegant look. It has a living/dining room measuring 32' by 13', large indeed. It is fully appointed with a traditional fireplace and built-in shelves, flanked by diagonally paned windows. There's much more! There is a family room with a raised hearth fireplace and sliding glass doors that open onto the terrace. A U-shaped kitchen has lots of built-ins . . . a range, an oven, a desk. Plus a separate breakfast nook. The sleeping facilities consist of three family bedrooms plus an elegant master bedroom suite. A conveniently located laundry with a folding counter is in the service entrance. Adjacent to the laundry is a washroom. The corner of the plan has a study or make it a fifth bedroom if you prefer.

Design 22746 2,790 Sq. Ft.; 57,590 Cu. Ft.

● This impressive one-story will be the talk-of-the-town. And not surprisingly, either. It embodies all of the elements to assure a sound investment and years of happy family livability. The projecting living room with its stucco, simulated wood beams and effective window treatment adds a dramatic note. Sunken by two steps, this room will enjoy privacy. The massive double front doors are sheltered by the covered porch and lead to the spacious entry hall. The interior is particularly well-zoned. The large, rear gathering room will cater to the family's gregarious instincts. Outdoor enjoyment can be obtained on the three terraces. Also, a study is available for those extra quiet moments. Be sure to observe the plan closely for all of the other fine features.

Design 22620

2,048 Sq. Ft.; 42,000 Cu. Ft.

● An enclosed courtyard! That sets this home apart right from the start. There are more unusual features inside. Like the 21' by 15' keeping room . . . complete with a wet bar, built-in bookcase, fireplace/woodbox combination. Plus sliding glass doors leading to the terrace. That's the kind of space you need for family life as well as entertaining! There's a formal dining room, too! And a well-designed kitchen. U-shaped for efficiency, with a built-in oven and range. Plus a separate breakfast room. Around the corner, the first floor laundry. That puts all the work areas together, saving you time and energy. Four large bedrooms grouped together for privacy. Ideal planning throughout.

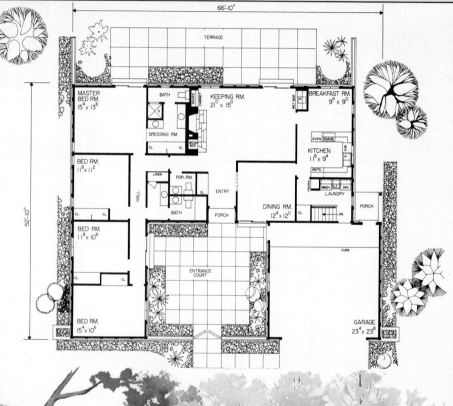

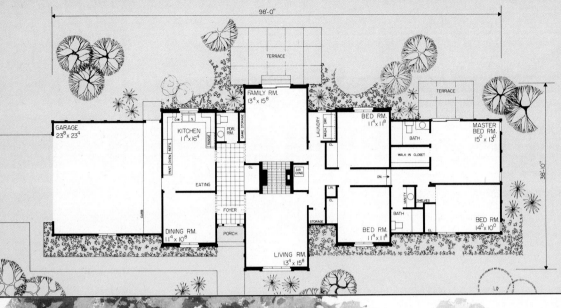

Design 22385
2,100 Sq. Ft.; 27,205 Cu. Ft.

● The charm of Tudor styled exterior adaptations is difficult to beat. Here is a hip-roof version which highlights the effective use of stucco, patterned brick and exposed beam work. The varying roof planes and the massive chimney, along with the recessed front entrance enhance the appeal. A study of the floor plan is most revealing. Excellent zoning is readily apparent.

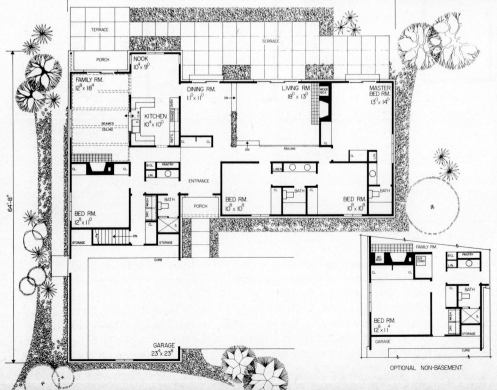

Design 22613
2,132 Sq. Ft.; 38,328 Cu. Ft.

● A classic Tudor! With prominent wood and stucco styling. And unique features throughout. Start with the sunken living room where an attractive railing has replaced the anticipated hallway wall. For more good looks, a traditional fireplace with an attached woodbox and sliding glass doors that open onto the terrace. There's a formal dining room, too, also with access onto the terrace. Together these rooms form a gracious center for entertaining! For casual times, a family room with a beamed ceiling, fireplace and summer porch. And a work-efficient kitchen plus a roomy breakfast nook.

15

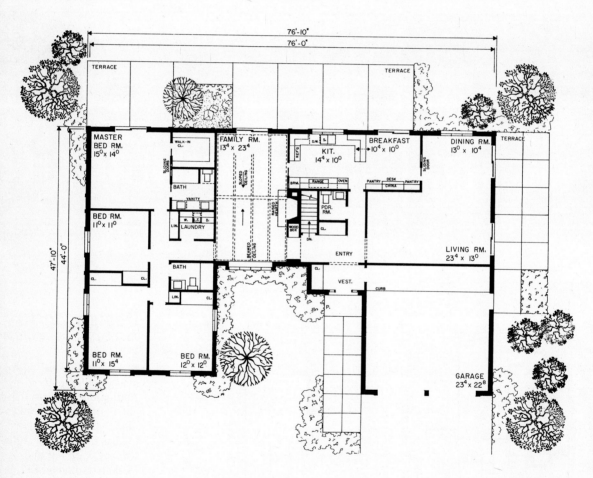

Design 22142 2,450 Sq. Ft.; 43,418 Cu. Ft.

● Adaptations of Old England have become increasingly popular in today's building scene. And little wonder; for many of these homes when well-designed have a very distinctive charm. Here is certainly a home which will be like no other in its neighborhood. Its very shape adds an extra measure of uniqueness. And inside, there is all the livability the exterior seems to fortell. The sleeping wing has four bedrooms, two full baths and the laundry room — just where the soiled linen originates. The location of the family room is an excellent one. It is convenient for children because their traffic usually flows between family room and bedrooms. The spacious formal living and dining area will enjoy its privacy and be great fun to furnish.

Design 22317 *3,161 Sq. Ft.; 57,900 Cu. Ft.*

● Here's a rambling English manor with its full measure of individuality. Its fine proportions and irregular shape offer even the most casual of passersby delightful views of fine architecture. The exterior boasts an interesting use of varying materials. In addition to the brick work, there is vertical siding, wavy-edged horizontal siding and stucco. Three massive chimneys provide each of the three major wings with a fireplace. The overhanging roof provides the cover for the long front porch. Note the access to both the foyer as well as the service hall. The formal living room, with its sloping beamed ceiling, and fireplace flanked by book shelves and cabinets, will be cozy, indeed. Study rest of plan. It's outstanding. Don't miss the three fireplaces and three full baths.

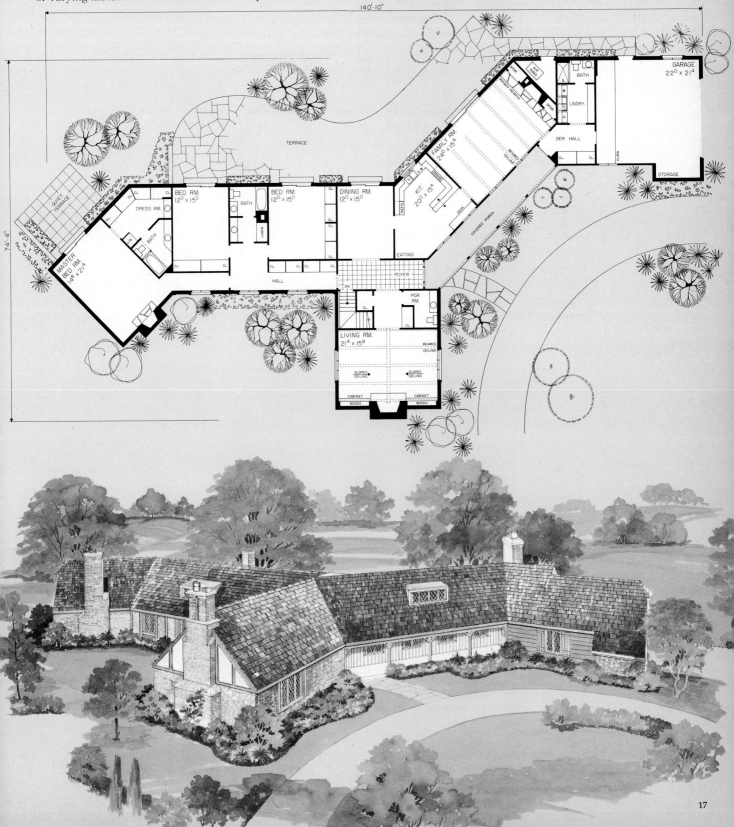

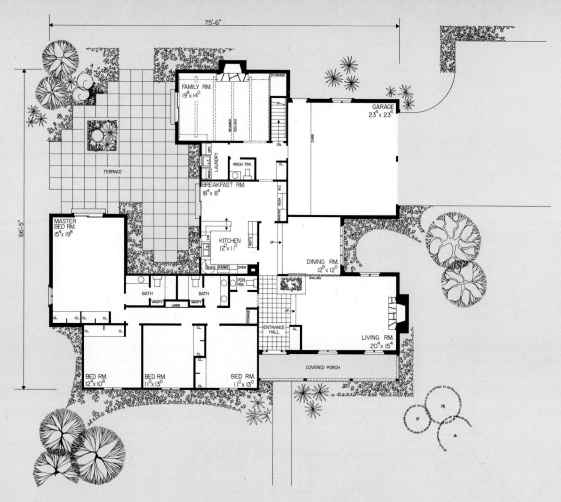

Design 22387 2,744 Sq. Ft.; 41,682 Cu. Ft.

● This rambling Tudor design will not fail to excite even the most casual of visitors. Its inviting facade is enhanced by its distinctive configuration. But such an appealing exterior is only a prelude to what the interior has to offer. Zoned for privacy, the four bedroom, 2½ bath sleeping area is outstanding. To the right of the entrance hall is the sunken living room which has a most commanding fireplace. The efficient kitchen effectively services the sunken dining room and the spacious breakfast room. Far removed from the sleeping and formal living areas is the beamed ceiling family room. Indoor-outdoor living relationships are delightfully maintained with utilization of those sliding glass doors to the strategically located terrace. Observe laundry, washroom and basement.

Design 22350 *3,044 Sq. Ft. — Excluding Atrium; 60,900 Cu. Ft.*

● This commanding Tudor adaptation has a distinctive character all its own. The interesting roof design, the contrasting brick and stucco, the diamond lite windows, the recessed double front doors, the carriage lamps, and massive chimneys are features which contribute to the charm of this impressive facade. And the extraordinary appeal of this design carries right on inside. The atrium is strategically located for full enjoyment from all living areas. A recessed terrace is directly accessible from the wonderful master suite as well as from the family room and breakfast nook. High ceilings add to the dramatic spaciousness of the formal living area. Note that the living room is sunken, has a raised hearth fireplace. The library is isolated and has its own fireplace.

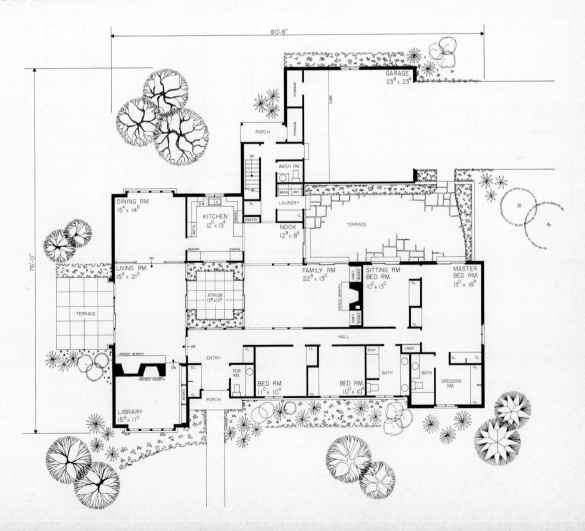

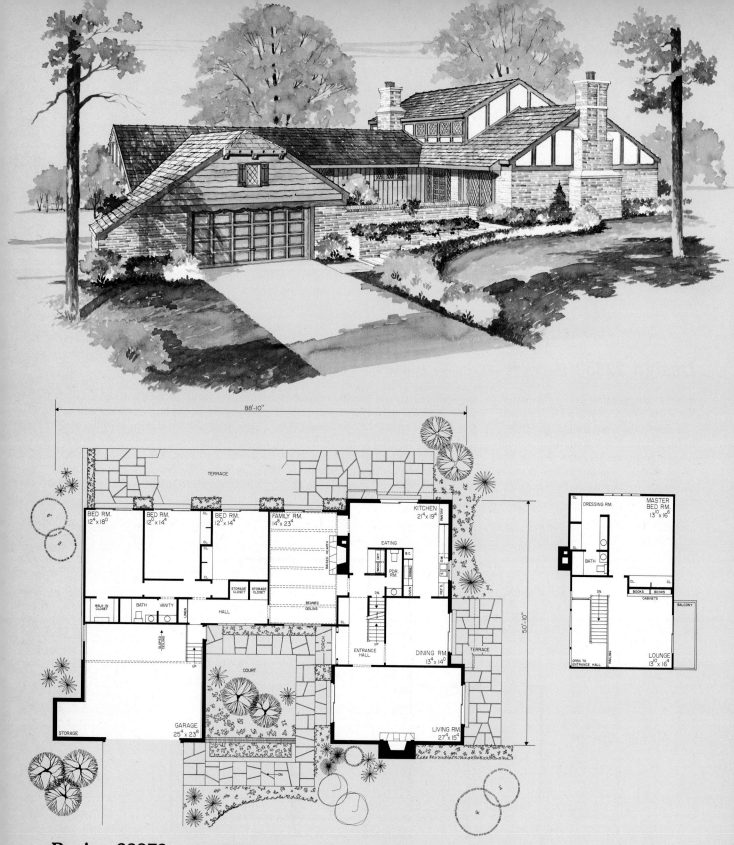

Design 22372 2,634 Sq. Ft. - First Floor; 819 Sq. Ft. - Second Floor; 47,867 Cu. Ft.

● What a wonderfully different and imposing two-story design this is! The Tudor styling and the varying roof planes, along with its U-shape, add to the air of distinction. From the driveway, steps lead past a big raised planter up to the enclosed entrance court. A wide overhanging roof shelters the massive patterned double doors flanked by diamond paned sidelites. The living room is outstanding. It is located a distance from other living areas and is quite spacious. The centered fireplace is the dominant feature, while sliding-glass doors open from each end onto outdoor terraces. The kitchen, too, is spacious and functions well. Two eating areas are nearby. It is worth noting that each of the major first floor rooms have direct access to the outdoor terraces. Note second floor suite which includes a lounge with built-in book cabinets.

Design 22391   *2,496 Sq. Ft. - First Floor; 958 Sq. Ft. - Second Floor; 59,461 Cu. Ft.*

● Here is a stately English adaptation that is impressive, indeed. The two-story octagonal foyer strikes a delightfully authentic design note. The entrance hall with open staircase and two-story ceiling is spacious. Clustered around the efficient kitchen are the formal living areas and those catering to informal activities. The family room with its beamed ceiling and raised hearth fireplace functions, like the formal living/dining zone, with the partially enclosed outdoor terrace. Three bedrooms with two baths comprise the first floor sleeping zone. Each room will enjoy its access to the terrace. Upstairs there are two more bedrooms and a study. Notice the sliding glass doors to the balcony and how the study looks down into the entrance hall. The three-car garage is great. Your own list of favorite features will surely be lengthy.

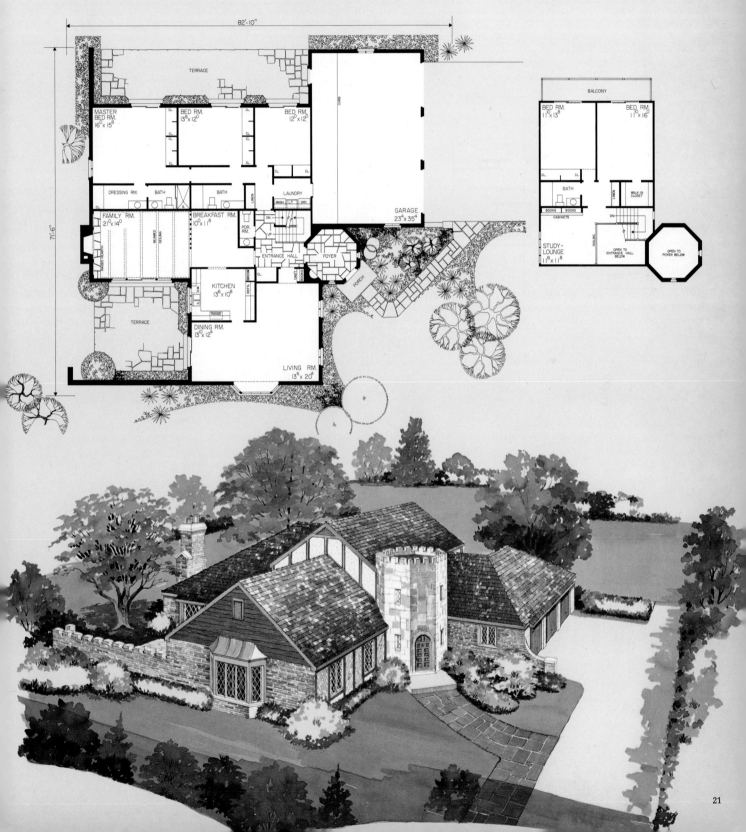

Design 22274 1,941 Sq. Ft. - First Floor; 1,392 Sq. Ft. - Second Floor; 32,580 Cu. Ft.

● Imagine having a second floor playroom! But, that's only the beginning. Imagine having such a distinctive and charming Tudor adaptation as this irregularly shaped story-and-a-half. Imagine how you and your family will enjoy the outdoor living on the entrance court and the terraces. Or then, imagine the fun of living with such outstanding features as those found inside. Study the location of the work center area and how it relates to the formal dining room and the informal family room. Notice the privacy afforded the living room. There are four bedrooms – two downstairs and two up. The playroom isn't the only multipurpose area, there is a sewing/study area. Don't miss the four full baths and extra washroom. Blueprints include optional basement.

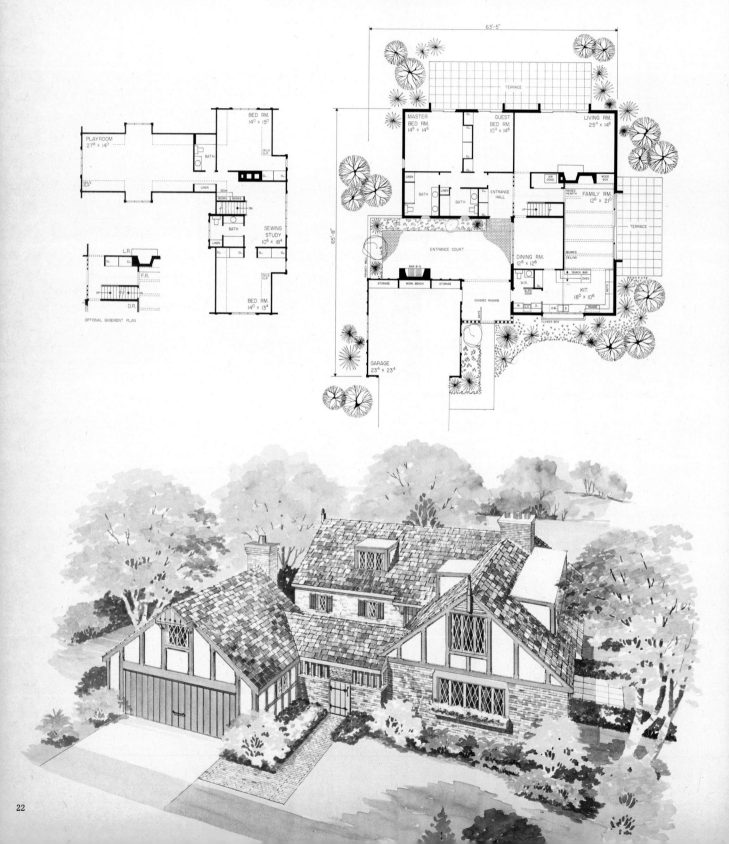

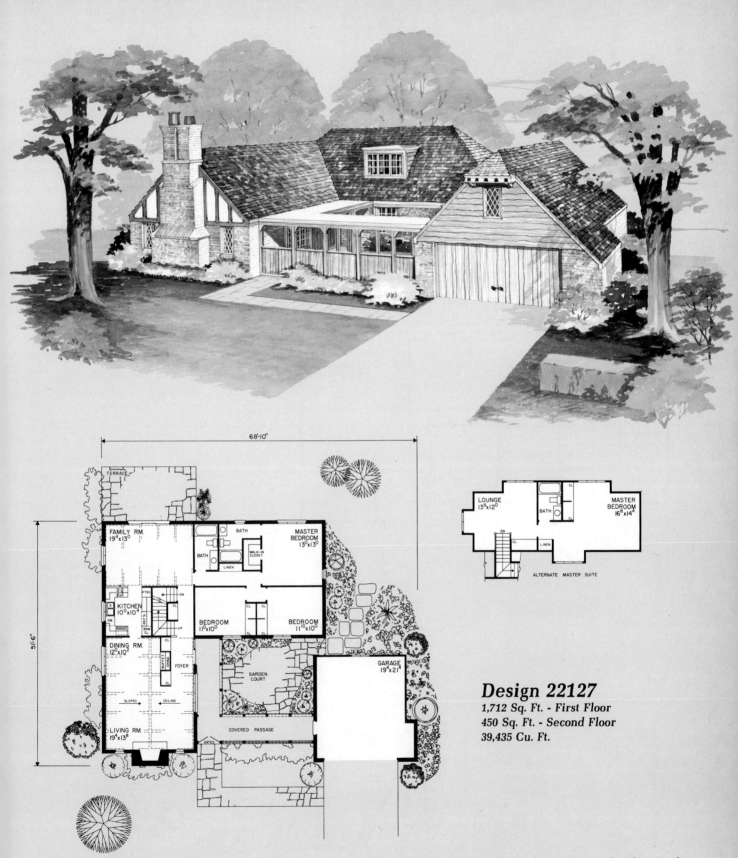

Design 22127

1,712 Sq. Ft. - First Floor
450 Sq. Ft. - Second Floor
39,435 Cu. Ft.

● Here is a basic one-story home with three bedrooms and two full baths, plus a bonus second floor under its high pitched roof. Features are plenty - both inside and out. A list of the exterior design highlights is most interesting. It begins with the character created by the impressive roof surfaces. The U-shape creates a unique appeal and results in the formation of a front, garden court. Exterior detailing of the projecting wings is delightful, indeed. The massive chimney is worthy of particular note. Inside, the living room features a sloping, beamed ceiling. It also has space left over for the formal dining. The family room has a flat, beamed ceiling. Sleeping facilities are exceptional. Upstairs there is an optional master bedroom suite if you choose to develop this area.

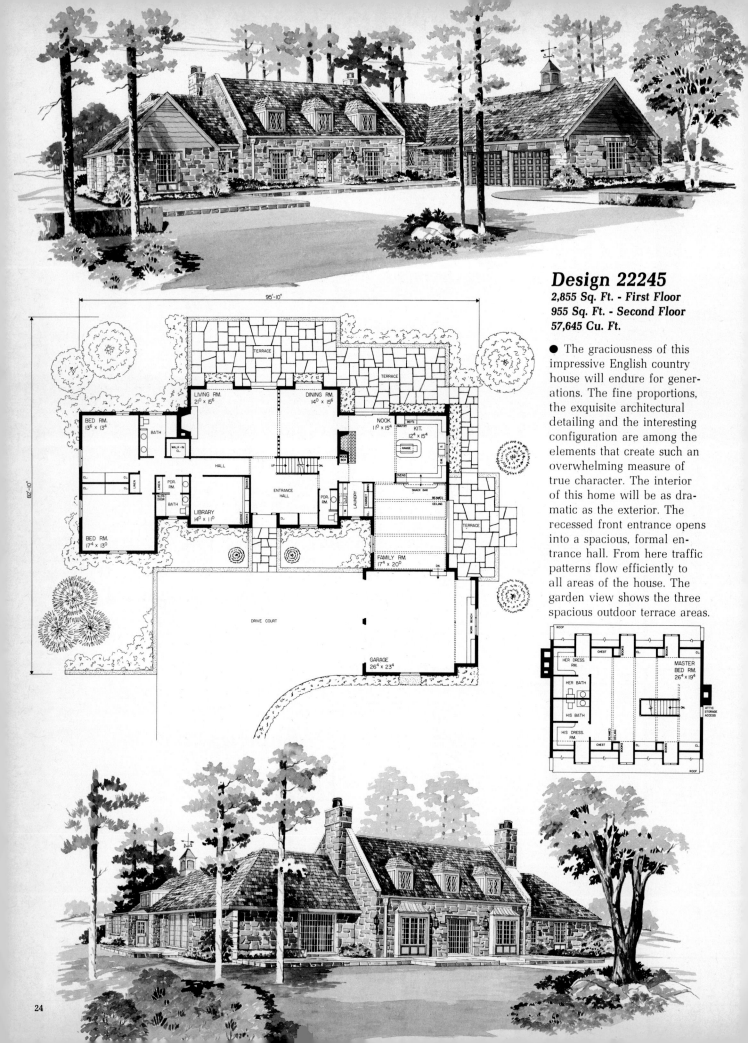

Design 22245
2,855 Sq. Ft. - First Floor
955 Sq. Ft. - Second Floor
57,645 Cu. Ft.

● The graciousness of this impressive English country house will endure for generations. The fine proportions, the exquisite architectural detailing and the interesting configuration are among the elements that create such an overwhelming measure of true character. The interior of this home will be as dramatic as the exterior. The recessed front entrance opens into a spacious, formal entrance hall. From here traffic patterns flow efficiently to all areas of the house. The garden view shows the three spacious outdoor terrace areas.

Design 22278 *1,804 Sq. Ft. - First Floor; 939 Sq. Ft. - Second Floor; 44,274 Cu. Ft.*

● This cozy Tudor adaptation is inviting. Its friendly demeanor seems to say, "welcome". Upon admittance to the formal front entrance hall, even the most casual of visitors will be filled with anticipation at the prospect of touring the house. And little wonder, too. Traffic patterns are efficient. Room relationships are excellent. A great feature is the location of the living, dining, kitchen and family rooms across the back of the house. Each enjoys a view of the rear yard and sliding glass doors provide direct access to the terrace. Another outstanding feature is the flexibility of the sleeping patterns. This may be a five bedroom house, or one with three bedrooms with study and lounge. Don't miss the three fireplaces and three baths.

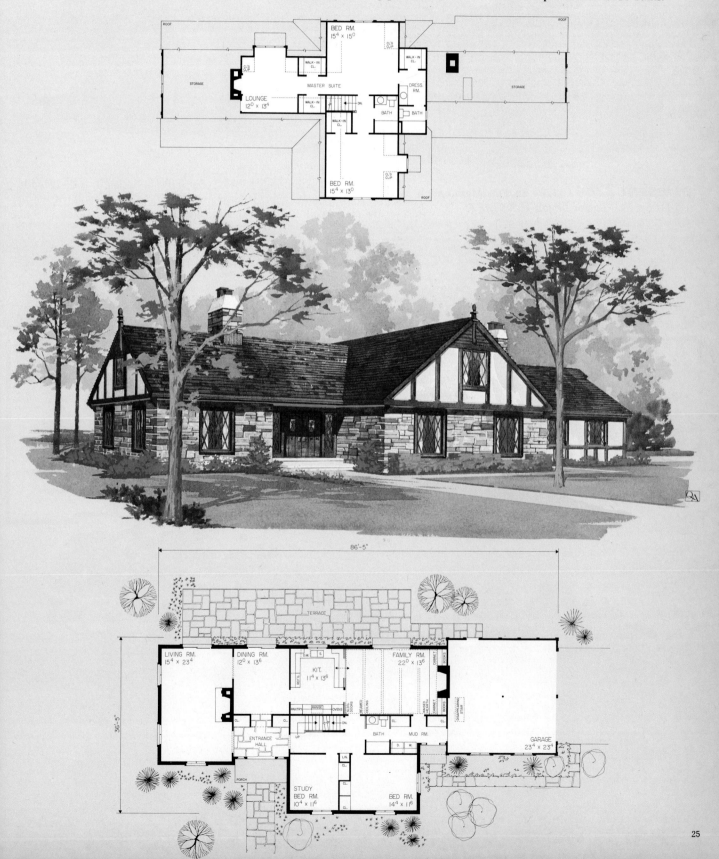

Design 22847
1,874 Sq. Ft. - Main Level
1,131 Sq. Ft. - Lower Level; 44,305 Cu. Ft.

● This is an exquisitely styled Tudor, hillside design. It is designed to serve its happy occupants for many years. Complete livability is on the main level. Bonus space will be found on the lower level.

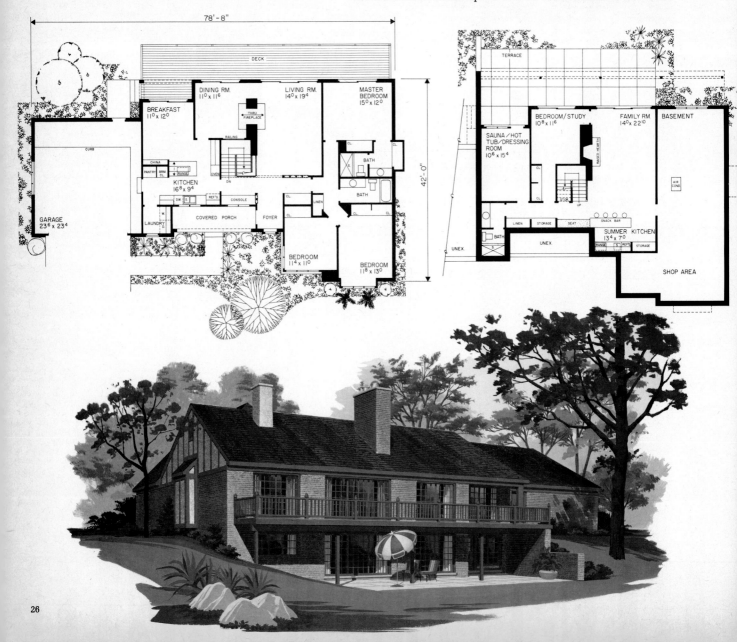

Design 22678
1,971 Sq. Ft.; 42,896 Cu. Ft.

● This delightful Tudor design has the option of two efficient floor plans. Design 22277 has its formal and informal area broken down into a living room and a family room. Where Design 22678 has a living room and an informal area of a large country kitchen. This design also has a basement. Both plans have three bedrooms.

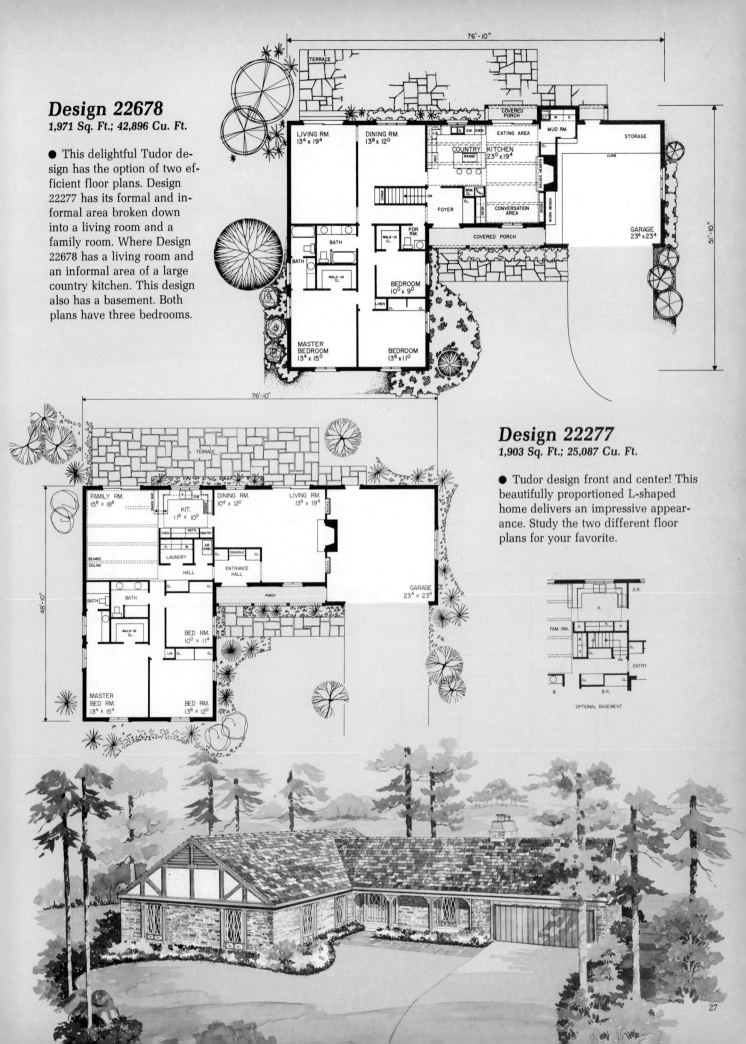

Design 22678 (floor plan labels)
76'-10"
51'-10"
TERRACE
LIVING RM. 13⁴ x 19⁴
DINING RM. 13⁸ x 12⁰
COVERED PORCH
EATING AREA
MUD RM.
STORAGE
COUNTRY KITCHEN 23⁰ x 19⁴
RANGE
D.W. OVEN
RAISED HEARTH
CURB
GARAGE 23⁴ x 23⁴
FOYER
CONVERSATION AREA
WORK BENCH
COVERED PORCH
BATH
BATH
WALK-IN CL.
PDR. RM.
WALK-IN CL.
BEDROOM 10⁰ x 9⁰
LINEN
MASTER BEDROOM 13⁴ x 15⁰
BEDROOM 13⁸ x 11⁰

Design 22277
1,903 Sq. Ft.; 25,087 Cu. Ft.

● Tudor design front and center! This beautifully proportioned L-shaped home delivers an impressive appearance. Study the two different floor plans for your favorite.

Design 22277 (floor plan labels)
76'-10"
48'-10"
TERRACE
FAMILY RM. 15⁸ x 18⁸
KIT. 11⁸ x 10⁰
DINING RM. 10⁴ x 12⁰
LIVING RM. 13⁸ x 19⁴
OVEN
REF'S
PANTRY
AIR COND.
LAUNDRY
BEAMED CEILING
HALL
CONSOLE
ENTRANCE HALL
GARAGE 23⁴ x 23⁴
PORCH
BATH
BATH
WALK-IN CL.
BED RM. 10⁰ x 11⁴
LIN. CL.
MASTER BED RM. 13⁴ x 15⁴
BED RM. 13⁸ x 12⁰

OPTIONAL BASEMENT
D.R.
K.
FAM. RM.
ENTRY
B.
B.R.

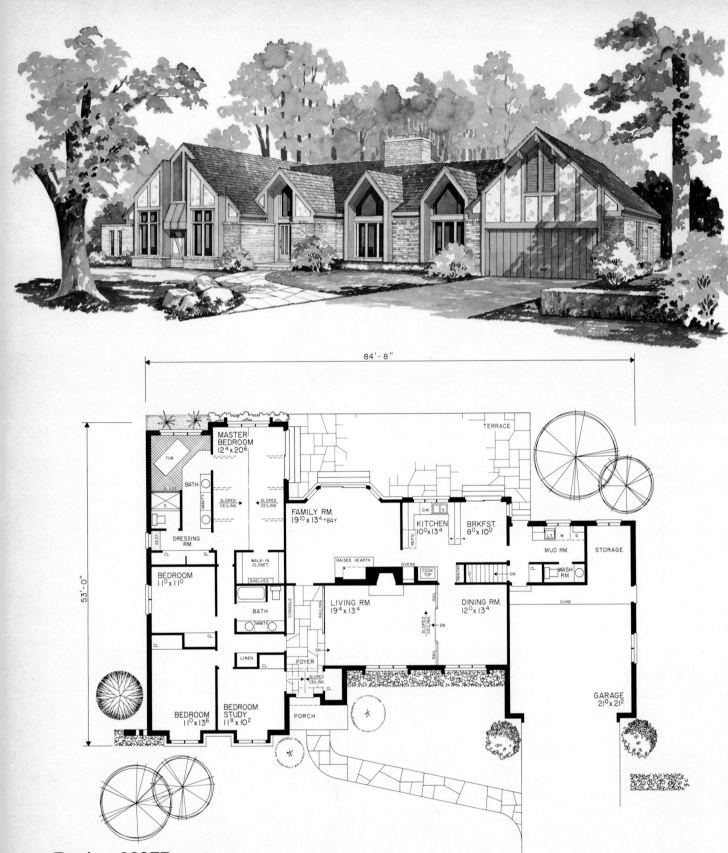

Design 22877 2,612 Sq. Ft.; 67,175 Cu. Ft.

● Here's a dramatic, Post-Modern exterior with a popular plan featuring an outstanding master bedroom suite. The bedroom itself is spacious, has a sloped ceiling, a large walk-in closet and sliding glass doors to the terrace. Now ex- amine the bath and dressing area. Two large closets, twin vanities, built-in seat and a dramatically presented corner tub are present. The tub will be a great place to spend the evening hours after a long, hard day. Along with this bed- room, there are three more served by a full bath. The living area of this plan has the formal areas in the front and the informal areas in the rear. Both have a fireplace. The spacious work center is efficiently planned.

TRADITIONAL EXTERIORS . . . *as highlighted in*

this section feature the variety of design characteristics to be found in classic forms of earlier periods of American architecture. These characteristics include: Double-hung, muntined windows, shutters, window bays, raised panelled doors, massive chimneys, cupolas, frame, stone, masonry exteriors, dovecotes and gabled roofs. When tastefully used, picket (or rail) fences, carriage lamps and flower boxes help complete a picture of warmth and charm that is, indeed, most inviting and pleasing to the eye. Any study of the floor plans should take note of the living, sleeping and work center zoning which is so important to practical living patterns.

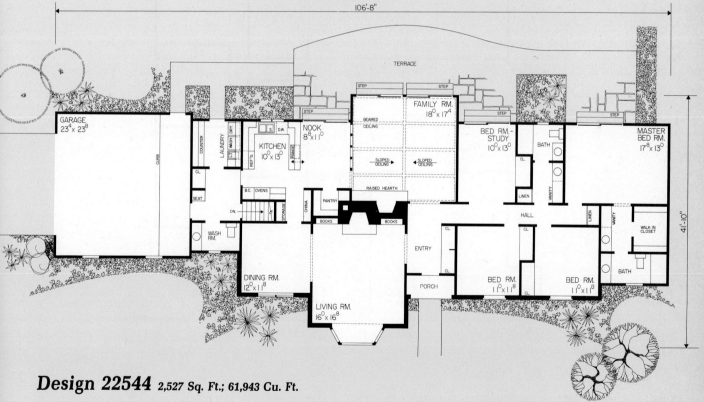

Design 22544 2,527 Sq. Ft.; 61,943 Cu. Ft.

● A blend of exterior materials enhance the beauty of this fine home. Here, the masonry material used is fieldstone to contrast effectively with the horizontal siding. You may substitute brick or quarried stone if you wish. Adding to the appeal are the various projections and their roof planes, the window treatment and the recessed front entrance. Two large living areas highlight the interior. Each has a fireplace. The homemaking effort will be easily and enjoyably dispatched with such features as the efficient kitchen, the walk-in pantry, the handy storage areas, the first floor laundry and extra washroom. The sleeping zone has four bedrooms, two baths with vanities and good closet accommodations. There's a basement for additional storage and recreation activities.

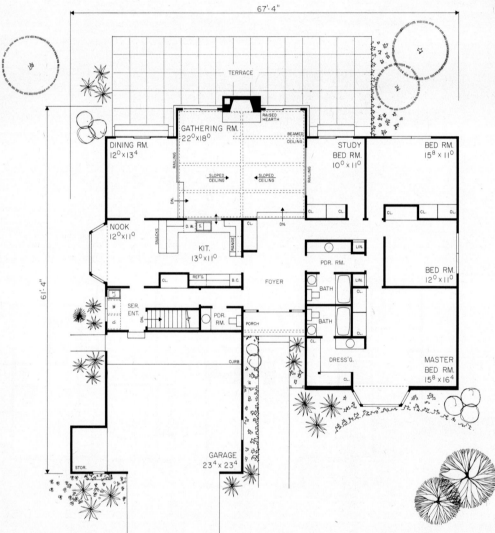

Design 22527 2,392 Sq. Ft.; 42,579 Cu. Ft.

● Vertical boards and battens, field-stone, bay window, a dovecote, a gas lamp and a recessed front entrance are among the appealing exterior features of this U-shaped design. Through the double front doors, flanked by glass side lites, one enters the spacious foyer. Straight ahead is the cozy sunken gathering room with its sloping, beamed ceiling, raised hearth fireplace and two sets of sliding glass doors to the rear terrace. To the right of the foyer is the sleeping wing with its three bedrooms, study (make it the fourth bedroom if you wish) and two baths. To the left is the strategically located powder room and large kitchen with its delightful nook and bay window.

● What a pleasing, traditional exterior! And what a fine, convenient living interior! The configuration of this home leads to interesting roof planes and even functional, outdoor terrace areas. The front court and the covered porch strike an enchanting note. The gathering room will be just that. It will be the family's multi-purpose living area. Sunken to a level of two steps, its already spacious feeling is enhanced by its open planning with the dining room and study. This latter room may be closed off for more privacy if desired. Adjacent to the foyer, the open stairwell leads to the basement level. This area has the possibility of being developed into recreation space.

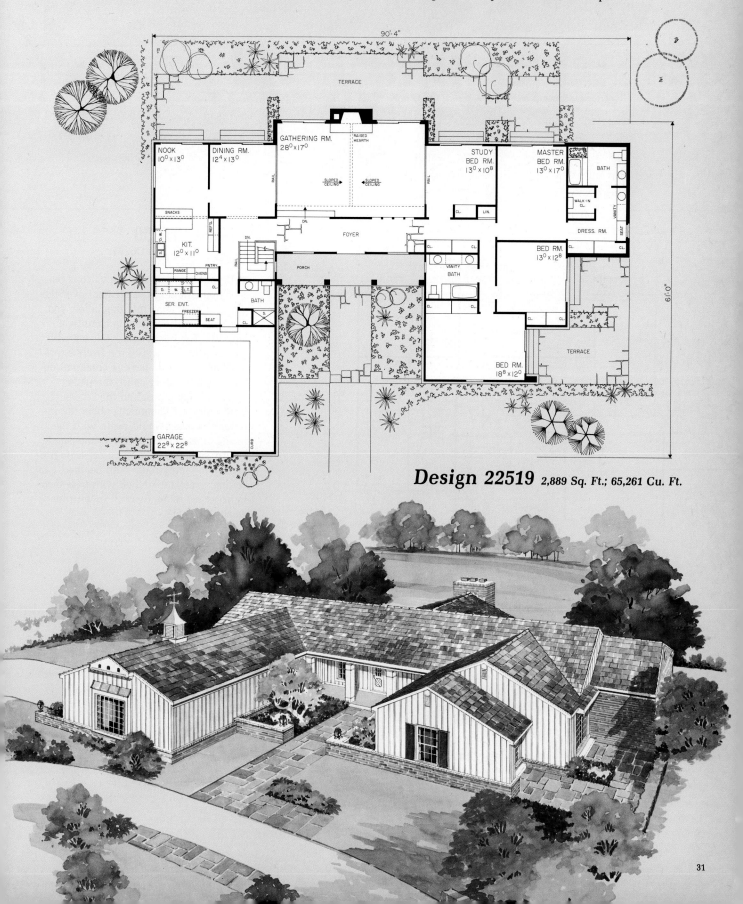

Design 22519 2,889 Sq. Ft.; 65,261 Cu. Ft.

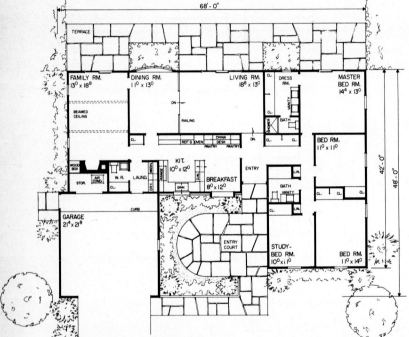

Design 21950
2,076 Sq. Ft.; 27,520 Cu. Ft.

● If you were to count the various reasons that will cause excitement over the prospect of moving into this home, you would certainly be able to compile a long list. You might head your list with the grace and charm of the front exterior. You'd certainly have to comment on the delightful entry court, the picket fence and lamp post and the recessed front entrance. Comments about the interior obviously would begin with the listing of such features as: spaciousness galore; sunken living room; separate dining room; family room with beamed ceiling; excellent kitchen with pass-thru to breakfast room; two full baths, plus washroom, etc.

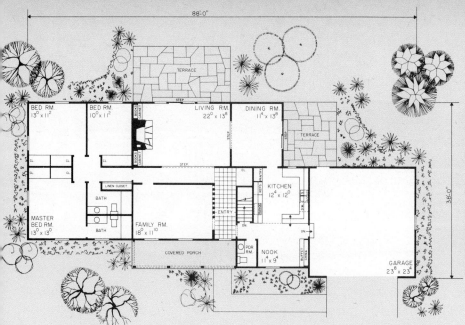

Design 22360
1,936 Sq. Ft.; 37,026 Cu. Ft.

● The charming characteristics of this traditional one-story are many. Fine proportion and pleasing lines assure a long and rewarding study. A list of them may begin with the fine window treatment, the covered front porch with its columns, the raised panelled door, the carriage lamp, the horizontal siding and the cupola. Inside, the family's everyday routine will enjoy all the facilities which will guarantee pleasurable living. The formal, sunken living room and the dining room function with their own terraces. A 3½ foot high wall with turned wood posts on top separate the excellent family room from the entry hall.

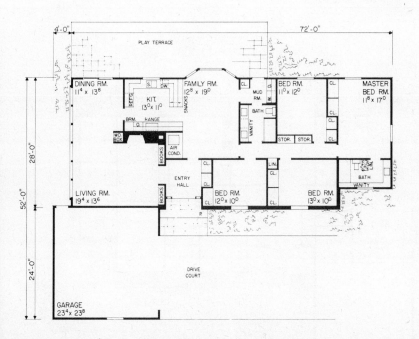

Design 21170
2,000 Sq. Ft.; 24,840 Cu. Ft.

● Footnote to perfection! This L-shaped traditional design tells a fine story of excellent proportion. Its appeal is its delightful simplicity. The large family will find its living patterns admirably taken care of by this attractive home. A family with many members needs well-organized space in which to move around. Here, traffic circulation will be orderly. The double front doors are recessed and protected by the roof overhang. Traffic can flow directly to the living room, the family room-kitchen area or to the sleeping area from the formal entry hall. The kitchen serves both the dining and family rooms equally. The inside bath is conveniently accessible from the living areas and the bedrooms.

Design 22766

2,711 Sq. Ft.; 59,240 Cu. Ft.

● A sizable master bedroom has a dressing area featuring two walk-in closets, a twin lavatory and compartmented bath. The two-bedroom children's area has a spacious, full bath and supporting study. Formal living and dining zone is separated by a thru-fireplace. A spacious kitchen-nook is cheerfully informal with a sun room just a step away through sliding glass doors. The service area has a laundry, storage closet, washroom and stairs to basement. An array of sliding glass doors lead to outdoor living on the various terraces. These are but some of the highlights of this appealing, L-shaped traditional home. Be sure to note the large number of sizable closets for a variety of uses.

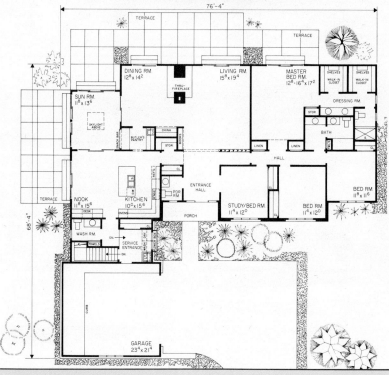

Design 22778

2,761 Sq. Ft.; 41,145 Cu. Ft.

● No matter what the occasion, family and friends alike will enjoy this sizable gathering room. A spacious 20' x 23', this room has a thru fireplace to the study and two sets of sliding glass doors to the large, rear terrace. Indoor-outdoor living also can be enjoyed from the dining room, study and master bedroom. There is also a covered porch accessible through sliding glass doors in the dining room and breakfast nook.

Design 22784
2,980 Sq. Ft.; 41,580 Cu. Ft.

● The projection of the master bedroom and garage create an inviting U-shaped area leading to the covered porch of this delightful traditionally styled design. After entering through the double front doors, the gallery will lead to each of the three living areas: the sleeping wing of two bedrooms, full bath and study; the informal area of the family room with raised hearth fireplace and sliding glass doors to the terrace and the kitchen/nook area (the kitchen has a pass-thru snack bar to the family room); and the formal area consisting of a separate dining room with built-in china cabinets and the living room. Note the privacy of the master bedroom.

Design 21149

2,040 Sq. Ft.; 35,290 Cu. Ft.

● The very shape of this traditional adaptation seems to spell, "welcome". A study of the floor plan reflects excellent zoning. The sleeping area consists of four bedrooms and two full baths. The formal area, located to the front of the house, consists of a separate dining room with built-in china cabinet and living room with fireplace and accompanying woodbox. Study the work center of the kitchen, laundry and wash room. An informal family room. It is only a couple of steps from the kitchen and functions with the outdoor terrace.

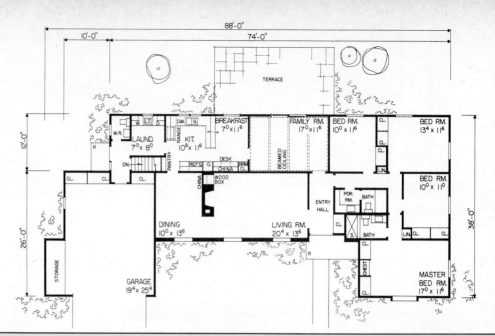

Design 22316

2,000 Sq. Ft.; 25,242 Cu. Ft.

● Here is a basic floor plan which is the favorite of many. It provides for the location, to the front of the plan, of the more formal areas (living and dining rooms); while the informal areas (family room and kitchen) are situated to the rear of the plan and function with the terrace. To the left of the center entrance is the four bedroom, two bath sleeping zone. Adjacent to the kitchen is the utility room with a wash room nearby. The garage features a storage room and work shop area with more storage.

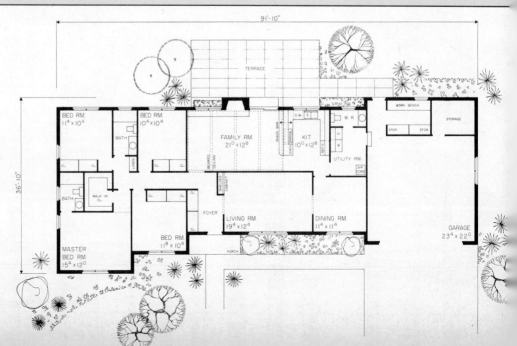

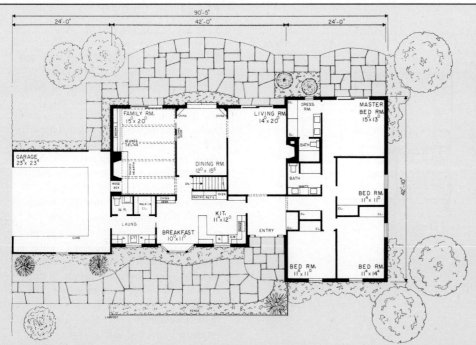

Design 22144
2,432 Sq. Ft.; 42,519 Cu. Ft.

● Have you ever wished you lived in a house in which the living, dining and family rooms all looked out upon the rear terrace? Further, have you ever wished your home had its kitchen located to the front so that you could see approaching callers? Or, have you ever wished for a house where traffic in from the garage was stopped right in the laundry so that wet, snowy, dirty and muddy apparel could be shed immediately? If these have been your wishes, this plan may be just for you.

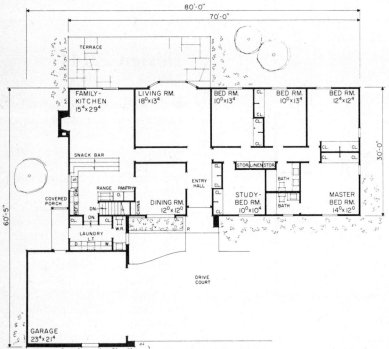

Design 21872
2,212 Sq. Ft.; 35,164 Cu. Ft.

● If exceptional exterior appeal means anything to interior living potential then this traditional home should have unlimited livability. And, indeed, it has! There are five bedrooms (and a study if you so wish), two full baths and loads of storage in the sleeping wing. The formal living zone highlights a quiet living room and separate dining room. Each completely free of cross-room traffic. For informal living there is the family-kitchen with a snack bar, fireplace and sliding glass doors to the terrace. The work center is outstanding with laundry and wash room nearby. There are plenty of cupboards and lots of counter space. The laundry, with more cupboards and twin closets, is nearby. Note wash room and covered side porch.

Design 21238
2,290 Sq. Ft.; 32,827 Cu. Ft.

● A popular floor plan concept housed in a charming, traditional exterior. The angular plan is one which functions most efficiently, for it is zoned for true convenience. The formal living and dining zone acts as a buffer between the quiet sleeping zone and the informal living and work center. The spacious center entry hall looks down into the sunken living room. The durable and attractive slate floor carries into the separate dining room from the entry hall.

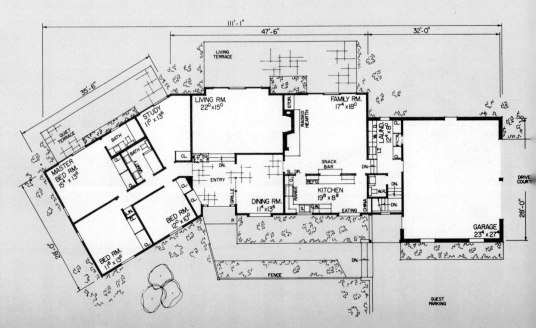

Design 21102

2,348 Sq. Ft.; 39,706 Cu. Ft.

● This quietly impressive home with curving front drive, covered front porch, delightful muntined windows, and panelled door flanked by patterned side-lites, houses a fine floor plan. The center entry hall joins another hall which runs the width of the home and routes traffic directly to each room. There are four bedrooms, two full baths, and plenty of storage potential in sleeping area. A covered rear porch off the master bedroom will be nice on hot, summer evenings. The living and dining rooms are sure to enjoy their privacy. The focal point of the plan, is perhaps the 27 foot family-kitchen. Don't miss the strategic location of the mud room. A snack bar provides a handy spot for the enjoyment of quick and easy meals.

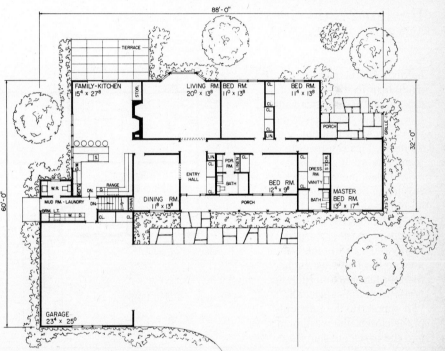

Design 22204
2,016 Sq. Ft.; 34,289 Cu. Ft.

● Your life's investment hardly could be more wisely made than for the choice of this delightful design as your family's next home. Over the years its charm will not diminish. This is a favorite plan of many. It establishes a quiet sleeping zone, a formal living-dining zone and an informal family-kitchen zone. Sliding glass doors permit the master bedroom, family room and breakfast nook to have easy access to the rear terrace. Entering the house from the garage, all will appreciate the proximity of the closets, the washroom and the basement stairs.

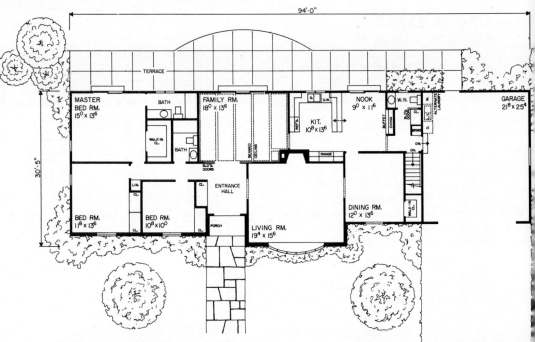

Design 22268
2,183 Sq. Ft.; 23,475 Cu. Ft.

● Reminiscent of Florida, yet this appealing design does not need to be built with a palm tree nearby to complete the picture. In fact, with minor modifications it would adapt to the more northerly climates. The wide overhanging roof functions as a sun visor for the shuttered window. A delightful measure of appeal is added by the long, low planting areas. The double front doors open to the center entrance hall. It is here that efficient traffic patterns become apparent. Looking out upon the rear yard are two living areas. They are partially, and effectively, separated by the fireplace wall.

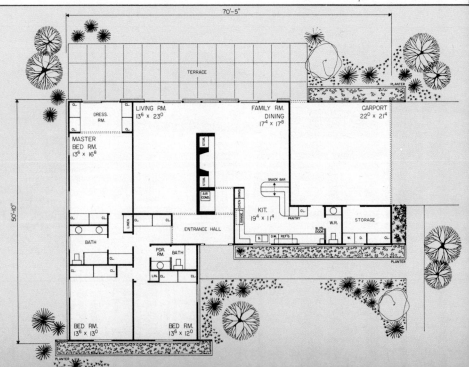

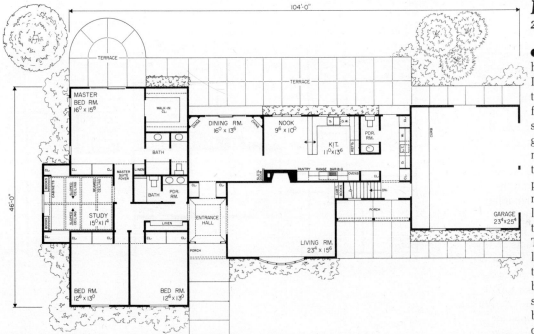

Design 22208
2,522 Sq. Ft.; 32,939 Cu. Ft.

● You really won't need a half acre to build this home. Its very breadth will guarantee plenty of space to the front, thus providing a fine setting. The pedimented gables, horizontal siding, corner boards, window and door treatment, two covered porches and the cupola set the note of distinction. An excellent feature is the service entrance, adjacent to the garage. The bedroom wing is positively outstanding. In addition to the three bedrooms and two baths, there is the private study. It has a sloping, beamed ceiling, bookshelves, cabinets and two closets.

Design 21835
2,144 Sq. Ft.; 33,310 Cu. Ft.

● Cedar shakes and quarried natural stone are the exterior materials which adorn this irregularly shaped traditional ranch home. Adding to the appeal of the exterior are the cut-up windows, the shutters, the pediment gable, the cupola and the double front doors. The detail of the garage door opening adds further interest. Inside, this favorite among floor plans, reflects all the features necessary to provide complete livability for the large family. The sleeping zone is a 24' x 40' rectangle which contains four bedrooms and two full baths. A dressing room with a vanity and a wall of wardrobe storage highlights the master bedroom. Both the informal family room and the formal living room have a fireplace.

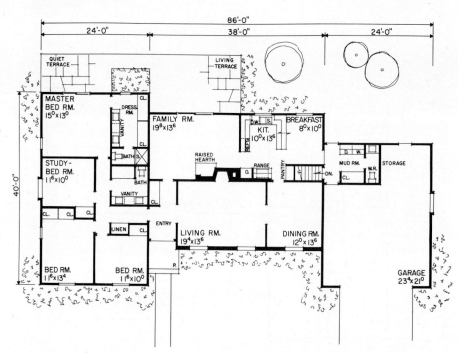

● Whatever the setting, here is a traditional, one story home that is truly impressive. Zoned in a most practical manner, the floor plan features an isolated bedroom wing, formal living and dining rooms and, across the rear of the house, the informal living areas.

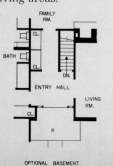

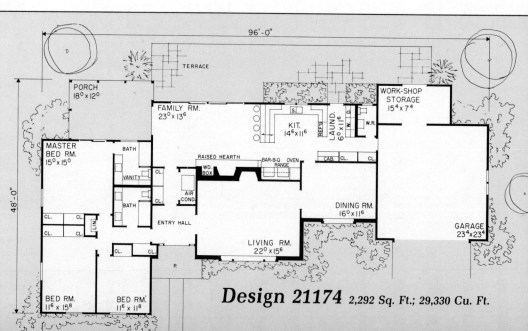

Design 21174 2,292 Sq. Ft.; 29,330 Cu. Ft.

Design 21786

2,370 Sq. Ft.; 37,170 Cu. Ft.

● Like this? If the answer is, yes, it is easy to understand. This is an extremely appealing design, highlighted by its brick masses, its window detailing, its interesting shape, and its inviting covered front entrance. The foyer is centrally located and but a step or two from all areas. The house, while it features all the facilities for family living, assures a full measure of privacy for all. The bedroom wing is distinctly defined. The quiet, sunken living room is off by itself. There is a separate, formal dining room. The family room is one which will function alone and cater to numerous activities. The kitchen, with its eating space, is of good size. The mud-room area is a true convenient living feature.

Design 22209
2,659 Sq. Ft.; 45,240 Cu. Ft.

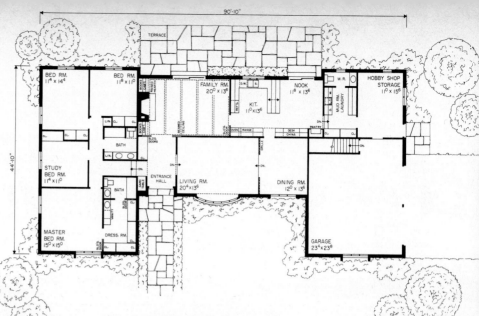

● Such an impressive home would, indeed, be difficult to top. And little wonder when you consider the myriad of features this one-story Colonial possesses. Consider the exquisite detailing, the fine proportions, and the symmetry of the projecting wings. The gracious and inviting double front doors are a prelude to the exceptional interior. Consider the four bedroom, two-bath sleeping wing. Formal entertaining can be enjoyed in the front living and dining rooms. For informal living there is the rear family room.

Design 22264
2,352 Sq. Ft.; 33,924 Cu. Ft.

● This U-shaped traditional will be a welcomed addition on any site. It has living facilities which will provide your family with years of delightful livability. The two living areas are located to the rear and function with the outdoor terrace. The outstanding kitchen is strategically located handy to the family room and the eating areas. A separate laundry area with fine storage and nearby powder room is a favorite feature. Note garage size and storage potential. Also notice stairway to attic.

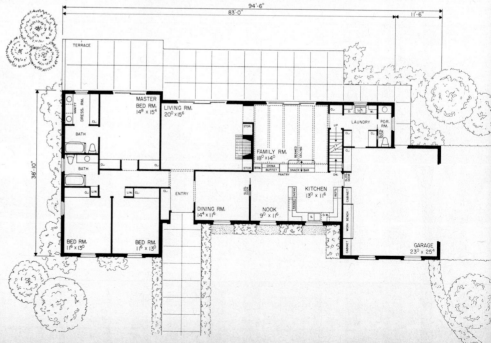

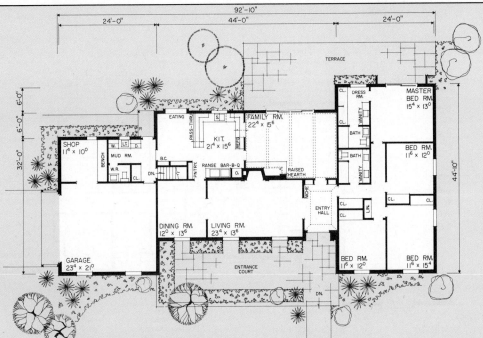

Design 21761
2,548 Sq. Ft.; 43,870 Cu. Ft.

● Low, strong roof lines and solid, enduring qualities of brick give this house a permanent, here-to-stay appearance. Bedroom wing is isolated, and the baths and closets deaden noise from the rest of the house. Center fireplaces in family and living rooms make furniture arrangement easy. There are a number of extras – a workshop, an unusually large garage, and an indoor barbecue. Garage has easy access to both basement and kitchen area. There are two eating areas – a formal dining room and a breakfast nook next to the delightful kitchen.

Design 22270

2,505 Sq. Ft.; 33,916 Cu. Ft.

● Four bedrooms and two baths make up the sleeping area of this delightful design. There are spacious living areas, too. The family room will serve the informal, family needs; while the living room is available for those more formal times. Both formal and informal dining areas are available to serve every family occasion. They both have easy access to the U-shaped kitchen. Complimenting the work center, an adjacent laundry and washroom will be appreciated. Outstanding storage facilities will be found throughout the plan. These are but some of the highlights of this family-oriented design.

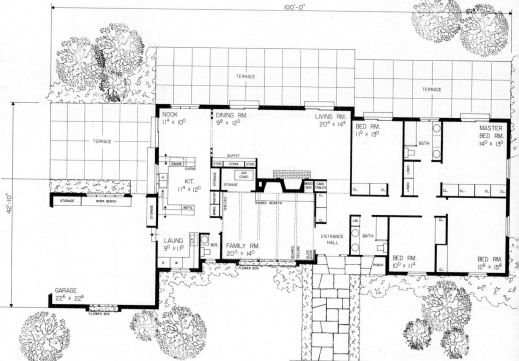

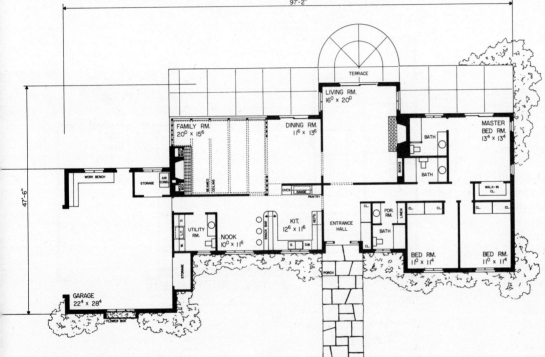

Design 22271
2,317 Sq. Ft.; 30,115 Cu. Ft.

● Here's a plan with both formal and informal living areas functioning with the rear terrace. Why let the beauty of your backyard be wasted on the laundry room? This puts the kitchen in the front of the plan. Working in the kitchen, you will be able to see approaching visitors. Among the other features, there are two fireplaces, three full baths, three bedrooms, nook and snack bar and extra garage storage. List the other features that will serve your family.

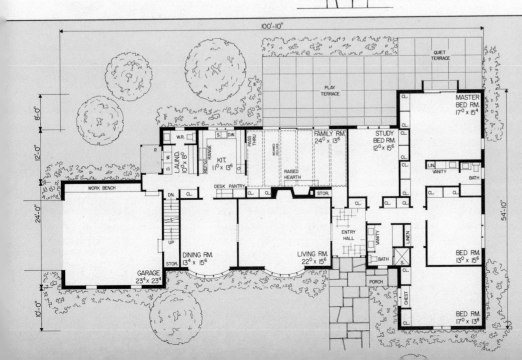

Design 21201
2,960 Sq. Ft.; 48,274 Cu. Ft.

● If it's formal living you are after, then the elegance and spaciousness of this richly detailed design should meet your specifications. The large bow windows, the overhanging roof, the massive chimney and the ornamental cupola give this house a stately facade. As you study the plan, note the generous size of the various rooms. Observe the excellence of the zoning and how the elements of each zone - sleeping, formal and informal living and work area - function together smoothly.

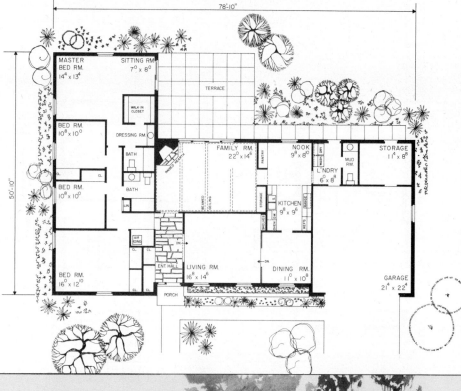

Design 22353

2,302 Sq. Ft.; 40,610 Cu. Ft.

● Here is an inviting Colonial Ranch home with matching pediment gables projecting toward the street. Deep double-hung windows flanked by shutters enhance the exterior charm. The massive chimney, the raised planter, the panelled front door, and the patterned garage door add their extra measure of appeal. The interior offers loads of livability. Note the sunken living room, the beamed-ceilinged family room, and the efficient kitchen strategically located between the breakfast nook and the formal dining room.

Design 22362
2,166 Sq. Ft.; 38,537 Cu. Ft.

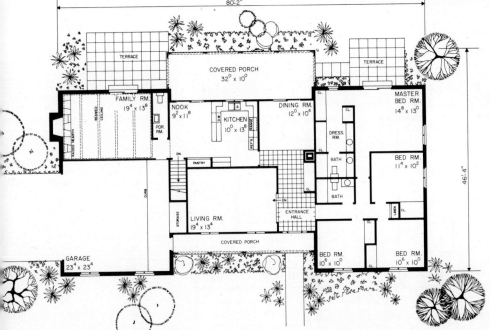

● Here is a ground-hugging, traditional adaptation with plenty of exterior appeal and a fine functioning floor plan. Observe the interior zoning. The sunken living room will have plenty of privacy. The four bedroom sleeping area is a wing by itself. The U-shaped kitchen is strategically flanked by the two eating areas. Study the exceptional family room. Note powder room. The indoor-outdoor living relationships are excellent. The covered rear porch will be a popular spot for summer outdoor eating and relaxation.

Design 22352
2,179 Sq. Ft.; 26,917 Cu. Ft.

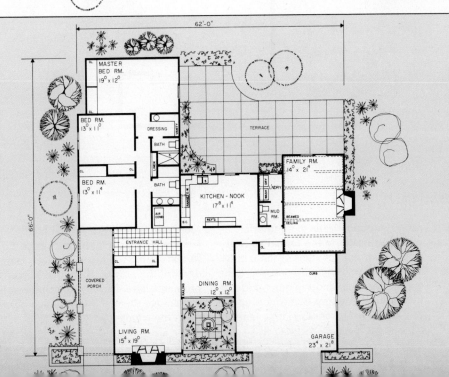

● This enchanting hip-roof traditional has a distinctive air of its own. From the recessed gardening area between the living room and garage to the master bedroom vanity, this plan is replete with features. Notice the covered front porch, the spacious kitchen, the quiet living room, the beamed ceilinged family room, the laundry/mud room, the sliding glass doors to terrace, etc. The planting court, so completely visible from the formal living and dining rooms, will be great fun for the amateur horticulturist during the warm months.

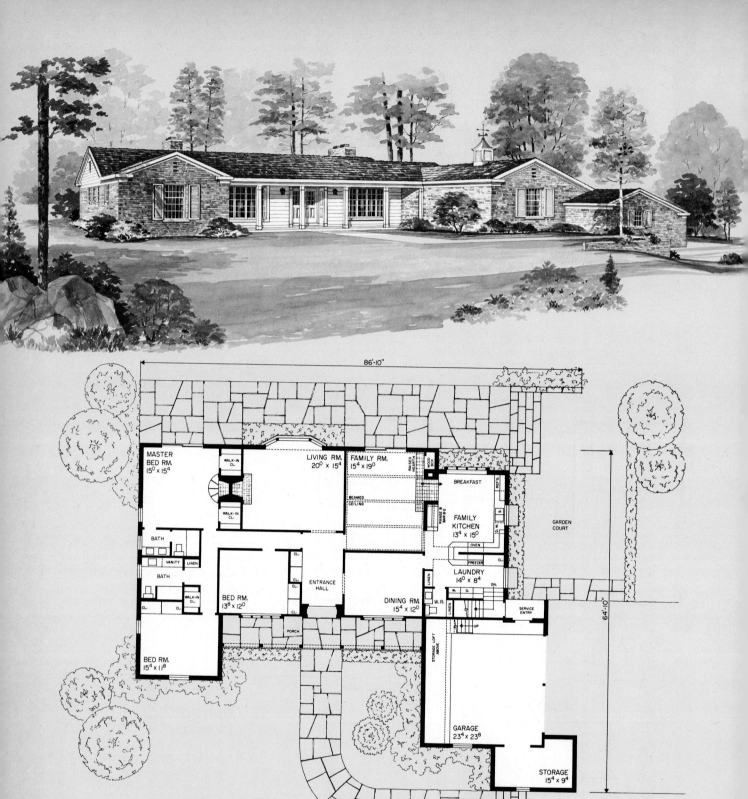

Design 21295 *2,520 Sq. Ft.: 38,328 Cu. Ft.*

● A custom home is one tailored to fit the needs and satisfy the living patterns of a particular family. Here is a traditional home which stands ready to serve its occupants ideally. The overhanging roof creates the covered porch with its attractive wood columns. The center entrance leads to an interior which will cater to the formal as well as the informal activities of the family. Two fireplaces, back-to-back, serve the master bedroom and the quiet, formal living room. Another two-way fireplace can be enjoyed from the large, family room and the gaily, informal family kitchen. Adjacent to the kitchen is the formal dining room, the spacious laundry and the powder room. No storage problems here. Of particular interest is the storage room and the storage balcony in the garage.

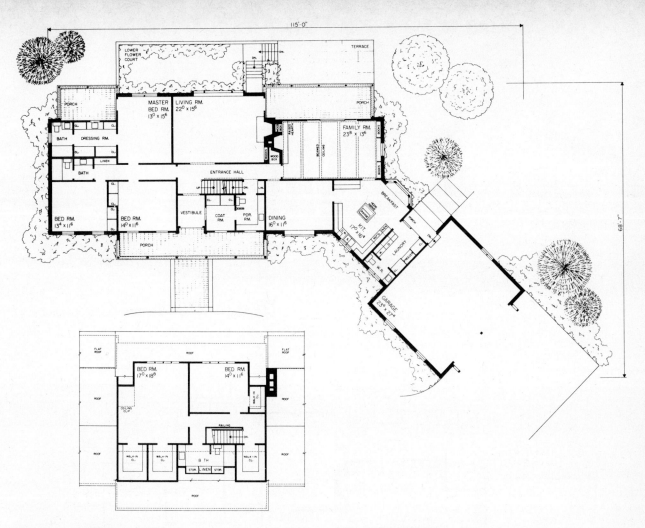

Design 21711 *2,580 Sq. Ft. - First Floor; 938 Sq. Ft. - Second Floor; 46,788 Cu. Ft.*

● If the gracious charm of the Colonial South appeals to you, this may be just the house for you. There is something solid and dependable in its well balanced facade and wide, pillared front porch. Much of the interest generated by this design comes from its interesting expanses of roof and angular projection of the kitchen and garage. The feeling of elegance is further experienced upon stepping inside, through double doors, to the spacious entrance hall. Here, there is the separate coat room. Adjacent, the powder room is also convenient from the living areas. The work area, consisting of the kitchen and laundry room, is truly outstanding. Designed as a five bedroom house, each is large. This home has complete livability on the first floor and bonus space upstairs.

Design 21924 2,504 Sq. Ft.; 42,498 Cu. Ft.

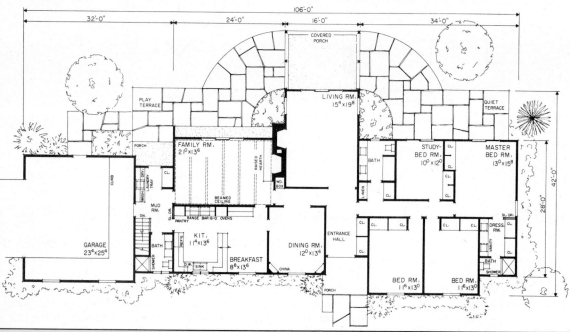

Design 21851 2,450 Sq. Ft.; 42,052 Cu. Ft.

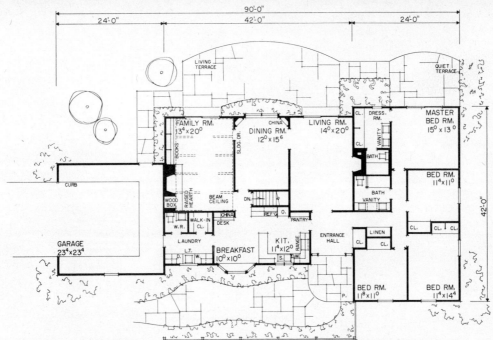

Design 21886 2,352 Sq. Ft.; 41,244 Cu. Ft.

Floor plan labels (Design 21886):

- 90'-0"
- 24'-0"
- 42'-0"
- 24'-0"
- 42'-0"
- LIVING TERRACE
- QUIET TERRACE
- FAMILY RM. 13⁴ x 20⁰
- DINING RM. 12⁰ x 15⁶
- LIVING RM. 14⁰ x 20⁰
- CL.
- DRESS. RM.
- MASTER BED RM. 15⁰ x 13⁰
- CL.
- VANITY
- BATH
- BED RM. 11⁴ x 11⁰
- CURB
- WOOD BOX
- RAISED HEARTH
- BEAM CEILING
- SLDG. DR.
- CHINA
- BOOKS
- DN.
- REF'G.
- PANTRY
- BATH
- VANITY
- GARAGE 23⁴ x 23⁴
- W.R.
- WALK-IN CL.
- LAUNDRY
- CHINA
- DESK
- L.T.
- D. W.
- BREAKFAST 10⁰ x 10⁰
- KIT. 11⁴ x 12⁰
- RANGE
- S.
- D.W.
- ENTRANCE HALL
- LINEN
- CL.
- CL.
- CL. CL. CL.
- BED RM. 11⁸ x 11⁰
- BED RM. 11⁴ x 14⁴
- P.

Floor plan labels (second design):

- 82'-0"
- 24'-0"
- 42'-0"
- 44'-0"
- 68'-0"
- QUIET TERRACE
- LIVING TERRACE
- MASTER BED RM. 15⁰ x 15⁰
- VANITY
- CL.
- POOL
- LIVING RM. 20⁰ x 14⁸
- DINING RM 11⁴ x 13⁰
- BREAKFAST 9⁸ x 9⁸
- BED RM. 11⁴ x 11⁰
- S.
- BATH
- BATH
- VANITY
- STOR.
- STOR.
- STOR.
- RAISED HEARTH
- BAR-B-Q
- RANGE
- S.
- KIT. 11⁸ x 12⁸
- O.
- REF'G
- D.W.
- LIN. LIN.
- CL. CL.
- ENTRY HALL
- SNACKS
- CL. CL.
- BED RM. 11⁴ x 14⁴
- BED RM. 11⁸ x 9⁸
- FAMILY RM. 22⁰ x 13⁴
- PANTRY
- HI-FI
- UP
- DN.
- W.R.
- LAUNDRY
- PORCH
- GARAGE 23⁴ x 23⁸
- TOOL RM. 16⁴ x 7⁸

● Here are three designs each featuring four bedrooms and two plus baths. While each home has a basement, it also highlights a first floor laundry. The differing arrangements of the living, dining, and family rooms are most interesting. The kitchens function directly with the breakfast rooms, yet again, their locations vary. Raised hearth fireplaces are a focal point of the family rooms, while a second fireplace can be found in the living rooms. Note the side opening garages. Design 21851 has a handy tool room for heavy equipment.

Design 22777
2,006 Sq. Ft.; 44,580 Cu. Ft.

● Many years of delightful living will be enjoyed in this one-story traditional home. The covered, front porch adds a charm to the exterior as do the paned windows and winding drive. Inside, there is livability galore. An efficient kitchen with island range and adjacent laundry make this work area very pleasing. A breakfast nook with bay window and built-in desk will serve the family when informal dining is called upon. A formal dining room with sliding glass doors leads to the rear terrace. The large gathering room with raised hearth fireplace can serve the family on any occasion gracefully. The sleeping wing consists of two bedrooms and a study (or make it three bedrooms). The master bedroom includes all of the fine features one would expect: a huge walk-in closet, a vanity, a bath and sliding glass doors to a private terrace.

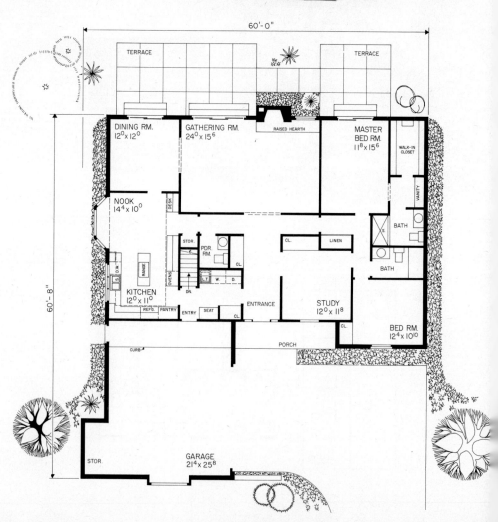

Design 22867 2,388 Sq. Ft.; 49,535 Cu. Ft.

● A live-in relative would be very comfortable in this home. This design features a self-contained suite (473 sq. ft.) consisting of a bedroom, bath, living room and kitchenette with dining area. This suite is nestled behind the garage away from the main areas of the house. The rest of this traditional, one-story house, faced with fieldstone and vertical wood siding, is also very livable. One whole wing houses the four family bedrooms and bath facilities. The center of the plan has a front, U-shaped kitchen and breakfast room. The formal dining room and large gathering room will enjoy the view, and access to, the backyard. The large, covered porch will receive much use.

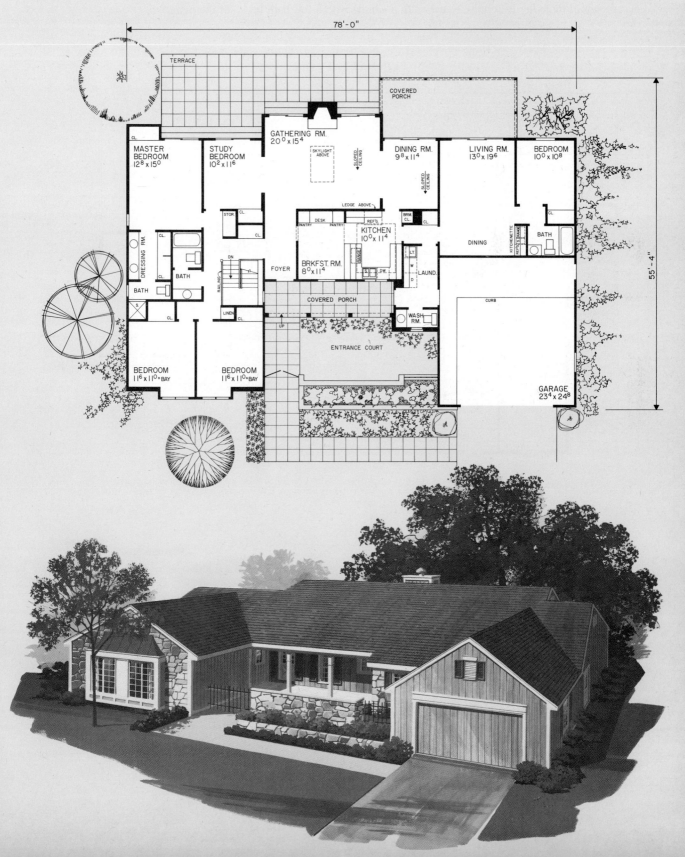

Design 21952 *2,705 Sq. Ft.; 41,582 Cu. Ft.*

● This delightful home has been designed for country-estate living. L-shaped, this traditional will be a worthy addition to any building site. Its pleasing proportions are almost breathtaking. They seem to foretell the tremendous amount of livability its inhabitants are to enjoy. The interior zoning hardly could be improved upon. The children's bedrooms function together in a wing with their own bath. There is a large master bedroom suite. It features Mr. and Mrs. dressing rooms, each with a vanity, with a full bath in the middle. The dining room is nestled between the living and family rooms. Both of these living areas have a beamed ceiling and a fireplace. All of the work area, kitchen, breakfast room, laundry and washroom, is in the front of the plan.

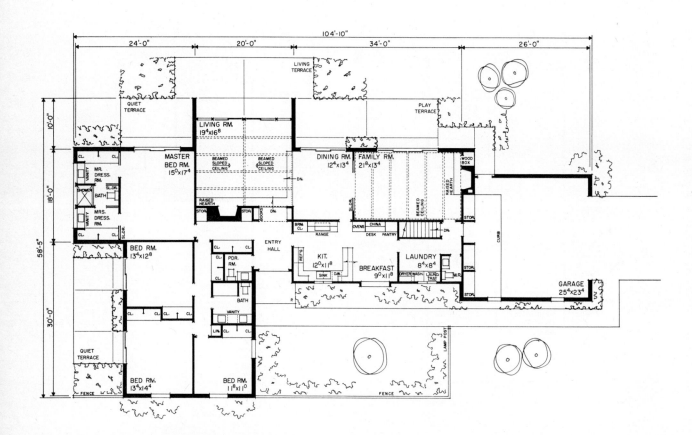

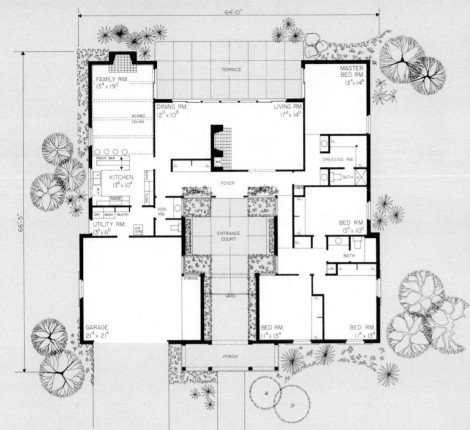

Floor plan labels:

64'-10"
66'-5"

FAMILY RM. 13⁴ x 19⁰
BEAMED CEILING
TERRACE
MASTER BED RM. 13⁴ x 14⁸
DINING RM. 12⁰ x 10⁸
LIVING RM. 17⁴ x 14⁰
CL
DRESSING RM.
WB
CL
BATH
SNACK BAR
KITCHEN 13⁴ x 10⁴
RANGE
FOYER
LINEN
CL
BED RM. 13⁴ x 10⁰
DRY WASH PANTRY
PDR. RM.
AIR COND.
UTILITY RM. 13⁴ x 6⁰
ENTRANCE COURT
BATH
LIN
STORAGE
GATES
GARAGE 21⁴ x 21⁴
BED RM. 11⁴ x 13⁴
BED RM. 11⁴ x 13⁴
PORCH

Design 22371
2,389 Sq. Ft.; 29,220 Cu. Ft.

● Here is a unique, brick veneer traditional home with a completely surrounded entrance court. The covered front porch with its well-proportioned columns, provides extra shelter for the covered walk-way to the court. This pleasant area provides an effective approach to the double front doors. Glass panels foster the enjoyment of the planting areas from inside. The configuration of this house as it envelopes the court gives rise to interesting roof planes. The interior features an abundance of highlights. They include: two fireplaces, plenty of closets, two full baths plus powder room, beamed ceilinged family room, snack bar with pass-thru to efficient kitchen, utility room, and interior planting units. The recessed rear terrace is accessible through sliding glass doors from the four major rooms (family, living, dining and master bedroom).

Design 21929 2,312 Sq. Ft.; 26,364 Cu. Ft.

● There's more to this U-shaped, traditional adaptation than meets the eye. Much more! And, yet, what does meet the eye is positively captivating. The symmetry of the pediment gables, the window styling, the projecting garden wall, the iron gates, and the double front doors, are extremely pleasing. Once inside, a quick tour reveals plenty of space and a super-abundance of features. Each of the rooms is extra large and allows for fine furniture placement. In addition to the raised hearth fireplace, the family room highlights built-in book shelves, sliding glass doors and beamed ceilings.

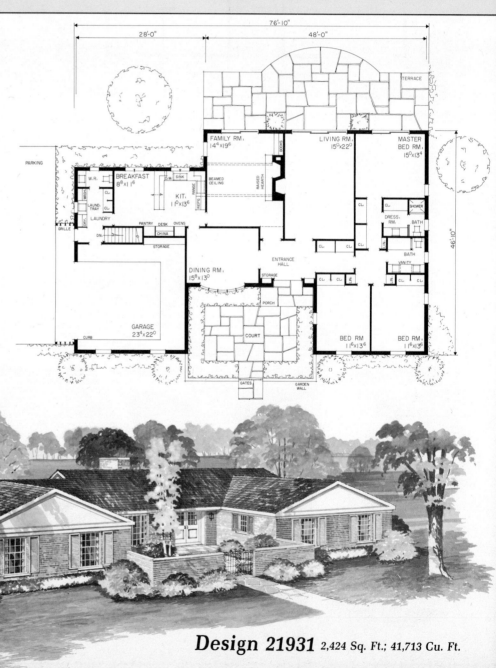

Design 21931 2,424 Sq. Ft.; 41,713 Cu. Ft.

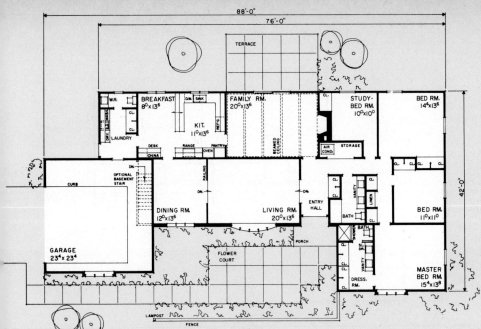

● This home will lead the hit parade in your new subdivision. Its sparkling, traditionally styled exterior will be the favorite of all that pass. And, once inside, friends will marvel at how the plan just seems to cater to your family's every activity. When it comes to eating, you can eat in the informal breakfast room or the formal dining room. As you come in the front door you may sit down and relax in the sunken living room or the beamed ceiling family room. Two full baths with built-in vanities, plus the extra wash room will more than adequately serve the family.

● Here is an exquisite U-shaped home that has an exciting story to tell about pleasureable indoor-outdoor living relationships. Wherever you may be standing in this four bedroom home, you will be a few steps from a set of sliding glass doors which open to outdoor terraces. The formal dining room, with its large bay of windows, will be a most pleasant place to eat. Also an informal breakfast nook with built-in pantry and china cabinets.

Design 21880 2,336 Sq. Ft.; 26,070 Cu. Ft.

Design 22259
2,016 Sq. Ft.; 43,337 Cu. Ft.

● Here is a 28 x 72 foot basic rectangle which houses 2,016 square feet of livability. Because of its rectangular shape it will be most economical to build. The projecting garage adds delightfully to the overall appeal and permits the utilization of a smaller building site. The covered front porch provides sheltered passage between the house and the garage. Inside there is a whale of a lot of livabiltiy. There are four bedrooms, two baths, laundry area, family room, large kitchen, spacious living and dining area. There is a fireplace flanked by book shelves and sliding glass doors to terraces.

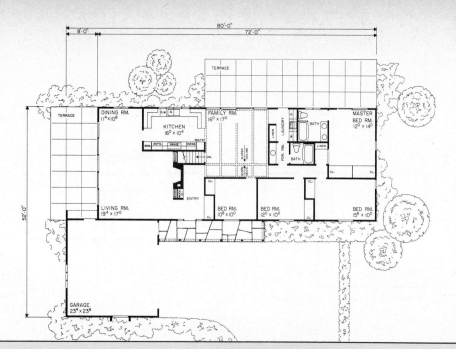

Design 22233
2,166 Sq. Ft.; 43,217 Cu. Ft.

● An L-shaped traditional with more than its full share of charm. There are features galore to recommend this home to the active family. In many ways the floor plan is unique. For instance, the covered front porch provides sheltered access to the garage from the foyer. Further, the location of the basement stairs makes that area equally accessible from house and garage. Also, observe the positioning of the laundry. It is, indeed a strategic one. Then, there is the placement of the kitchen only a step or two from the breakfast nook, and the family and dining rooms. While the family room with its beamed ceiling, and raised hearth fireplace will be in constant use, the living room will be a favorite spot, too. No cross room traffic in this floor plan.

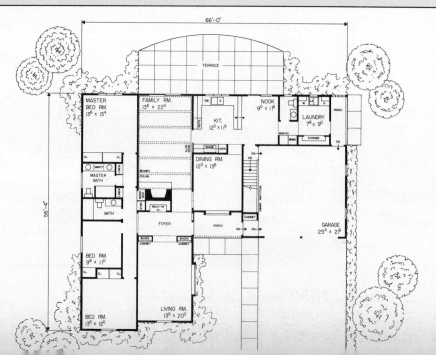

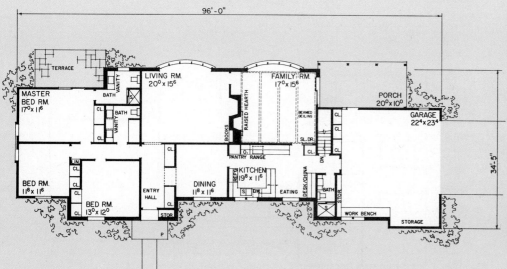

96'-0"

34'-5"

TERRACE

MASTER BED RM.
17⁰ x 11⁶

VANITY

BATH

CL

BATH

VANITY

CL

LIVING RM.
20⁰ x 15⁶

RAISED HEARTH

BOOKS

FAMILY RM.
17⁰ x 15⁶

BEAMED CEILING

SL. DR.

PORCH
20⁰ x 10⁰

GARAGE
22⁴ x 23⁴

CL

CL

CL

DN

BED RM.
11⁸ x 11⁶

LIN
CL

CL

CL

BED RM.
13⁰ x 12⁰

ENTRY HALL

STOR

CL

PANTRY RANGE

DINING
11⁸ x 11⁶

REF
KITCHEN
19⁸ x 11⁶

S

DW

DESK/CHINA

EATING

BATH

STOR

WORK BENCH

STORAGE

P

Design 21144
2,064 Sq. Ft.; 29,579 Cu. Ft.

● Natural quarried stone, an interesting roof line, delightful window treatment, and a recessed front entrance give this traditional home an aura of quiet charm. Of particular interest inside are the multiple dining arrangements. There's a separate dining room for formal diners, a breakfast nook, and a snack bar. Both the family room and master bedroom have their outdoor living areas. Three full baths, two with stall showers, provide ample facilities. Each of the living areas feature an attractive fireplace — one with a raised hearth.

Design 22260
2,041 Sq. Ft.; 41,248 Cu. Ft.

● Upon entering thru the front door of this hip-roof traditional, you will view the built-in planter atop a practical storage cabinet. A look into the living room reveals an attractive fireplace flanked by bookshelves, cabinet and wood box. A step into the master bedroom brings into view the twin walk-in closets and sliding glass doors to the rear terrace. Moving into the kitchen, the fine counter and cupboard space will be appreciated. This efficient work area is but a step from the informal nook and the formal dining room. Behind the garage is a large, covered screened porch.

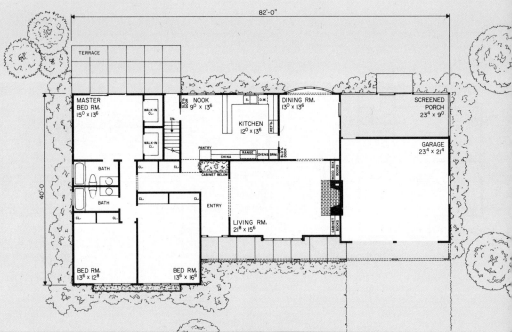

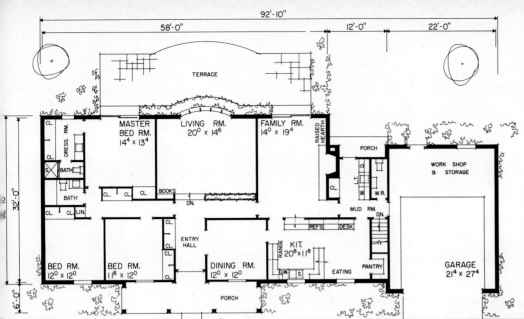

Design 21788
2,218 Sq. Ft.; 36,002 Cu. Ft.

● "Charm" is one of the many words which may be used to correctly describe this fine design. In addition to its eye-appeal, it has a practical and smoothly functioning floor plan. The detail of the front entrance, highlighted by columns supporting the projecting pediment gable, is outstanding. Observe the window treatment and the double, front doors. Perhaps the focal point of the interior will be the formal living room. It is, indeed, dramatic with its bay window overlooking the backyard. Three bedrooms and two baths are in the private area.

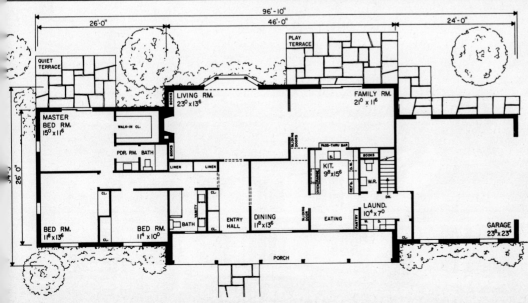

Design 22109
2,054 Sq. Ft.; 38,392 Cu. Ft.

● Long and low are characteristics of this traditional one-story. The main portion of the house is highlighted by the porch with its columns. The shuttered windows and doors add their note of distinction. The breadth of this design is emphasized by the addition of the two wings. One comprises the attached two-car garage. The other, the sleeping area made up of three bedrooms and two full baths. The master bedroom has its own compartmented bath, the huge walk-in closet, and sliding glass doors to its quiet terrace.

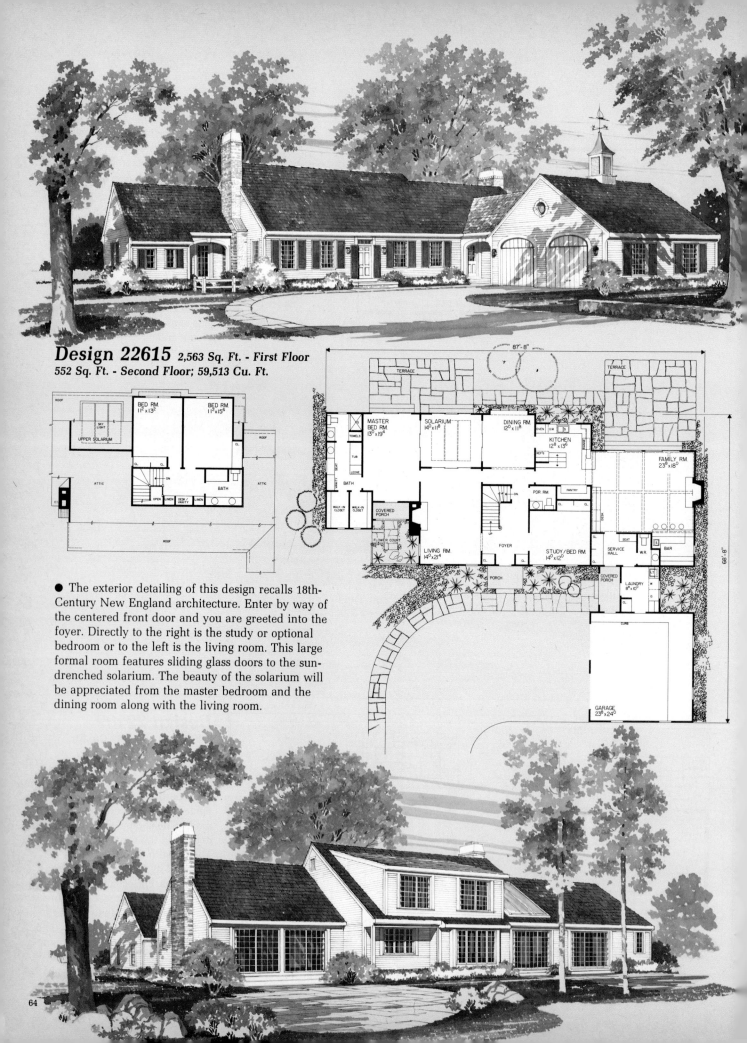

Design 22615 2,563 Sq. Ft. - First Floor
552 Sq. Ft. - Second Floor; 59,513 Cu. Ft.

- The exterior detailing of this design recalls 18th-Century New England architecture. Enter by way of the centered front door and you are greeted into the foyer. Directly to the right is the study or optional bedroom or to the left is the living room. This large formal room features sliding glass doors to the sun-drenched solarium. The beauty of the solarium will be appreciated from the master bedroom and the dining room along with the living room.

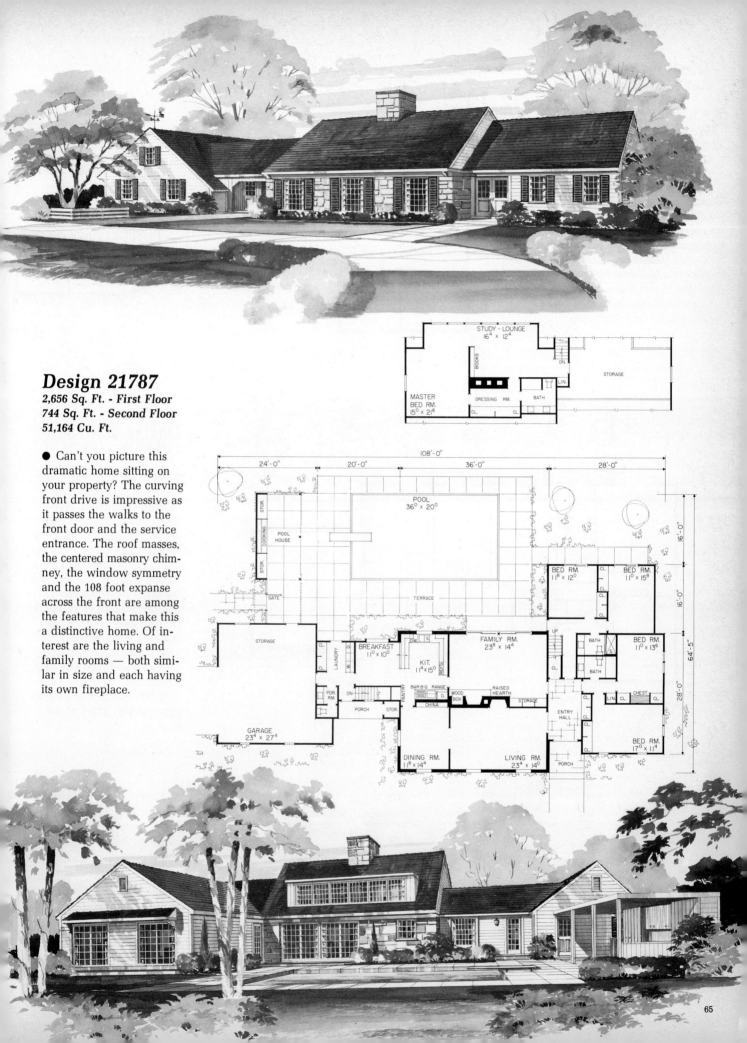

Design 21787

2,656 Sq. Ft. - First Floor
744 Sq. Ft. - Second Floor
51,164 Cu. Ft.

● Can't you picture this dramatic home sitting on your property? The curving front drive is impressive as it passes the walks to the front door and the service entrance. The roof masses, the centered masonry chimney, the window symmetry and the 108 foot expanse across the front are among the features that make this a distinctive home. Of interest are the living and family rooms — both similar in size and each having its own fireplace.

STUDY - LOUNGE 16⁴ x 12⁴

MASTER BED RM. 15⁰ x 21⁶

DRESSING RM.

BATH

STORAGE

BOOKS

DN.

LIN.

CL. **CL.**

108'-0"

24'-0" 20'-0" 36'-0" 28'-0"

16'-0"

16'-0"

64'-5"

28'-0"

POOL 36⁰ x 20⁰

POOL HOUSE

STOR. **COOKING** **STOR.**

GATE

TERRACE

STORAGE

CL.

LAUNDRY **W. D.**

BREAKFAST 11⁸ x 10⁰

DW. **S**

KIT. 11⁴ x 15⁰

PREP'G

FAMILY RM. 23⁸ x 14⁴

UP

BATH

BATH

S

CL.

BED RM. 11⁸ x 12⁰

BED RM. 11⁰ x 15⁸

CL.

CL.

BED RM. 11⁰ x 13⁶

CL.

PDR. RM.

DN.

PANTRY

BAR-B-Q **RANGE**

O.

WOOD BOX

RAISED HEARTH

STORAGE

CL. **LIN.** **CL.** **CHEST** **CL.**

PORCH **STOR.**

CHINA

ENTRY HALL

GARAGE 23⁴ x 27⁴

DINING RM. 11⁸ x 14⁴

LIVING RM. 23⁴ x 14⁰

PORCH

CL.

BED RM. 17⁰ x 11⁴

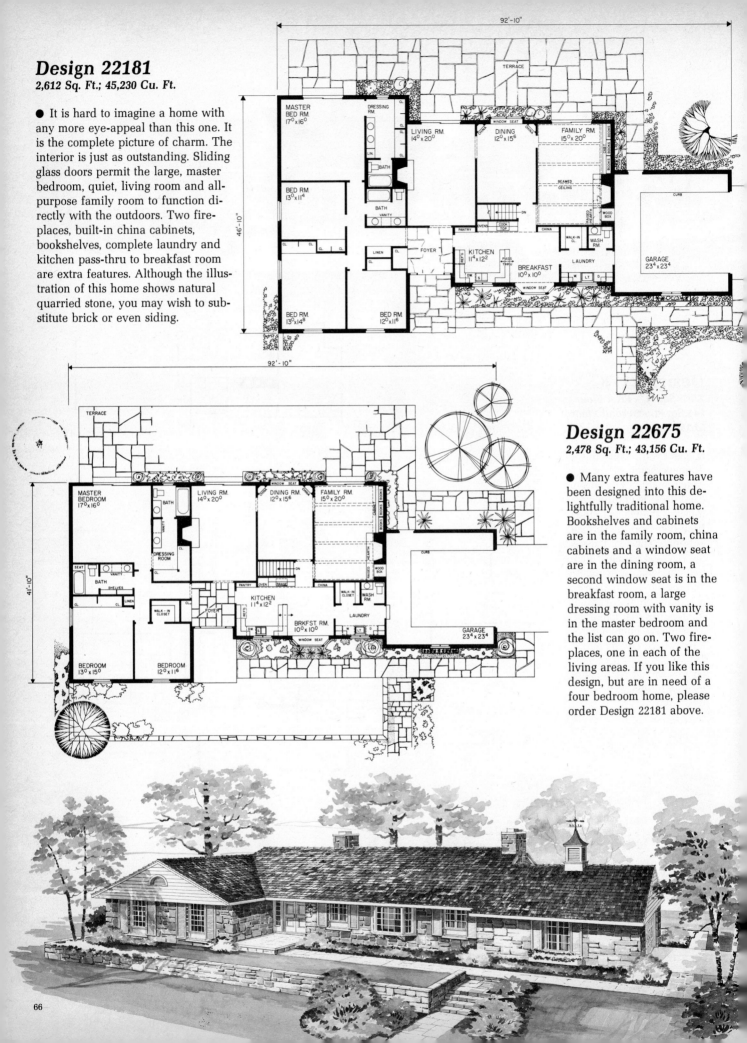

Design 22181
2,612 Sq. Ft.; 45,230 Cu. Ft.

● It is hard to imagine a home with any more eye-appeal than this one. It is the complete picture of charm. The interior is just as outstanding. Sliding glass doors permit the large, master bedroom, quiet, living room and all-purpose family room to function directly with the outdoors. Two fireplaces, built-in china cabinets, bookshelves, complete laundry and kitchen pass-thru to breakfast room are extra features. Although the illustration of this home shows natural quarried stone, you may wish to substitute brick or even siding.

Design 22675
2,478 Sq. Ft.; 43,156 Cu. Ft.

● Many extra features have been designed into this delightfully traditional home. Bookshelves and cabinets are in the family room, china cabinets and a window seat are in the dining room, a second window seat is in the breakfast room, a large dressing room with vanity is in the master bedroom and the list can go on. Two fireplaces, one in each of the living areas. If you like this design, but are in need of a four bedroom home, please order Design 22181 above.

SPANISH & WESTERN VARIATIONS . . .

can be found to offer a delightful change of pace wherever built. The appealing exterior design highlights include stucco surfaces, arched window heads, porch or courtyard columns, flared chimneys, exposed rafter tails, tiled roofs, window grilles, massive panelled doors, wide over-hanging roofs, covered porches and private courtyards. Sloping and beamed ceilings are often among the focal points of these spacious interiors. The rambling nature of the floor plan configurations is consistent with the wide, open spaces from which these designs emanated. This, of course, results in a selection of houses with virtually unlimited livability potential.

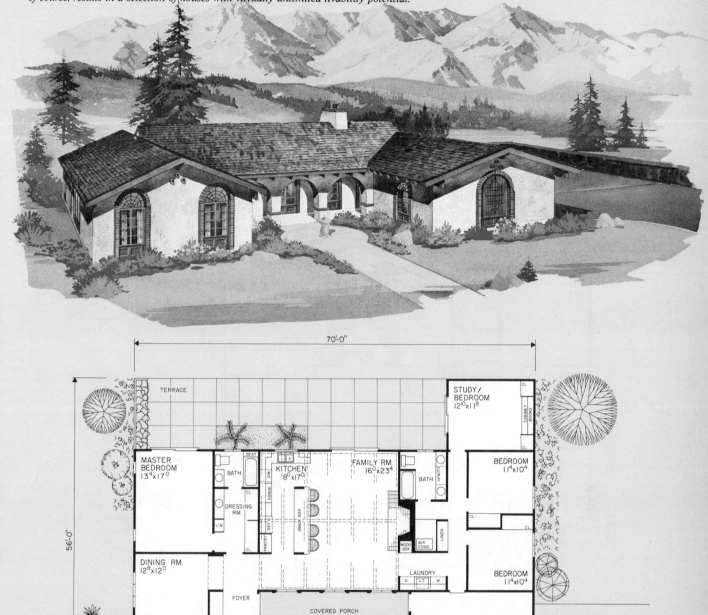

Design 22236 2,307 Sq. Ft.; 28,800 Cu. Ft.

● Living in this Spanish adaptation will truly be fun for the whole family. It will matter very little whether the backdrop matches the mountains above, becomes the endless prairie, turns out to be the rolling farmland, or is the backdrop of a suburban area. A family's flair for distinction will be satisfied by this picturesque exterior, while its requirements for everyday living will be gloriously catered to. The hub of the plan will be the kitchen-family room area. The beamed ceiling and raised hearth fireplace will contri-bute to the cozy, informal atmosphere. The separate dining room and the sunken living room function together formally. The master bedroom will enjoy its privacy from the three children's rooms located at the opposite end of the plan.

Design 22820 2,261 Sq. Ft.; 46,830 Cu. Ft.

● A privacy wall around the courtyard with pool and trellised planter area is a gracious area by which to enter this one-story design. The Spanish flavor is accented by the grillework and the tiled roof. Interior livability has a great deal to offer. The front living room has slid-ing glass doors which open to the entrance court; the adjacent dining room features a bay window. Informal activities will be enjoyed in the rear family room. Its many features include a sloped, beamed ceiling, raised hearth fireplace, sliding glass doors to the terrace and a snack bar for those very informal meals. A laundry and powder room are adjacent to the U-shaped kitchen. The sleeping wing can remain quiet away from the plan's activity centers. Notice the three-car garage with an extra storage area.

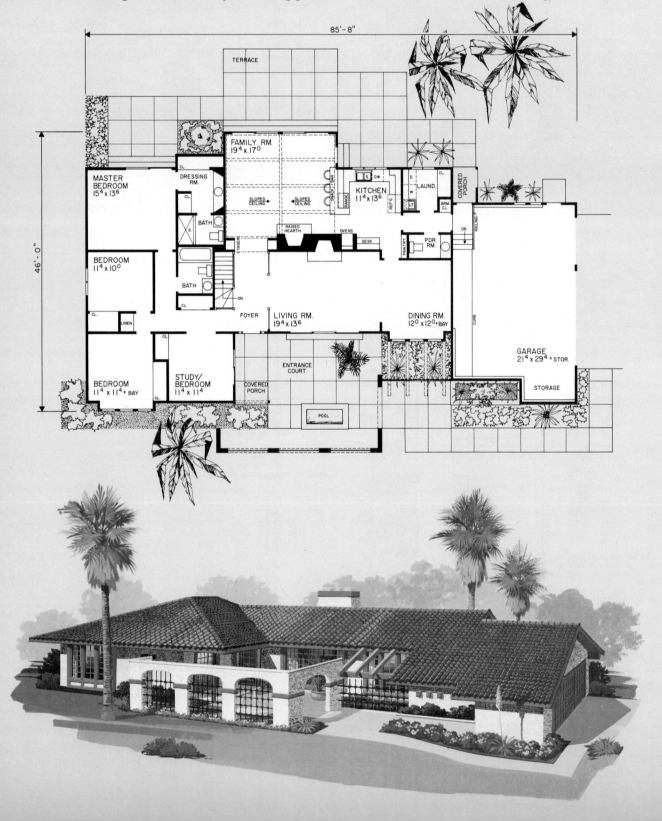

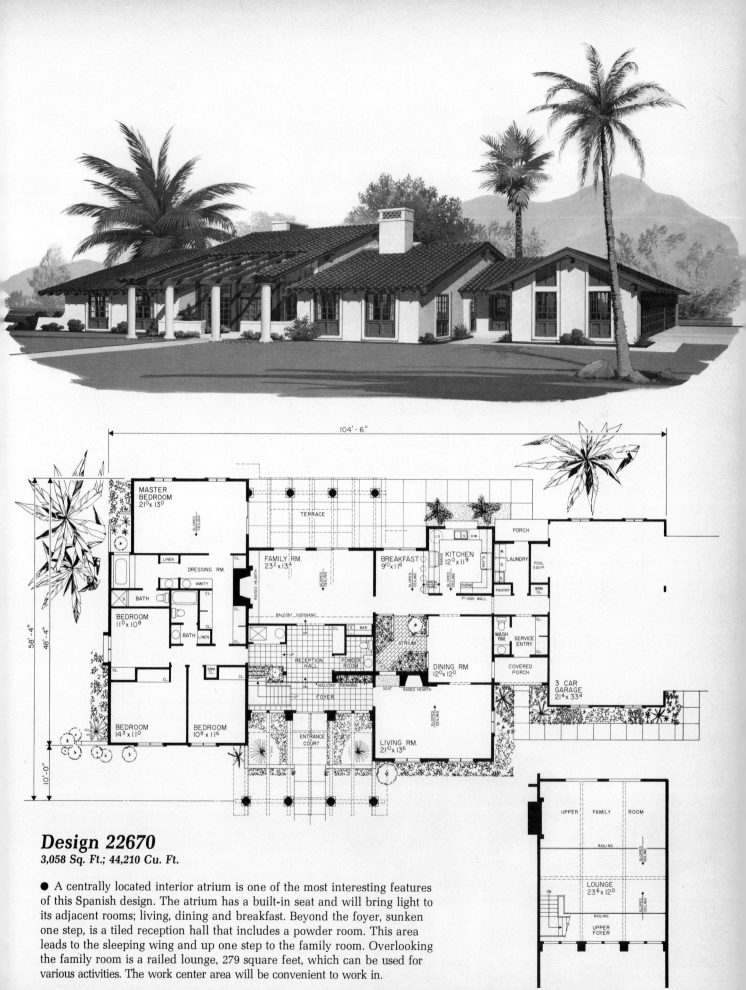

Design 22670
3,058 Sq. Ft.; 44,210 Cu. Ft.

● A centrally located interior atrium is one of the most interesting features of this Spanish design. The atrium has a built-in seat and will bring light to its adjacent rooms; living, dining and breakfast. Beyond the foyer, sunken one step, is a tiled reception hall that includes a powder room. This area leads to the sleeping wing and up one step to the family room. Overlooking the family room is a railed lounge, 279 square feet, which can be used for various activities. The work center area will be convenient to work in.

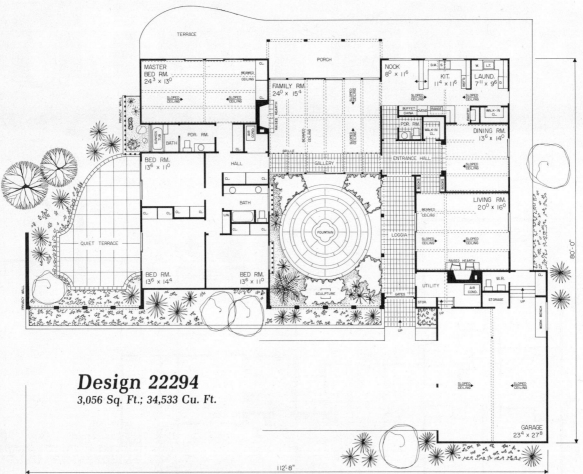

Design 22294
3,056 Sq. Ft.; 34,533 Cu. Ft.

Labels within floor plan:
TERRACE, PORCH, NOOK 8⁰ x 11⁶, KIT. 11⁴ x 11⁶, LAUND. 7¹¹ x 9⁶, MASTER BED RM. 24³ x 13⁰, BEAMED CEILING, SLOPED CEILING, FAMILY RM. 24⁰ x 15⁴, BUFFET CHINA, OVENS, RANGE, WALK-IN CL., PANTRY, DINING RM. 13⁶ x 14⁰, BATH, PDR. RM., AIR COND., PDR. RM., WALK-IN CL., BED RM. 13⁶ x 11⁰, HALL, GRILLE, GALLERY, ENTRANCE HALL, BOOKS, LIVING RM. 20⁰ x 16⁰, BEAMED CEILING, BATH, LIN., FOUNTAIN, LOGGIA, QUIET TERRACE, SCULPTURE, GATES, RAISED HEARTH, UTILITY, W.R., BED RM. 13⁶ x 14⁴, BED RM. 13⁶ x 11⁰, STOR., AIR COND., STORAGE, UP, WORK BENCH, GARAGE 23⁴ x 27⁸, PRIVACY WALL

Dimensions: 80'-0", 112'-8"

● Here is a western ranch with an authentic Spanish flavor. Striking a note of distinction, the arched privacy walls provide a fine backdrop for the long, raised planter. The low-pitched roof features tile and has a wide overhang with exposed rafter tails. The interior is wonderfully zoned. The all-purpose family room is flanked by the sleeping wing and the living wing. Study each area carefully for the planning is excellent and the features are many. Indoor-outdoor integration is outstanding. At left — the spacious interior court. The covered passage to the double front doors is dramatic, indeed.

Design 22335 2,674 Sq. Ft.; 41,957 Cu. Ft.

● Surely a winner for those who have a liking for the architecture of the Far West. With or without the enclosure of the front court, this home with its stucco exterior, brightly colored roof tiles, and exposed rafter tails will be impressive, indeed. The floor plan reflects a wonderfully zoned interior. This results in a fine separation of functions which helps assure convenient living. The traffic patterns which flow from the spacious foyer are most efficient. Study them. While the sleeping wing is angled to the front line of the house, the sunken living room projects, at an angle, from the rear. Worthy of particular notice are such highlights as the two covered porches, the raised hearth fireplaces, the first floor laundry, the partial basement and the oversized garage with storage space.

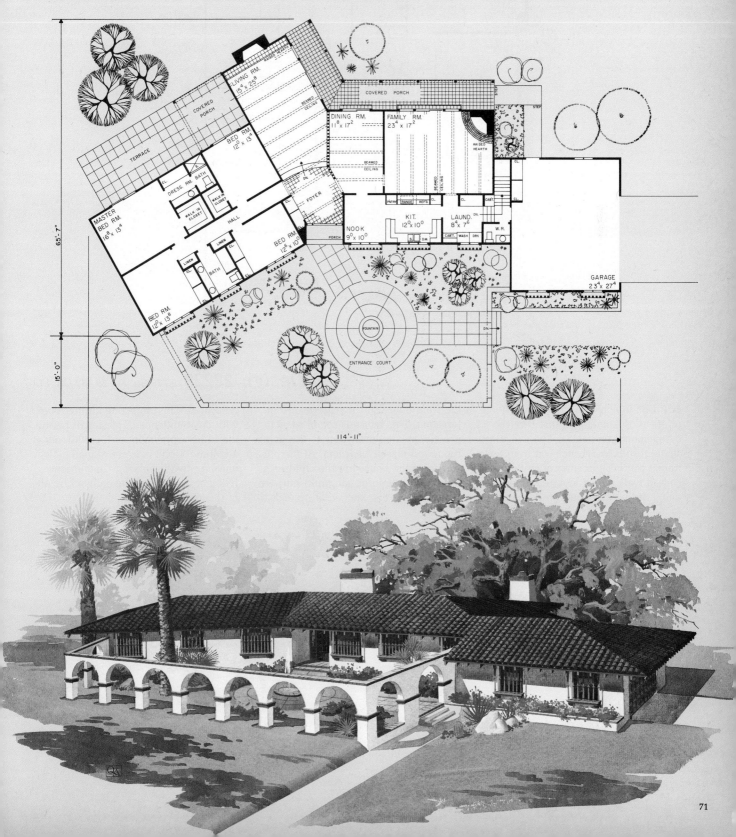

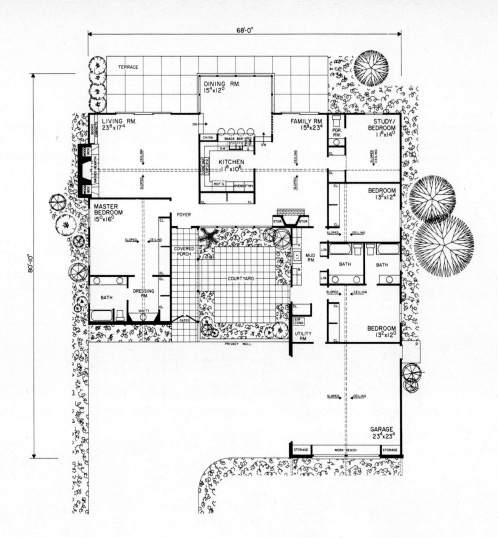

Design 22229 2,728 Sq. Ft.; 29,482 Cu. Ft.

● Rustic in character, this ranch home offers all the amenities that carefree living should be heir to. The irregular shape results in an enclosed front entrance court. Twin gates open to the coverd walk which looks out upon the delightful private court on its way to the front door. Traffic patterns are interesting. This house is zoned so as to provide maximum privacy to the living room and master bedroom. At the other end of the house are the children's rooms and the informal, multi-purpose family room. The kitchen is strategically located. The projecting dining room with its abundance of glass will permit the fullest enjoyment of the outdoors at mealtime. Don't miss the sloped ceilings and two fireplaces. Convenient living at its best will be enjoyed by all in this one-story design.

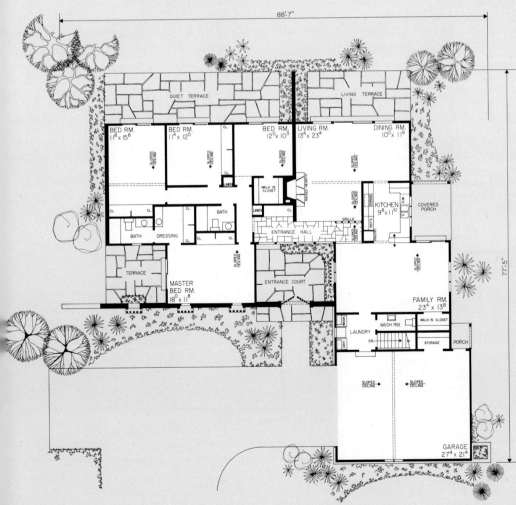

Design 22370
2,232 Sq. Ft.; 35,848 Cu. Ft.

● Whatever the setting - near mountains of the Far West, or in a subdivision of the Mid West - this L-shaped ranch home will deliver a lifetime of excellent livability. Behind the twin gates, opening from the drive court, is a delightful entrance court with massive beam-work above. A somewhat similar area provides the master bedroom with its own privacy terrace. Three additional bedrooms, each functioning through sliding glass doors with rear terrace. The open planning of the living and dining rooms provide a spacious and formal living zone. It, too, has its outdoor living area. A covered porch is adjacent to the family room and provides an excellent view of the kitchen.

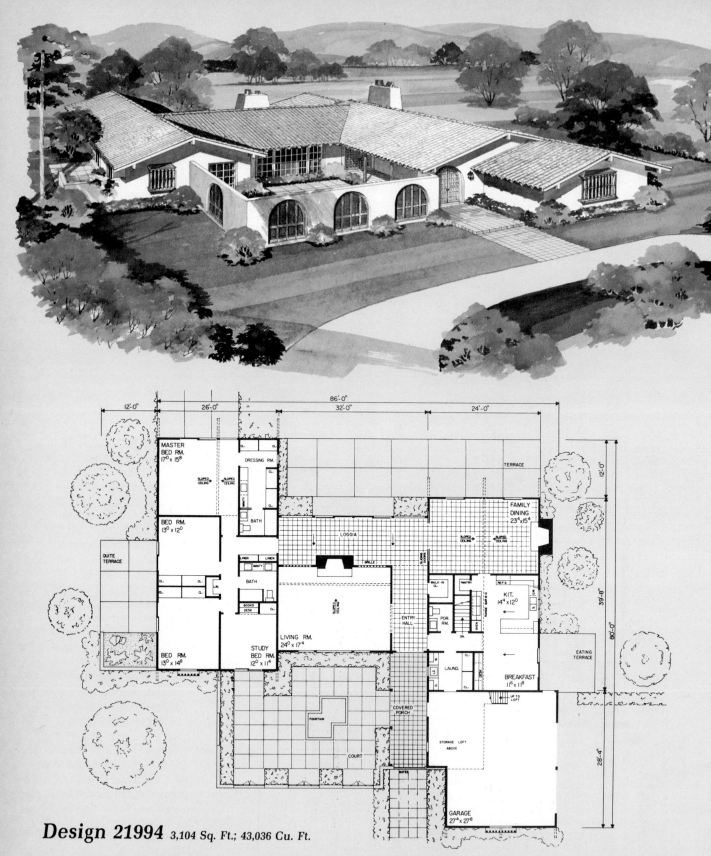

Design 21994 3,104 Sq. Ft.; 43,036 Cu. Ft.

● The Spanish flavor of the old Southwest is delightfully captured by this sprawling ranch house. Its L-shape and high privacy wall go together to form a wide open interior court. This will be a great place to hold those formal and/or informal garden parties. The plan itself is wonderfully zoned. The center portion of the house is comprised of the big, private living room with sloped ceiling. Traffic patterns will noiselessly skirt this formal area. The two wings—the sleeping and informal living—are connected by the well-lighted and spacious loggia. In the sleeping wing, observe the size of the various rooms and the fine storage. In the informal living wing, note the big family room and breakfast room that family members will enjoy.

● Echoing design themes of old Spain, this history house distills the essence of country houses built by rancheros in Early California. Yet its floor plan provides all the comfort and convenience essential to our contemporary living.

Among its charming features is a secluded court, or patio; a greenhouse tucked in behind the garage; a covered rear porch; a low-pitched wide overhanging roof with exposed rafter tails; sloping beamed ceilings. Contri-

buting to the authenticity of the design are the two sets of panelled doors. The covered walk to the front doors provides a sheltered area adjacent to the court. Once inside, the feeling of space continues to impress.

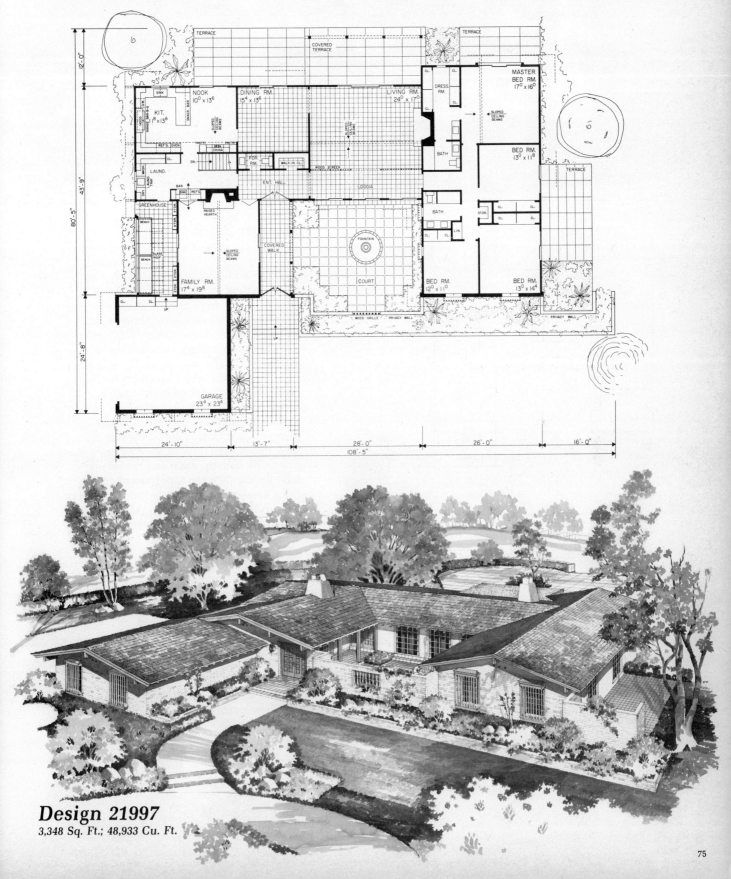

Design 21997
3,348 Sq. Ft.; 48,933 Cu. Ft.

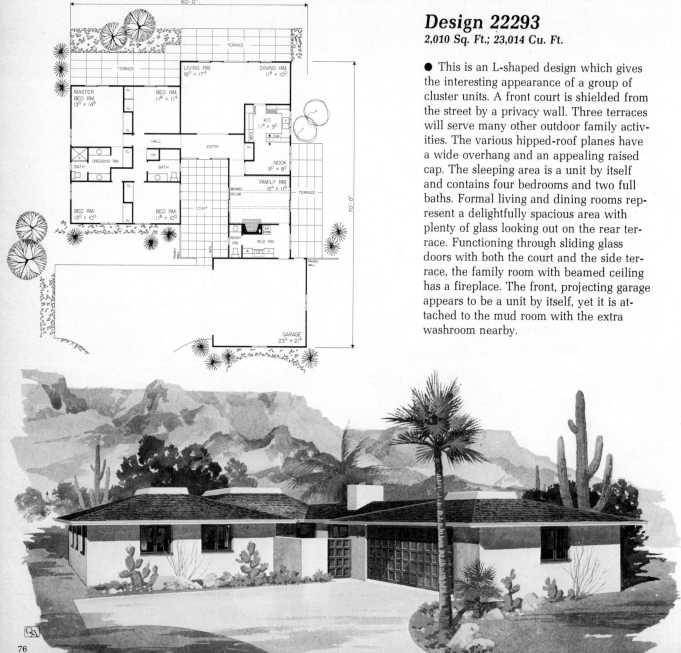

Design 22293
2,010 Sq. Ft.; 23,014 Cu. Ft.

● This is an L-shaped design which gives the interesting appearance of a group of cluster units. A front court is shielded from the street by a privacy wall. Three terraces will serve many other outdoor family activities. The various hipped-roof planes have a wide overhang and an appealing raised cap. The sleeping area is a unit by itself and contains four bedrooms and two full baths. Formal living and dining rooms represent a delightfully spacious area with plenty of glass looking out on the rear terrace. Functioning through sliding glass doors with both the court and the side terrace, the family room with beamed ceiling has a fireplace. The front, projecting garage appears to be a unit by itself, yet it is attached to the mud room with the extra washroom nearby.

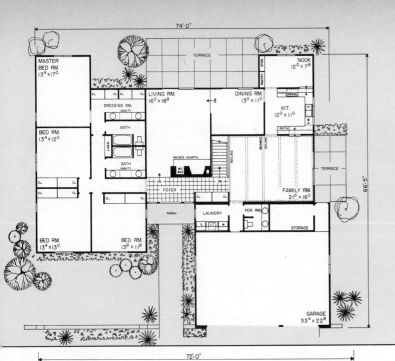

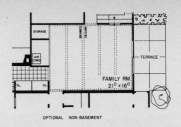

OPTIONAL NON-BASEMENT

Design 22269 2,652 Sq. Ft.; 29,470 Cu. Ft.

● This appealing home will be a favorite wherever built. Its wide, overhanging hip-roof engenders a pleasing, ground-hugging effect. While a stucco exterior is shown, other materials may be used depending upon your personal preferences and geographical location. The flared wing walls at the garage and the front wall add that extra measure of distinction. An open stairway leads to the basement.

Design 22386
1,994 Sq. Ft.; 22,160 Cu. Ft.

● This distinctive home may look like the Far West, but don't let that inhibit you from enjoying the great livability it has to offer. Wherever built, you will experience a satisfying pride of ownership. Imagine, an entrance court in addition to a large side courtyard! A central core is made up of the living, dining and family rooms, plus the kitchen. Each functions with an outdoor living area. The younger generation has its sleeping zone divorced from the master bedroom. The location of the attractive, attached garage provides direct access to the front entry. Don't miss the vanity, the utility room with laundry equipment, the snack bar and the raised hearth fireplace. Note three pass-throughs from the kitchen. Observe the beamed and sloping ceilings of the living areas.

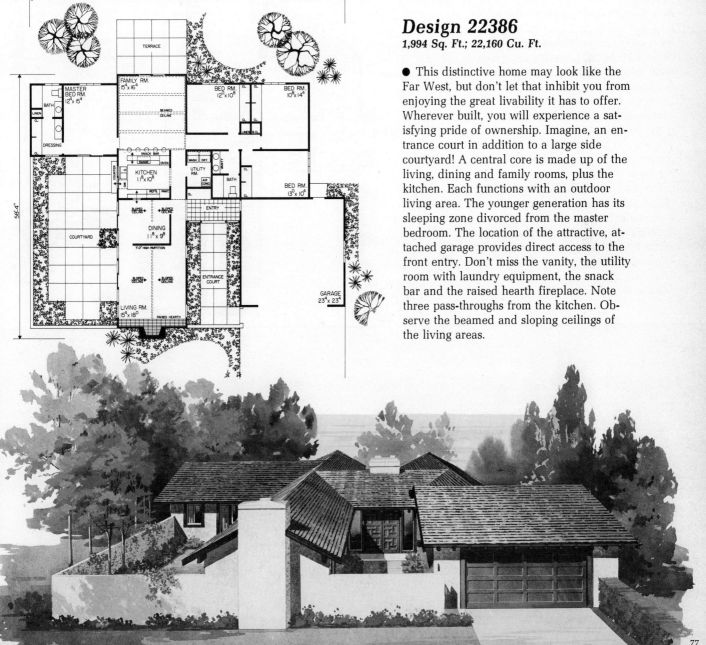

Design 22594
2,294 Sq. Ft.; 42,120 Cu. Ft.

● A spectacular foyer! It is fully 21' long and offers double entry to the heart of this home. Other highlights include a 21' by 21' gathering room complete with sloped ceiling, raised hearth fireplace and sliding glass doors. There's a formal dining room, too. Plus a well-located study which insures space for solitude or undisturbed work. The kitchen features a snack bar and a breakfast nook with another set of sliding doors. For more convenience, a pantry and first-floor laundry. In the master suite, a dressing room with entry to the bath, four closets and sliding doors onto the terrace! Two more bedrooms if you wish to convert the study or one easily large enough for two children with a dressing area and private entry to the second bath.

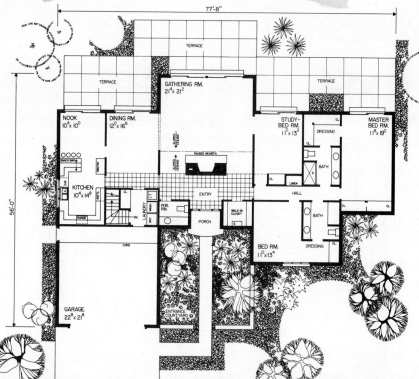

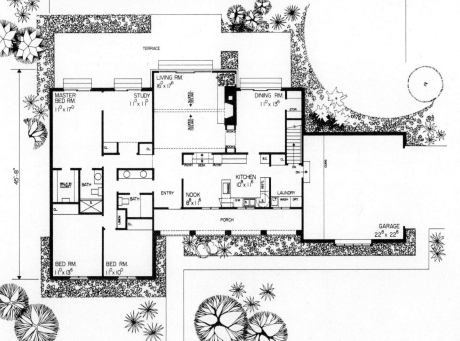

Design 22557
1,955 Sq. Ft.; 43,509 Cu. Ft.

● This eye-catching design with a flavor of the Spanish Southwest will be as interesting to live in as it will be to view from the street. The character of the exterior is set by the wide overhanging roof with its exposed beams; the massive arched pillars; the arching of the brick over the windows; the panelled door and the vertical siding that contrasts with the brick. The elegantly large master bedroom/study suite is a focal point of the interior. However, if necessary, the study could become the fourth bedroom. The living and dining rooms are separated by a massive raised hearth fireplace. All of the work center is in the front of the plan. It also has easy access to the garage and the basement.

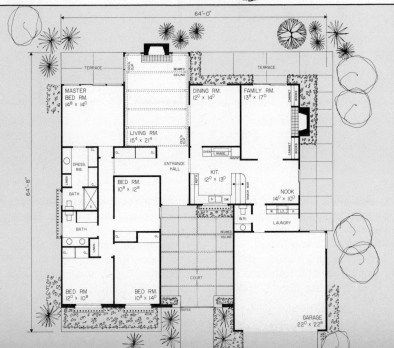

Design 22287
2,394 Sq. Ft.; 26,933 Cu. Ft.

● Here is a flat roof contemporary designed to be in harmony with the surroundings of the Far West. Yet, its fine proportions and sleek appearance would be a credit wherever built. Here, again, the covered court fosters a peaceful, welcoming atmosphere on the way to the front door. The center entrance hall routes traffic efficiently to the main areas. The kitchen is strategically located — handy to the front door, only a step from the two eating areas and just around the corner from the laundry and entrance from the garage. The formal, living room functions well with the dining room. The family room is ideally located, too. It is close to the kitchen and directly accessible to the outdoors. Study the sleeping area.

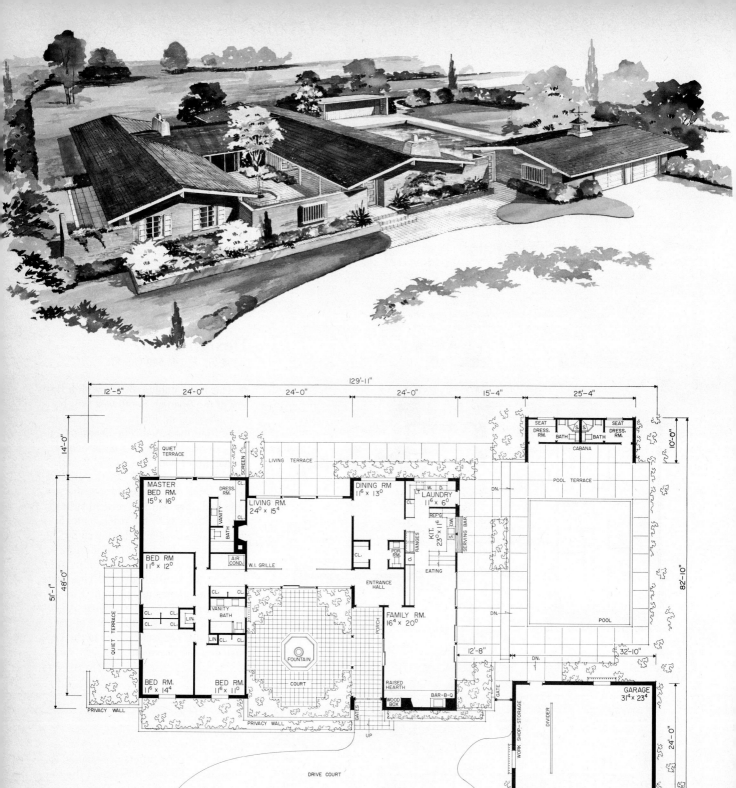

Design 21756 *2,736 Sq. Ft.; 29,139 Cu. Ft.*

● Reminiscent of the West and impressive, indeed. If you are after something that is luxurious in both its appearance and its livability this design should receive your consideration. This rambling ranch house, which encloses a spacious and dra- matic flower court, is designed for comfort and privacy indoors and out. Study the outdoor areas. Notice the seclusion each of them provides. Three bedrooms, plus a master suite with dressing room and bath form a private bedroom wing. Formal and informal living areas serve ideally for various types of entertaining. There is excellent circulation of traffic throughout the house. The kitchen is handy to the formal dining room and the informal family room. Don't miss raised hearth fireplace.

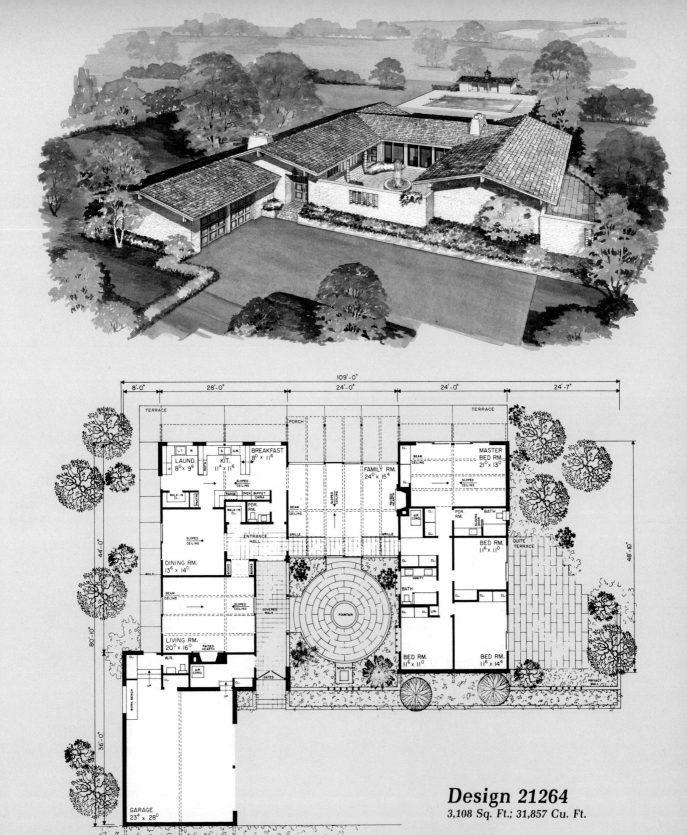

Design 21264
3,108 Sq. Ft.; 31,857 Cu. Ft.

● A romantic adaptation from the Spanish Southwest. This design is truly distinctive, both in its exterior styling and in its gracious floor plan. Its exterior beauty is characterized by the series of low-pitched, overhanging roofs, the extended rafter ends,

the blank masonry wall masses and the paneled double front gates. Behind the front privacy wall is the unique, enclosed court. The stroll up the covered walk to the entrance hall will be a delightful experience, indeed. The entrance hall routes traffic

to the formal dining and living rooms, the efficient work center and to the passageway between the family room and court to the four bedroom sleeping wing. Study the many other features. You will be able to make a long list.

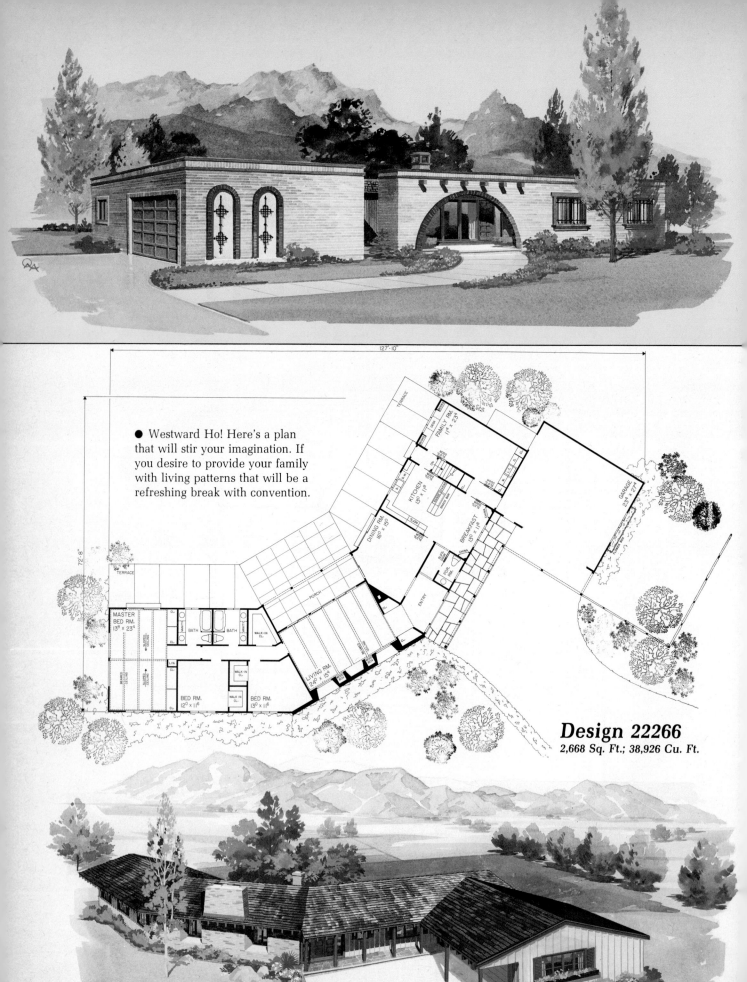

● Westward Ho! Here's a plan that will stir your imagination. If you desire to provide your family with living patterns that will be a refreshing break with convention.

Design 22266
2,668 Sq. Ft.; 38,926 Cu. Ft.

Floor plan labels:
- CORREDOR 42⁶ x 10⁴
- PATIO
- MAID'S RM.- HOBBY RM. 13⁸ x 10⁶
- KITCHEN 10⁰ x 15⁶
- NOOK 6⁰ x 15⁶
- FAMILY RM. 20⁰ x 15⁶
- SUNKEN TUB
- HER BATH
- MASTER BED RM. 17⁴ x 15⁶
- HIS BATH
- LAUNDRY
- UTILITY RM.
- AIR COND.
- BATH
- WALK-IN CLOSET
- DINING RM. 12⁰ x 13⁶
- LIVING RM. 19⁸ x 13⁶
- FOYER
- BATH
- GARAGE 23⁴ x 22⁸
- COVERED PORCH
- BED RM. 12⁰ x 13⁴
- BED RM. 12⁰ x 13⁴

Dimensions: 93'-2", 46'-6"

Design
2,740 Sq. Ft.;

● The features that will appeal to you about this flat-roofed Spanish hacienda are almost endless. Of course, the captivating qualities of the exterior speak for themselves. The extension of the front bedroom wall to form the inviting arch is distinctive. Once inside, any list of features will continue to grow rapidly. Both the family and living rooms are sunken. Private patio adjacent to the master suite.

Design 22258 2,504 Sq. Ft.; 26,292 Cu. Ft.

● Here's a real Western Ranch House with all the appeal of its forebears. As for the livability offered by this angular design, the old days of the rugged west never had anything like this.

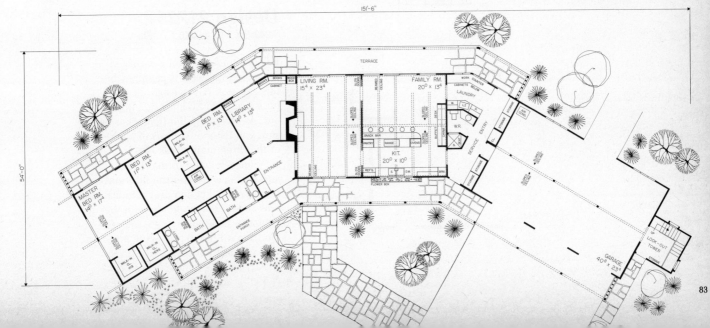

Floor plan labels:
- TERRACE
- LIVING RM. 15⁴ x 23⁴
- FAMILY RM. 20⁰ x 13⁴
- LIBRARY 14⁴ x 13⁶
- BED RM. 11⁰ x 15⁴
- LAUNDRY
- SERVICE ENTRY
- W.R.
- SNACK BAR
- PANTRY
- RANGE
- OVENS
- KIT. 20⁰ x 10⁰
- REF'S.
- MASTER BED RM. 14⁰ x 17⁴
- BED RM. 11⁰ x 13⁴
- BATH
- ENTRANCE
- ENTRANCE PORCH
- FLOWER BOX
- GARAGE 40⁶ x 23³
- LOOK-OUT TOWER

Dimensions: 151'-6", 54'-0"

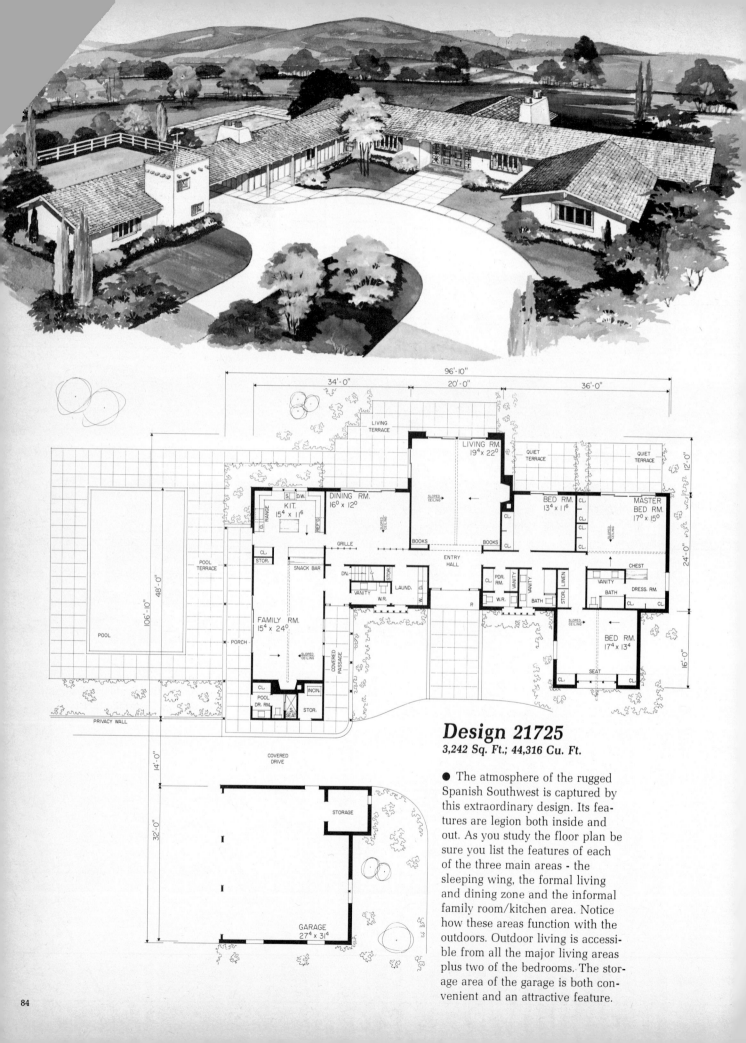

Design 21725
3,242 Sq. Ft.; 44,316 Cu. Ft.

● The atmosphere of the rugged Spanish Southwest is captured by this extraordinary design. Its features are legion both inside and out. As you study the floor plan be sure you list the features of each of the three main areas - the sleeping wing, the formal living and dining zone and the informal family room/kitchen area. Notice how these areas function with the outdoors. Outdoor living is accessible from all the major living areas plus two of the bedrooms. The storage area of the garage is both convenient and an attractive feature.

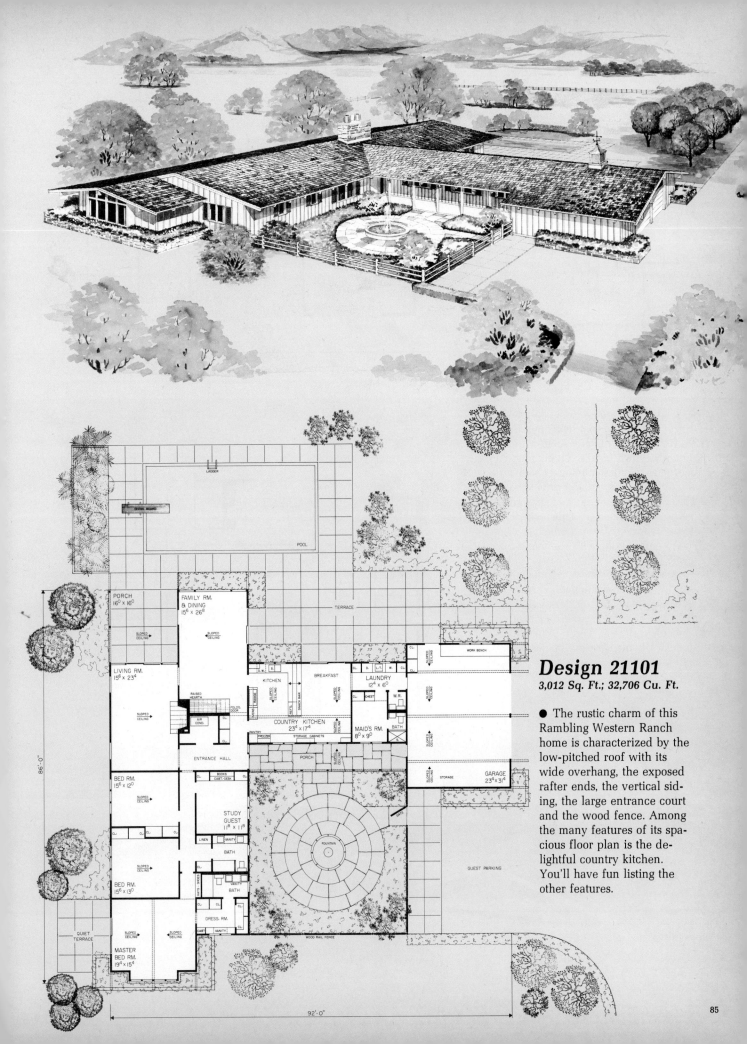

Design 21101
3,012 Sq. Ft.; 32,706 Cu. Ft.

● The rustic charm of this Rambling Western Ranch home is characterized by the low-pitched roof with its wide overhang, the exposed rafter ends, the vertical siding, the large entrance court and the wood fence. Among the many features of its spacious floor plan is the delightful country kitchen. You'll have fun listing the other features.

Floor plan labels:

LADDER

DIVING BOARD

POOL

PORCH 16⁶ x 16⁰

FAMILY RM. & DINING 15⁶ x 26⁸

TERRACE

WORK BENCH

LIVING RM. 15⁶ x 23⁴

SLOPED CEILING

RAISED HEARTH

KITCHEN

BREAKFAST

LAUNDRY 12⁴ x 6⁰

COUNTRY KITCHEN 23⁴ x 17⁴

MAID'S RM. 8⁰ x 9⁰

BATH

GARAGE 23⁴ x 31⁴

STORAGE

ENTRANCE HALL

PANTRY

FREEZER

STORAGE CABINETS

PORCH

BED RM. 15⁶ x 12⁰

BOOKS CABT.-DESK

STUDY GUEST 11⁸ x 11⁸

LINEN

VANITY

BATH

FOUNTAIN

BED RM. 15⁶ x 13⁰

BATH

VANITY

GUEST PARKING

DRESS. RM.

CABT. VANITY

QUIET TERRACE

MASTER BED RM. 19⁴ x 15⁴

WOOD RAIL FENCE

86'-0"

92'-0"

Design 21825

2,170 Sq. Ft.; 21,417 Cu. Ft.

● Five wonderful outdoor living areas headed by the front private court are highlights of this impressive U-shaped, four bedroom home. The low-pitched, wide overhanging roof, the exposed rafters, the grille work and the attractive gate are all features which remind one of the Spanish Southwest.

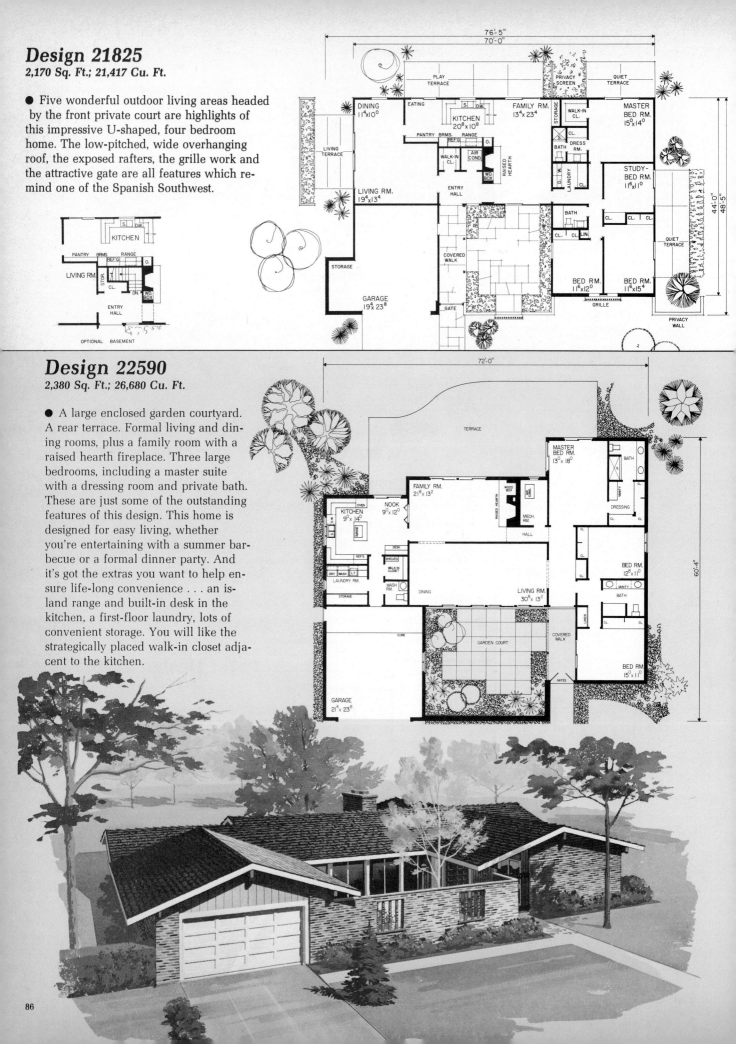

Design 22590

2,380 Sq. Ft.; 26,680 Cu. Ft.

● A large enclosed garden courtyard. A rear terrace. Formal living and dining rooms, plus a family room with a raised hearth fireplace. Three large bedrooms, including a master suite with a dressing room and private bath. These are just some of the outstanding features of this design. This home is designed for easy living, whether you're entertaining with a summer barbecue or a formal dinner party. And it's got the extras you want to help ensure life-long convenience . . . an island range and built-in desk in the kitchen, a first-floor laundry, lots of convenient storage. You will like the strategically placed walk-in closet adjacent to the kitchen.

Design 21754
2,080 Sq. Ft.; 21,426 Cu. Ft.

● Boasting a traditional Western flavor, this rugged U-shaped ranch home has all the features to assure grand living. The low-pitched, wide-overhanging roof with exposed rafters, the masses of brick, and the panelled doors with their carriage lamps above are among the exterior highlights which create this design's unique character. The private front flower court, inside the high brick wall, fosters a delightfully dramatic atmosphere which carries inside. The floor plan is positively unique and exceptionally livable. Wonderfully zoned, the three bedrooms enjoy their full measure of privacy. Observe the dressing room, walk-in closet and linen storage. The formal living and dining rooms function together in a most pleasing fashion. An attractive open railing separates the dining room from the sunken living room.

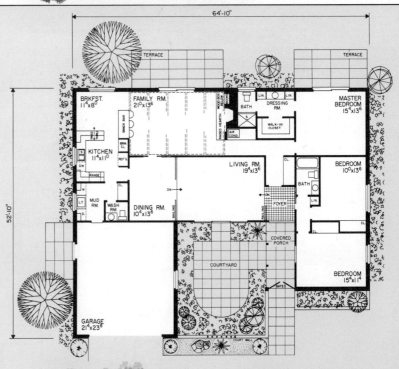

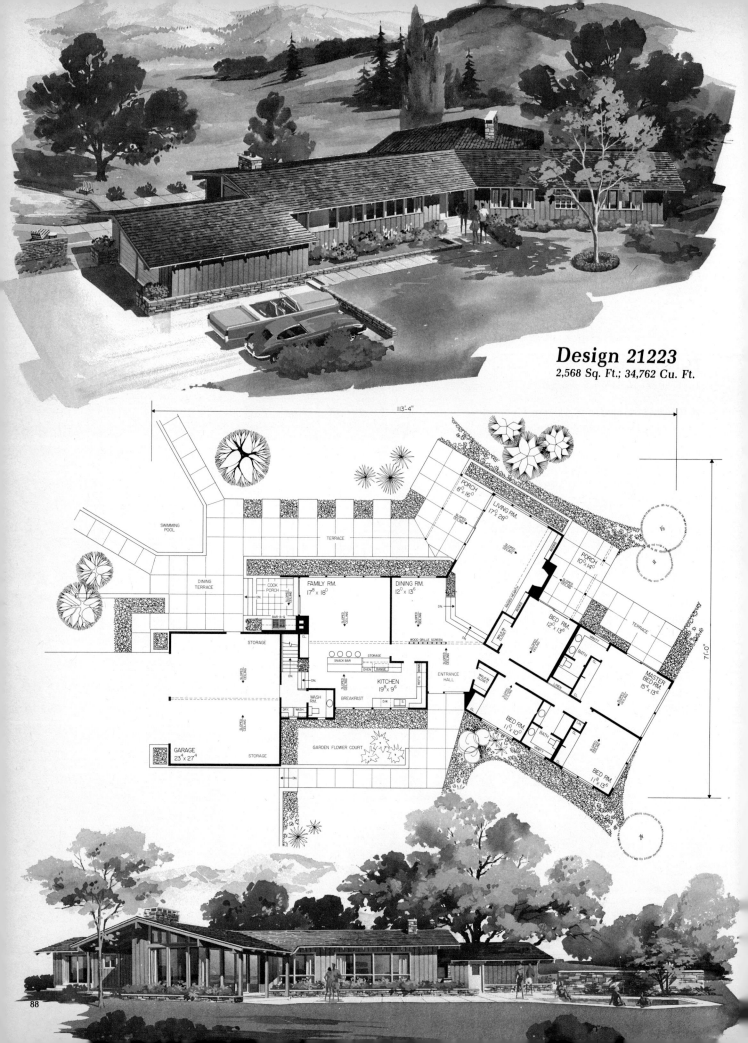

Design 21223
2,568 Sq. Ft.; 34,762 Cu. Ft.

FRENCH FACADES . . .

have an outstanding charm of their own. Their exterior appeal seems to announce a graciously formal lifestyle. The hip-roof is a distinguishing characteristic of the one-story French house. Shuttered casement windows, brick quoins at the corners of the house, cornice dentils, double front doors with raised panels, massive chimneys and cupolas are among other features that establish the style. In many cases arched window heads and shutters, recessed front entrances, wrought iron grillwork, carriage lamps and entry courts add an extra measure of appeal. In addition to the variety of interior living features, it is worth noting the outdoor living potential.

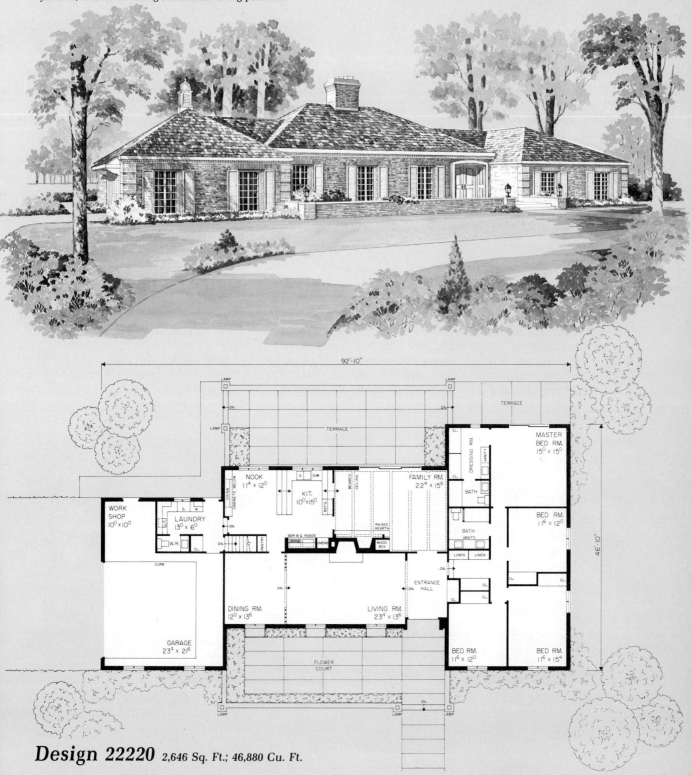

Design 22220 2,646 Sq. Ft.; 46,880 Cu. Ft.

● The gracious formality of this home is reminiscent of a popularly accepted French styling. The hip-roof, the brick quoins, the cornice details, the arched window heads, the distinctive shutters, the recessed double front doors, the massive center chimney, and the de-lightful flower court are all features which set the dramatic appeal of this home. This floor plan is a favorite of many. The four bedroom, two bath sleeping wing is a zone by itself. Further, the formal living and dining rooms are ideally located. For enter-taining they function well together and look out upon the pleasant flower court. Overlooking the raised living terrace at the rear are the family and breakfast rooms and work center. Don't miss the laundry, extra wash room and work shop in garage.

● You'll want life's biggest investment — the purchase of a home — to be a source of everlasting enjoyment. To assure such a rewarding dividend, make every effort to match your family's desired living patterns with a workable plan. Of course, you'll want your plan enveloped by a stunning exterior. Consider both the interior and exterior of this design. Each is impressive. The sleeping zone comprises a separate wing and is accessible from both living and kitchen areas. There are four bedrooms, two full baths and plenty of closets. The 32 foot wide living and dining area will be just great fun to decorate. Then, there is the large family room with its raised hearth fireplace and sliding glass doors to the terrace. Note the fine laundry with wash room nearby. The extra curb area in the garage is great for storing small garden equipment.

● This French design is surely impressive. The exterior appearance will brighten any area with its French roof, paned-glass windows, masonry brick privacy wall and double front doors. The inside is just as appealing. Note the unique placement of rooms and features. The entry hall is large and leads to each of the areas in this plan. The formal dining room is outstanding and guests can enter through the entry hall. While serving one can enter by way of the butler's pantry (notice it's size and that it has a sink). To the right of the entry is a sizable parlor. Then there is the gathering room with fireplace, sliding glass doors and adjacent study. The work center is also outstanding. There is the U-shaped kitchen, island range, snack bar, breakfast nook, pantry plus wash room and large laundry near service entrance. Basement stairs are also nearby.

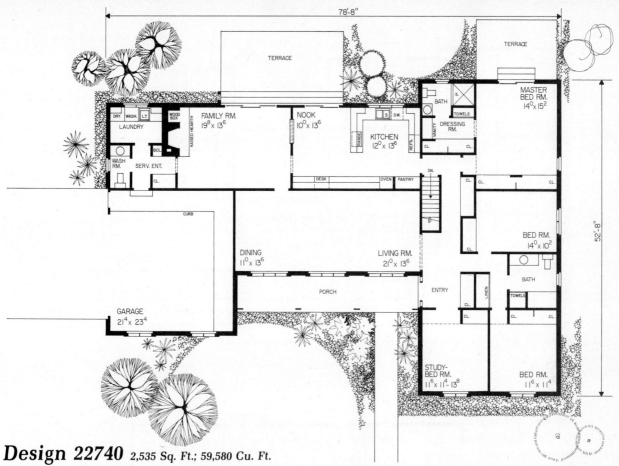

Design 22740 2,535 Sq. Ft.; 59,580 Cu. Ft.

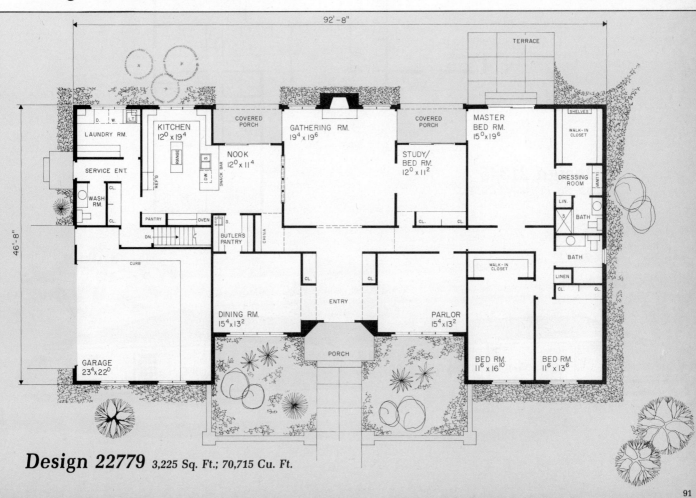

Design 22779 3,225 Sq. Ft.; 70,715 Cu. Ft.

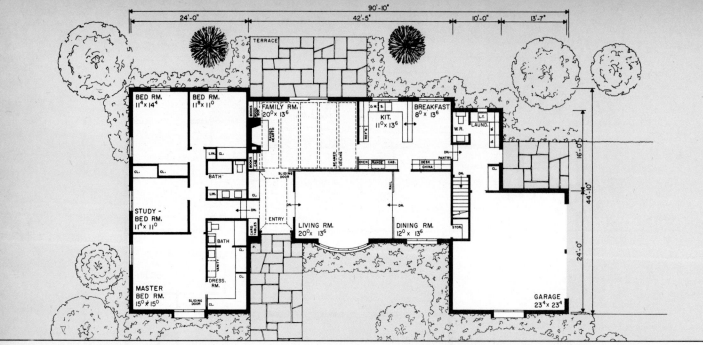

● Here are three delightful French Provincial adaptations, any one of which would surely be an impressive addition to a neighborhood. Each design features a sleeping wing of four bedrooms, two full baths, and plenty of closets. Further, each design has a separate first floor laundry with an adjacent wash room. Observe the sunken living room . . .

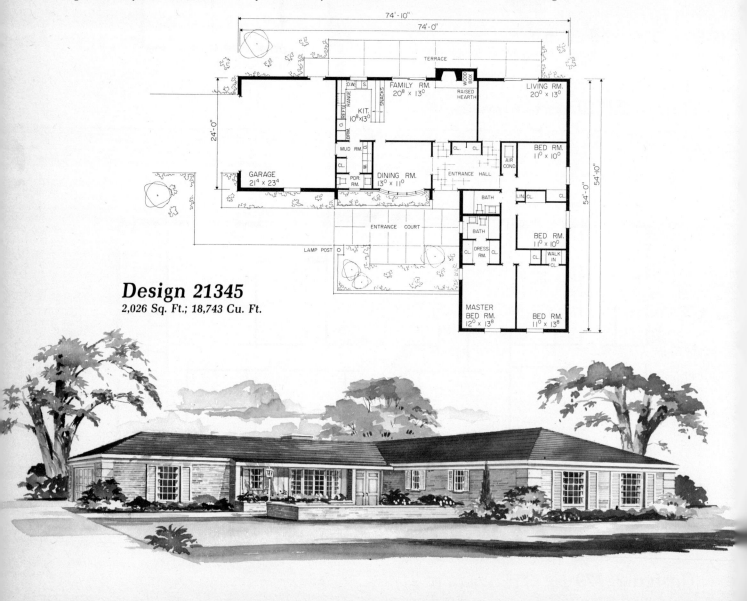

Design 21345
2,026 Sq. Ft.; 18,743 Cu. Ft.

Design 22134 2,530 Sq. Ft.; 44,458 Cu. Ft.

. . . and the beamed ceiling family room of Design 22134 above. Don't miss its big dressing room or raised hearth fireplace. Design 21345 has both its family and living rooms located to the rear and functioning with the terrace. Design 21054 has an efficient work area and a large formal dining room.

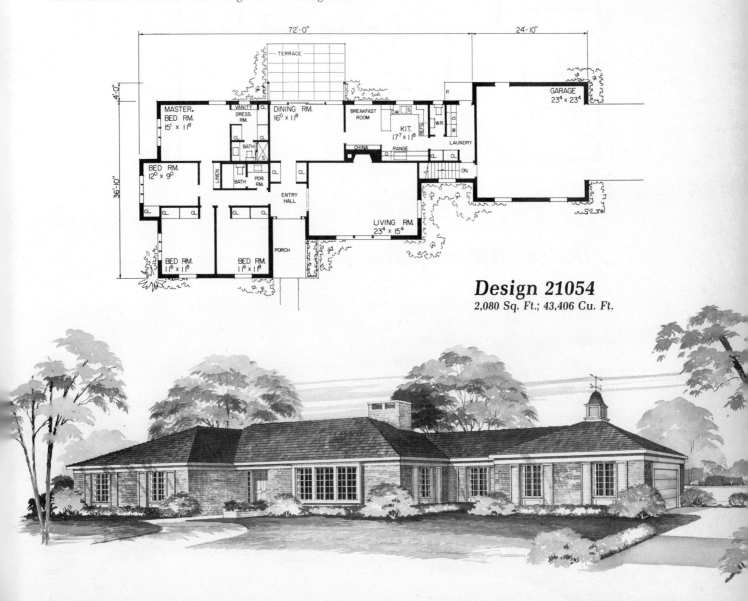

Design 21054
2,080 Sq. Ft.; 43,406 Cu. Ft.

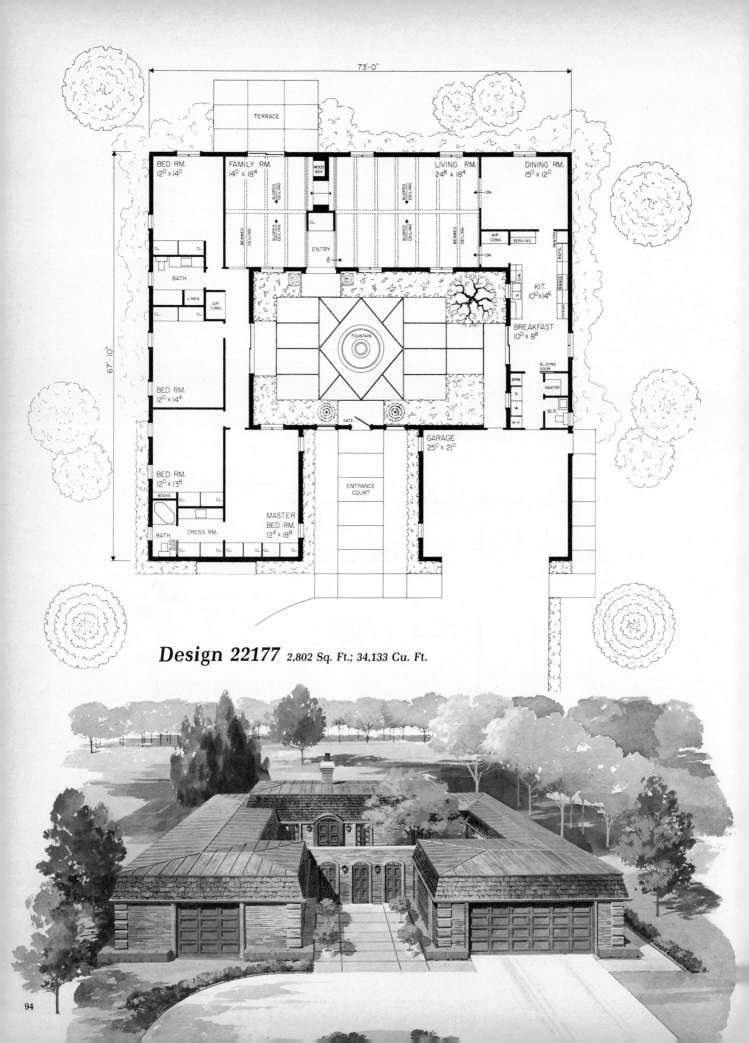

73'-0"

67'-10"

TERRACE

BED RM.
12⁰ x 14⁰

FAMILY RM.
14⁰ x 18⁴

WOOD BOX

LIVING RM.
24⁸ x 18⁴

DINING RM.
15⁰ x 12⁰

BEAMED CEILING

SLOPED CEILING

SLOPED CEILING

SLOPED CEILING

BEAMED CEILING

DN.

AIR COND.

SERVING

PANTRY

REFG'L

CL.

CL.

BATH

ENTRY

DN.

DN.

LINEN

AIR COND.

CL.

CL.

S.

D.W.

RANGE

OVENS

KIT.
10⁰ x 14⁶

FOUNTAIN

BREAKFAST
10⁰ x 8⁸

BED RM.
12⁰ x 14⁴

B.RM.
D.
W.

SLIDING DOOR

PANTRY

W.R.

W.H.

GATE

BED RM.
12⁰ x 13⁸

GARAGE
25⁰ x 21⁰

BOOKS

CL.

CL.

BATH

SLDG. DOOR

DRESS. RM.

CL.

CL.

CL.

MASTER BED RM.
12⁸ x 18⁸

ENTRANCE COURT

Design 22177 2,802 Sq. Ft.; 34,133 Cu. Ft.

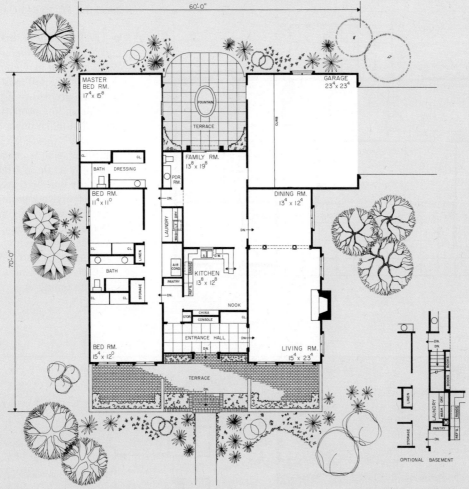

Design 22347 2,322 Sq. Ft.; 26,572 Cu. Ft.

● The regal character of this distinctive home is most inviting. The symmetry of the front exterior is enhanced by the raised terrace. The recessed front entrance shelters panelled double doors which open to the formal hall. Traffic may pass to the right directly into the sunken living room. To the left is the sunken three bedroom, two-bath sleeping area. The center of the plan features the efficient kitchen with nook space and the family room. The rear terrace, enclosed on three sides to assure privacy, is accessible from master bedroom, as well as family room, through sliding glass doors. Separating the formal living and dining rooms are finely proportioned, round wood columns. Don't overlook the first floor laundry. Blueprints include details for optional partial basement.

Design 22179
2,439 Sq. Ft.; 33,043 Cu. Ft.

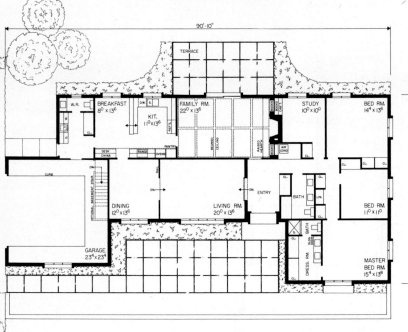

● The formality of this French adaptation is a pleasing picture to behold. Wherever you may choose to build it, this one-story will most assuredly receive the accolades of passers-by. It is the outstanding proportion and the fine detail that make this a home of distinction. What's inside is every bit as delightful as what is outside. Your family will enjoy its three sizable bedrooms. The study will be a favorite haven for those who wish a period of peace and quiet. The sunken living room and the informal family room offer two large areas for family living. For eating there is the breakfast and separate dining room. Two baths and extra wash room serve the family well.

Design 22851
2,739 Sq. Ft.; 55,810 Cu. Ft.

● This spacious one-story has a classic Country French hip roof. The front entrance creates a charming entry. Beyond the covered porch is an octagonal foyer. A closet, shelves and powder room are contained in the foyer. All of the living areas overlook the rear yard. Sliding glass doors open each of these areas to the rear terrace. Their features include a fireplace in the living room, skylight in the dining room and a second set of sliding glass doors in the family room leading to a side covered porch. An island range and other built-ins are featured in the spacious, front kitchen.

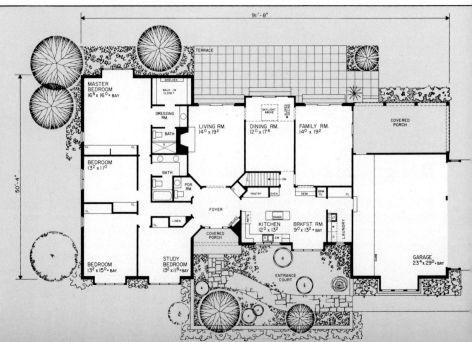

Design 21892

2,036 Sq. Ft.; 26,575 Cu. Ft.

● The romance of French Provincial is captured here by the hip-roof masses, the charm of the window detailing, the brick quoins at the corners, the delicate dentil work at the cornices, the massive centered chimney, and the recessed double front doors. The slightly raised entry court completes the picture. The basic floor plan is a favorite of many. And little wonder, for all areas work well together, while still maintaining a fine degree of separation of functions. The highlight of the interior, perhaps, will be the sunken living room. The family room, with its beamed ceiling, will not be far behind in its popularity. The separate dining room, mud room, efficient kitchen, complete the livability.

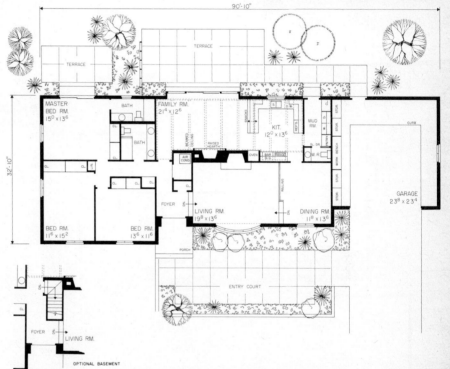

Design 21363

2,078 Sq. Ft.; 23,637 Cu. Ft.

● Picture this impressive L-shaped home with its French detailing sitting on your site just waiting for you and your family to move in. It will certainly be a glorious day. However, before the first shovel full of ground is turned you will have fun deciding upon the options this designs offers. As shown by the illustrations, you have your choice of building with or without a basement. Further, you may want to decide to have a fireplace flanked by bookshelves located in the living room. This family oriented design has four bedrooms. The master bedroom has its own private bath, while the three children's bedrooms are served by the main bath.

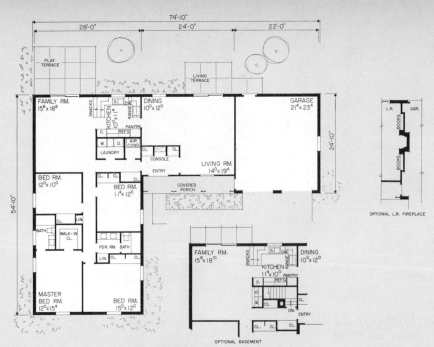

Design 21874

2,307 Sq. Ft.; 39,922 Cu. Ft.

● Certainly the exterior of this French adaptation with its hip-roof, wrought iron, attractive windows, brick quoins at the corners, and cupola, doesn't look familiar. Here is truly good design — in high style. Nor is the interior likely to look very familiar, either. Have you ever seen quite the livability this one-story has to offer? There are five bedrooms, 2½ baths, separate dining room, informal family room, efficient kitchen, convenient laundry, and an attached two-car garage. The storage is outstanding. There are plenty of wardrobe closets, linen storage, china cabinet, kitchen cupboard, and laundry cabinets. There is even a storage unit on the covered front porch.

Design 21881

2,472 Sq. Ft.; 44,434 Cu. Ft.

● Whether you park your car in the garage as the owner of this attractive home, or in the area reserved for guests, you'll be sure to appreciate all that this design has to offer. Its appealing exterior is one which will forever serve the family ideally. Once inside, you are but a few steps from the family and living rooms. The kitchen is but a couple of steps beyond the laundry and wash room with the informal family room just around the corner. Whether enjoyed to the front or the rear of this home, outdoor living will be gracious, indeed. Note the covered porch and the terraces in the rear. There are three of them!

Design 21228 2,583 Sq. Ft. - First Floor; 697 Sq. Ft. - Second Floor; 51,429 Cu. Ft.

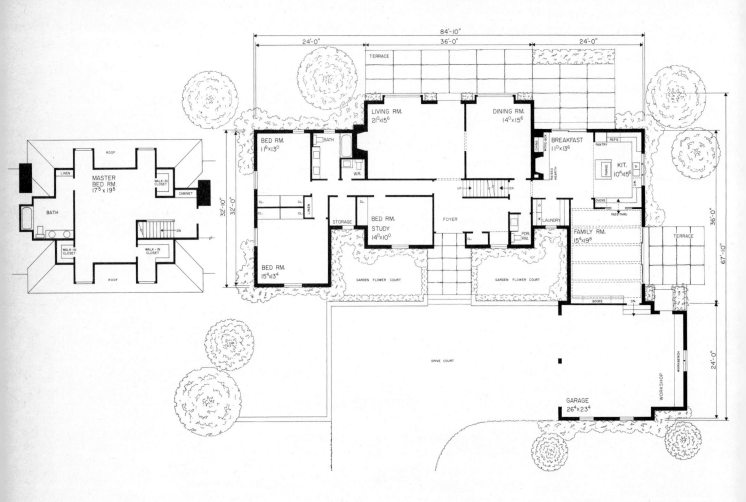

● This beautiful house has a wealth of detail taken from the rich traditions of French Regency design. The roof itself is a study in pleasant dormers and the hips and valleys of a big flowing area. A close examination of the plan shows the careful arrangement of space for privacy as well as good circulation of traffic. The spacious formal entrance hall sets the stage for good zoning. The informal living area is highlighted by the updated version of the old country kitchen. Observe the fireplace, and the barbecue. While there is a half-story devoted to the master bedroom suite, this home functions more as a one-story country estate design than as a 1½ story.

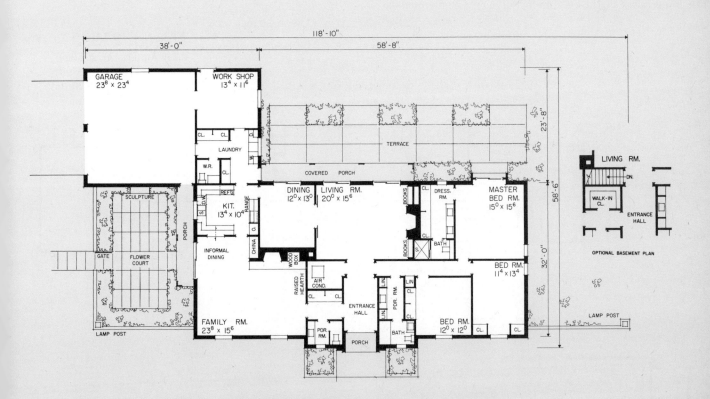

Design 21784 2,686 Sq. Ft.; 32,515 Cu. Ft.

● Truly impressive, and surely a home of which dreams are made. Yet, its basic rectangular shape, its economical use of space, its tremendous livability and its outstanding design make it a worthy lifetime investment. Consider the features which will serve you so well and make you such a proud home-owner for so many years to come. The pleasant formality of the front entrance invites one through the double front doors to a spacious interior. Study the zoning. The formal living and dining rooms will enjoy their deserved privacy and function with their own rear outdoor living facilities. The family room and kitchen function together and have an enclosed court.

● The elegance of pleasing proportion and delightful detailing has seldom been better exemplified than by this classic French country manor adaptation. Approaching the house across the drive court, the majesty of this multi-roofed structure is breathtaking, indeed. An outstanding feature is the maid's suite. It is located above the garage and is easily reached by use of the covered porch connecting the laundry room's service entrance to the garage. If desired, it would make an excellent studio, quiet retreat or even a game room.

Design 21993

2,658 Sq. Ft. - First Floor
840 Sq. Ft. - Master Suite
376 Sq. Ft. - Maid's Suite
57,057 Cu. Ft.

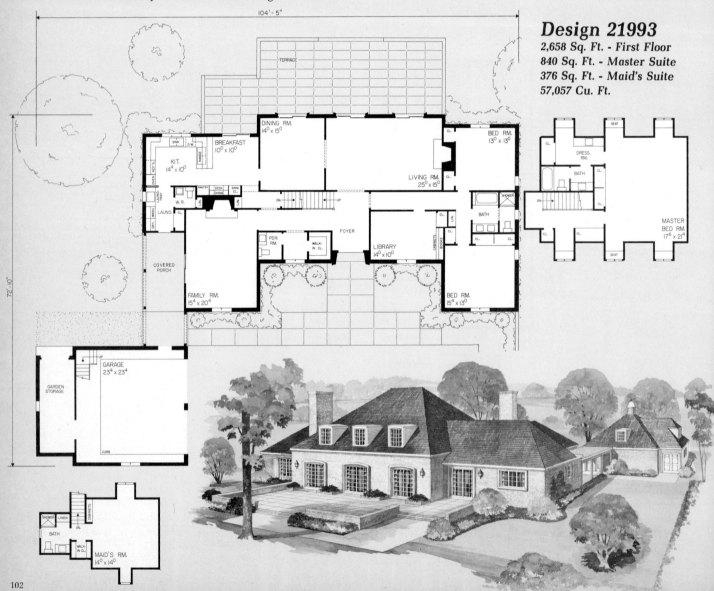

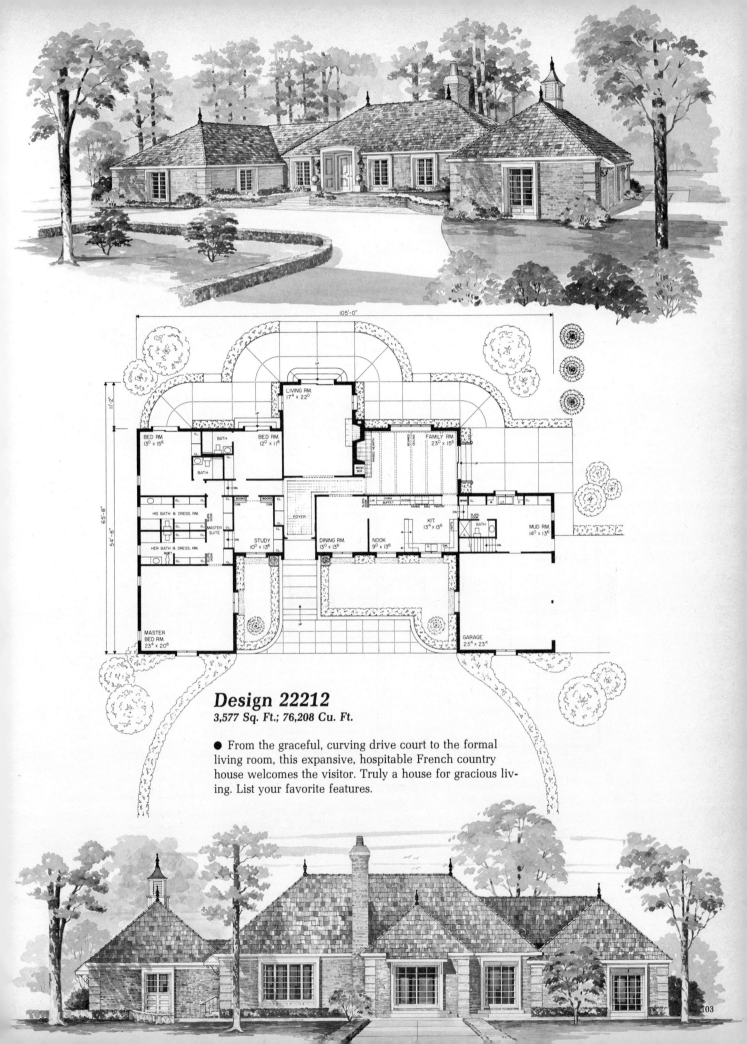

Design 22212
3,577 Sq. Ft.; 76,208 Cu. Ft.

● From the graceful, curving drive court to the formal living room, this expansive, hospitable French country house welcomes the visitor. Truly a house for gracious living. List your favorite features.

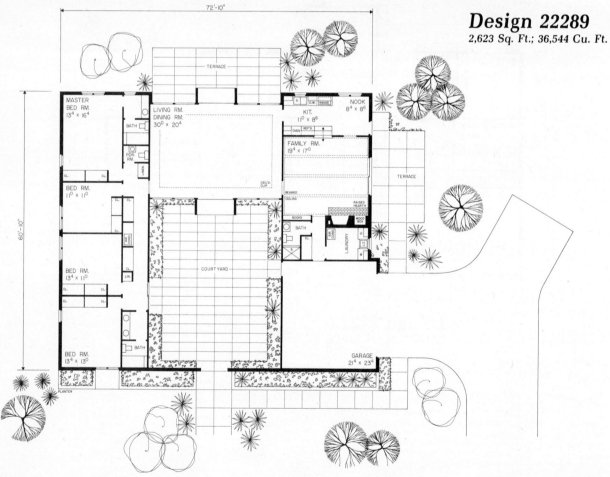

Design 22289

2,623 Sq. Ft.; 36,544 Cu. Ft.

● Impressive? You bet it is! And, as a matter of fact, it looks almost palatial. It is easy to guess that there will be as much fun (and maybe more) in that huge court yard as in any other part of the unique plan. The formality of the exterior is derived from the trim plant-ing areas and the contemporary adap-tation of the French Mansard roof. The two-story effect of the front entrance is, indeed, dramatic. Separating the peaceful sleeping wing is the formal living-dining area. Measuring 30 x 20 feet, this will be a real joy to furnish. With all that glass and the 17 foot ceil-ing, spaciousness will be the byword. The kitchen — family room — laundry area functions well. Don't miss the three full baths, the raised hearth fire-place or the breakfast nook. Note the pass-thru from kitchen to family room.

COUNTRY-ESTATE DESIGNS...

as high-lighted in this interesting section have both traditional and contemporary exteriors. Each design offers square footage between 3000 and 3809 sq. ft. In a couple of designs, bonus square footage and livability are picked-up by the addition of the upstairs sleeping quarters. These houses deliver all the livability potential and amenities one would want in a house designed for the unrestricted budget. Provisions are made for both formal and informal living patterns. Flexible and varied indoor-outdoor living relationships have been provided. The configurations of these floor plans are important for they represent, with thoughtful siting, the opportunity to enjoy solar orientation.

Design 22888
3,018 Sq. Ft.; 59,769 Cu. Ft.

● This is an outstanding Early American design for the 20th-Century. The exterior detailing with narrow clap boards, multi-paned windows and cupola are the features of yesteryear. Interior planning, though, is for today's active family. Formal living room, in-formal family room plus a study are present. Every activity will have its place in this home. Picture yourself working in the kitchen. There's enough counter space for two or three helpers. Four bedrooms are in the private area. Stop and imagine your daily routine if you occupied the master bedroom. Both you and your spouse would have plenty of space and privacy. The flower porch, accessible from the master bedroom, living and dining rooms, is a very delightful "plus" feature. Study this design's every detail.

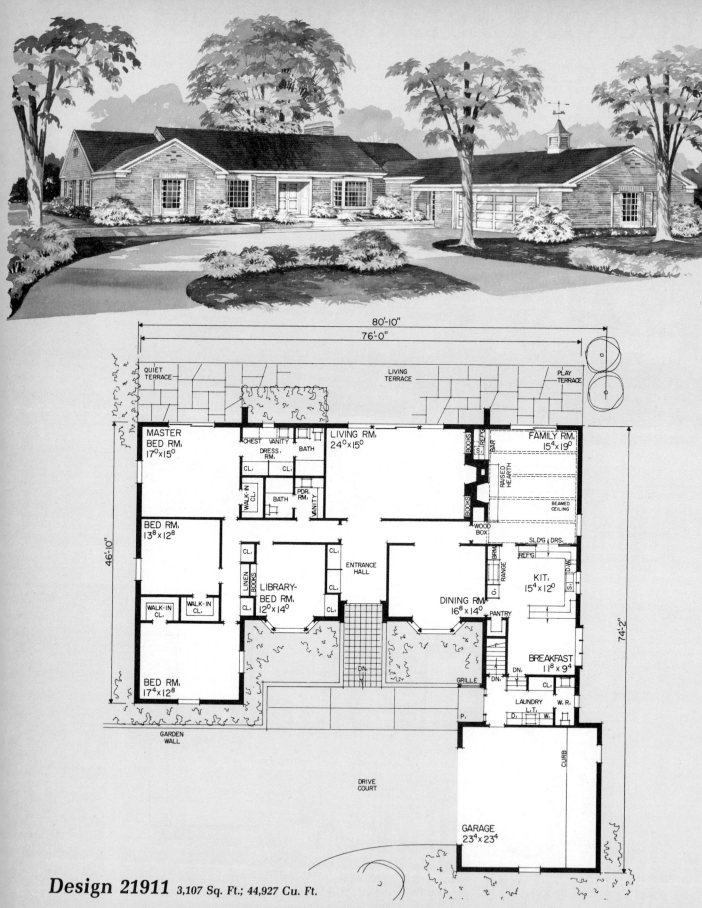

Design 21911 3,107 Sq. Ft.; 44,927 Cu. Ft.

● For luxurious, country-estate living it would be difficult to beat the livability offered by these two impressive traditional designs. To begin with, their exterior appeal is, indeed, gracious. Their floor plans highlight plenty of space, excellent room arrangements, fine traffic circulation, and an abundance of convenient living features. It is interesting to note that each design features similar livability facilities. Both may function as four bedroom homes . . .

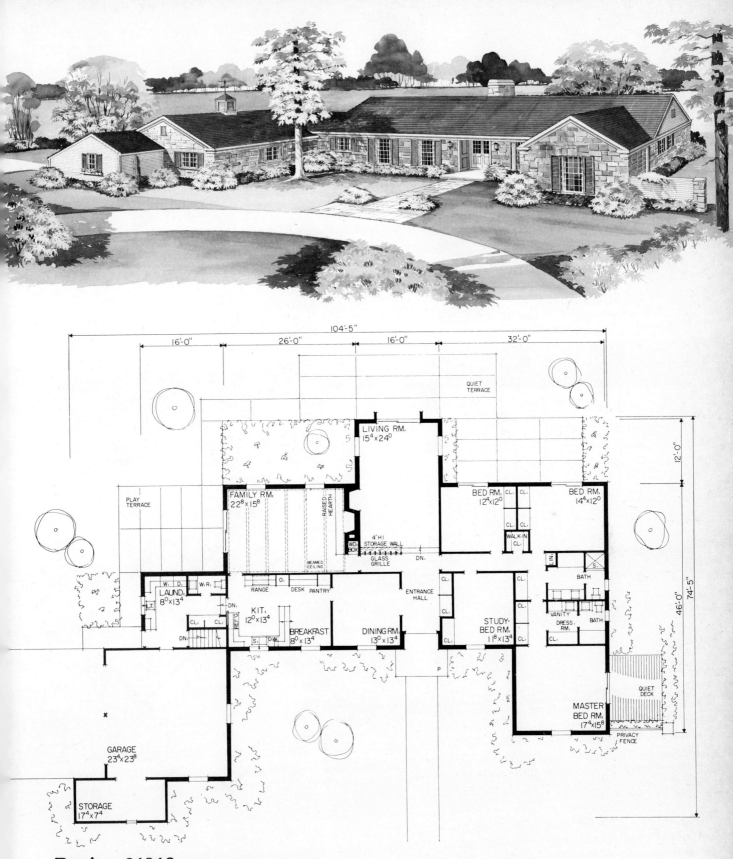

Design 21916 3,024 Sq. Ft.; 46,470 Cu. Ft.

● . . . or three bedroom with a study or library. There are first floor laundries, two fireplaces, formal and informal living and dining areas, fine storage potential, and delightful indoor-outdoor living relationships. You'll have fun listing the built-in features. The two family rooms have beamed ceilings and sliding glass doors to the play terraces. The two living rooms are spacious and enjoy a full measure of privacy. They are but a step from outdoor living.

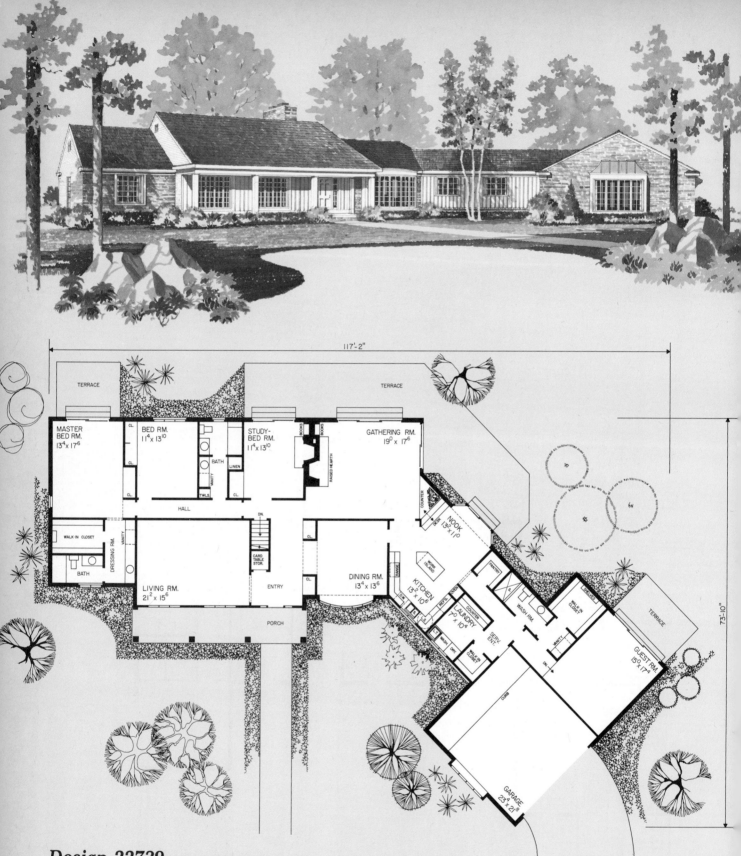

Design 22739 3,313 Sq. Ft.; 65,230 Cu. Ft.

● If you and your family are looking for new living patterns, try to envision your days spent in this traditionally styled home. Its Early American flavor is captured by effective window and door treatment, cornice work and porch pillars. Its zoning is interesting.

The spacious interior leaves nothing to be desired. There are three bedrooms and two full baths in the sleeping area. A quiet, formal living room is separated from the other living areas. The gathering and dining rooms are adjacent to each other and function with

the excellent kitchen and its breakfast eating area. Note work island, pantry and pass-thru. Then, there is an extra guest room sunken one step. A live-in relative would enjoy the privacy of this room. Full bath is nearby. This is definitely a home for all to enjoy.

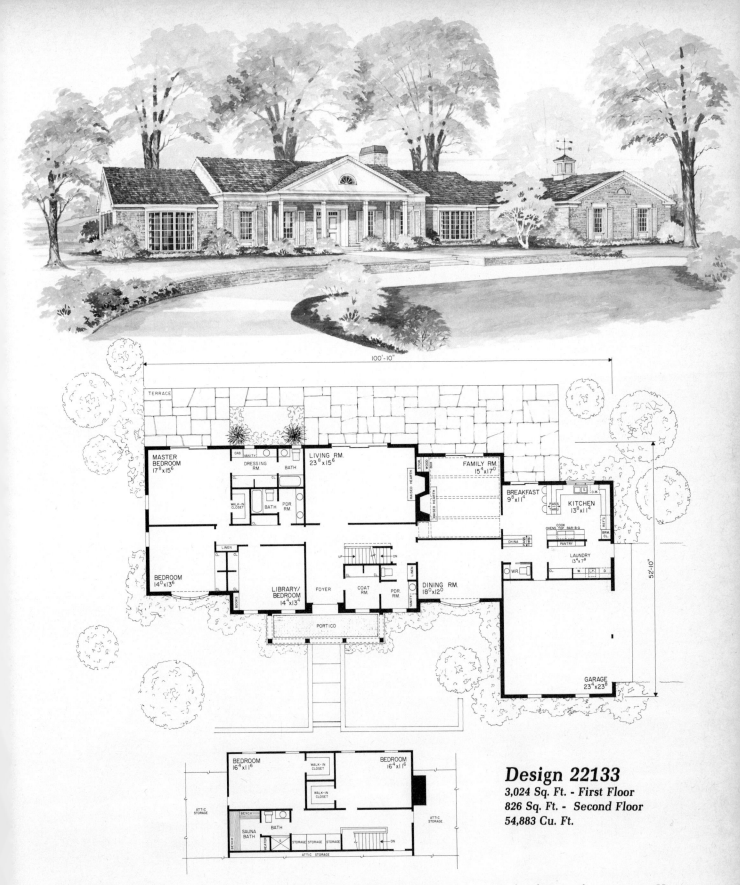

Design 22133

3,024 Sq. Ft. - First Floor
826 Sq. Ft. - Second Floor
54,883 Cu. Ft.

● A country-estate home which will command all the attention it truly deserves. The projecting pediment gable supported by the finely proportioned columns lends an aura of elegance. The window treatment, the front door detailing, the massive, capped, chimney, the cupola, the brick veneer exterior and the varying roof planes complete the characterization of this impressive home. Inside, there are 3,024 square feet on the first floor. In addition, there is a two bedroom second floor should its development be necessary. However, whether called upon to function as a one, or 1½ story home it will provide a lifetime of gracious living. Don't overlook the compartment baths, the laundry and the many built-ins available.

Design 22783

3,210 Sq. Ft.; 57,595 Cu. Ft.

● The configuration of this traditional design is outstanding indeed. The garage-bedroom wing on one side and the master bedroom on the other create an inviting, U-shaped entry court. This area is raised two steps from the driveway and has a 6 foot high masonry wall with coach lamps for an added attraction. Upon entrance through the double front doors, one will begin to enjoy the livability that this design has to offer. Each room is well planned and deserves praise. The sizable master bedroom has a fireplace and sliding glass doors to the entry court. Another sizable room, the gathering room, has access to the rear terrace, along with the dining room, family room and rear bedroom. An interior kitchen is adjacent to each of the major rooms.

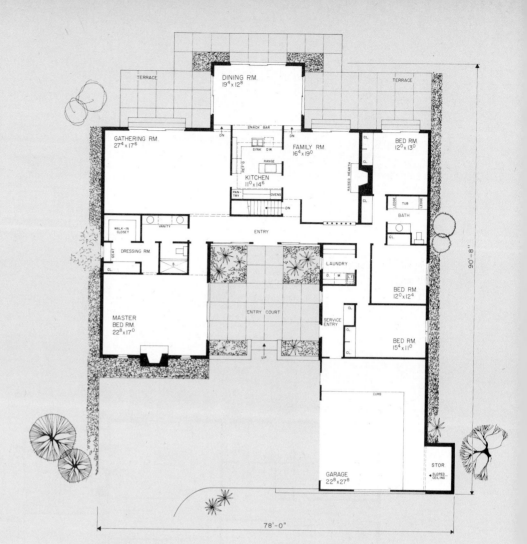

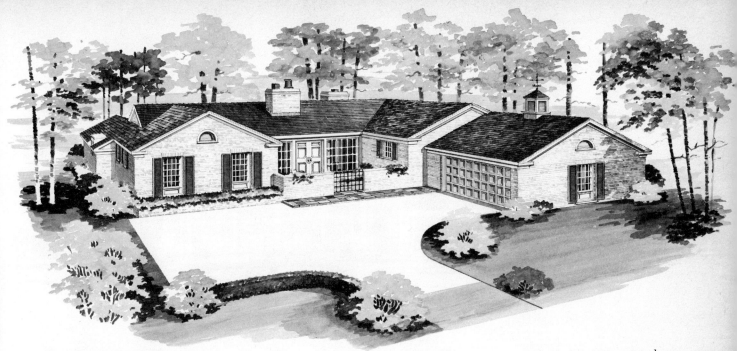

Design 22183 3,074 Sq. Ft.; 33,587 Cu. Ft.

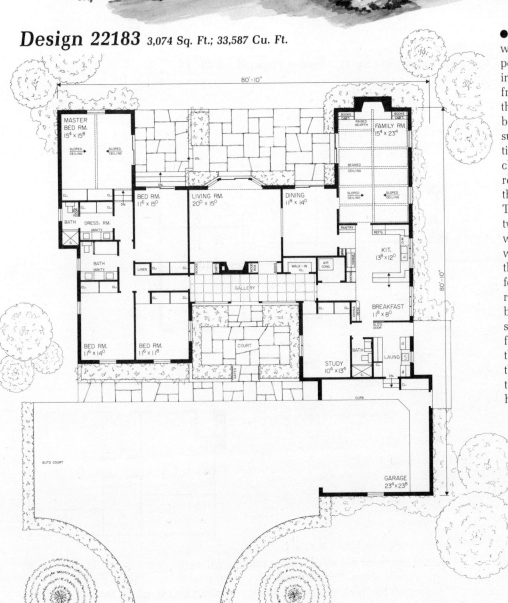

● A great country-estate home with unsurpassed exterior appeal and positively outstanding interior livability. The enclosed front courtyard is just one of the many features that contribute to the air of distinction surrounding this pleasing traditional design. The floor plan includes everything one would require to guarantee his family the ultimate in gracious living. There are four bedrooms and two full baths in the sleeping wing, a large rear living room with bay window overlooking the back yard, formal and informal dining, family room with raised hearth fireplace and built-in book cabinets plus a study. The members of your family will have fun making their own lists of the features that are most appealing to them. What are your favorite highlights of this design?

Design 21060 3,190 Sq. Ft. - First Floor; 1,024 Sq. Ft. - Second Floor; 52,189 Cu. Ft.

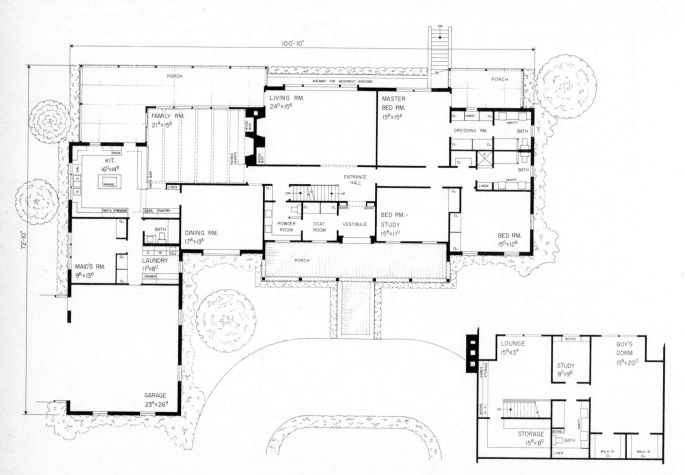

● Like some of the other designs of this section, this Colonial adaptation can be categorized as either a one or 1½ story home. However, you may opt to live in this home as a one-story. You may develop the second floor as sug-gested above, or not at all, except for attic storage space. Truly a home of distinction for the large family. Study this plan carefully. List its many fea-tures for this is certainly a unique home with unrestricted livability. It will serve your family's formal and in-formal living patterns during any occa-sion. Don't overlook the bath facilities, or the extra maid's room, adjacent to the laundry. It can be used as a family hobby room if you wish.

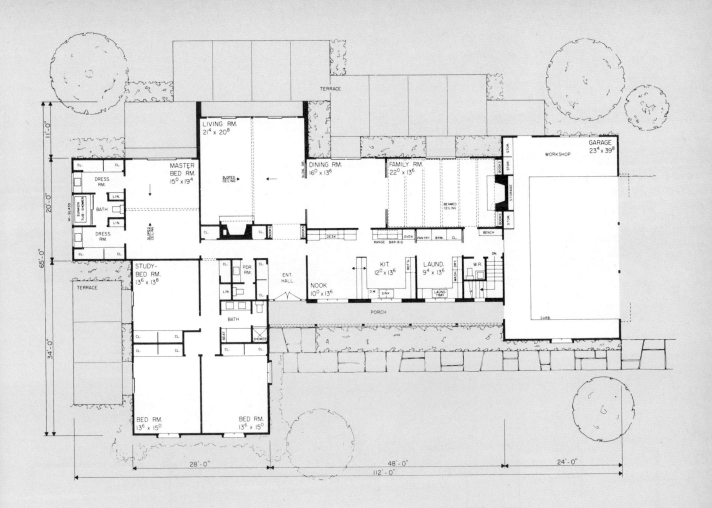

Design 21936 3,280 Sq. Ft.; 54,619 Cu. Ft.

● Country-estate living will be experienced in this 3,280 square foot home. The arrangement of the numerous rooms places the major living areas to the rear. They will enjoy their privacy and function with the outdoors. Count the sliding glass door units. Visualize the gracious indoor/outdoor living to be enjoyed by all the members of the family. Even the children's rooms have a terrace. The homemaker's work center overlooks the front yard and is efficient, indeed. There is a breakfast nook, a U-shaped kitchen, a separate laundry room, an extra washroom, and a whole wall of storage facilities. Be sure you notice the powder room near the entrance hall.

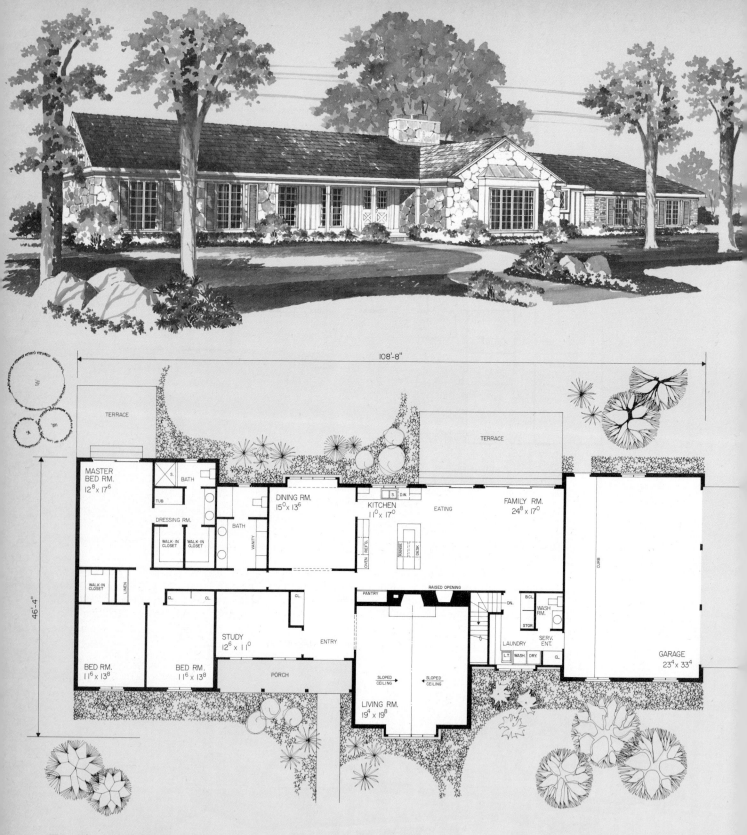

Design 22767 3,000 Sq. Ft.; 58,460 Cu. Ft.

● What a sound investment this impressive home will be. And while its value withstands the inflationary pressures of ensuing years, it will serve your family well. It has all the amenities to assure truly pleasurable living. The charming exterior will lend itself

to treatment other than the appealing fieldstone, brick and frame shown. Inside, the plan will impress you with large, spacious living areas, formal and informal dining areas, three large bedrooms, two full baths with twin lavatories, walk-in closets and a fine study.

The kitchen features an island work center with range and desk. The two fireplaces will warm their surroundings in both areas. Two separate terraces for a variety of uses. Note laundry, wash room and three-car garage with extra curb area.

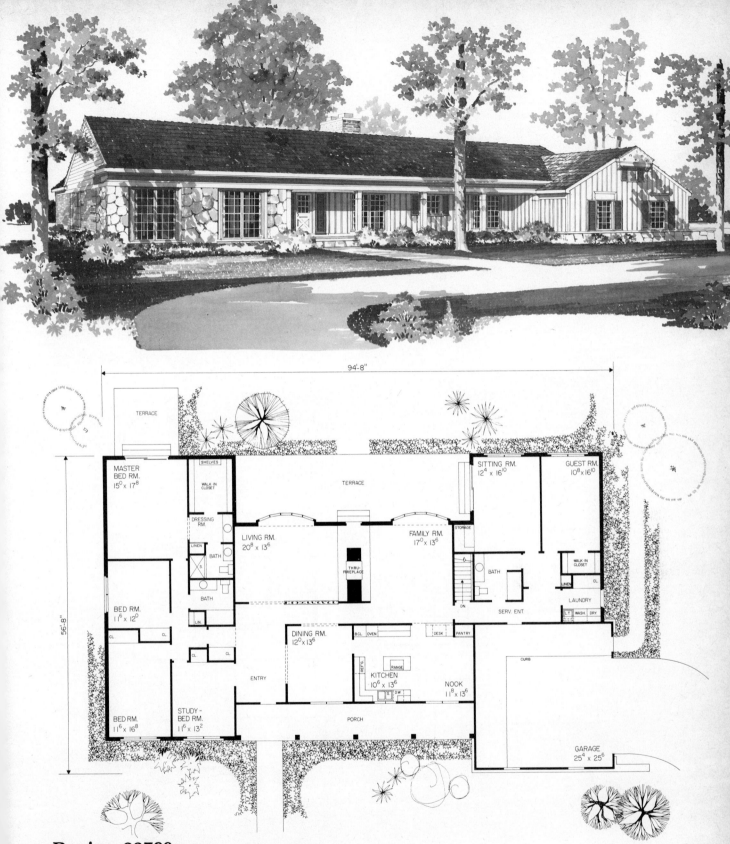

Design 22768 3,436 Sq. Ft.; 65,450 Cu. Ft.

● Besides its elegant traditionally styled exterior with its delightfully long covered front porch, this home has an exceptionally livable interior. There is the outstanding four bedroom and two-bath sleeping wing. Then, the efficient front kitchen with island range flanked by the formal dining room and the informal breakfast nook. Separated by the two-way, thru fireplace are the living and family rooms which look out on the rear yard. Worthy of particular note is the development of a potential live-in relative facility. These two rooms would also serve the large family well as a hobby room and library or additional bedrooms. A full bath is adjacent as well as the laundry. Note curb area in the garage for the storage of outdoor equipment.

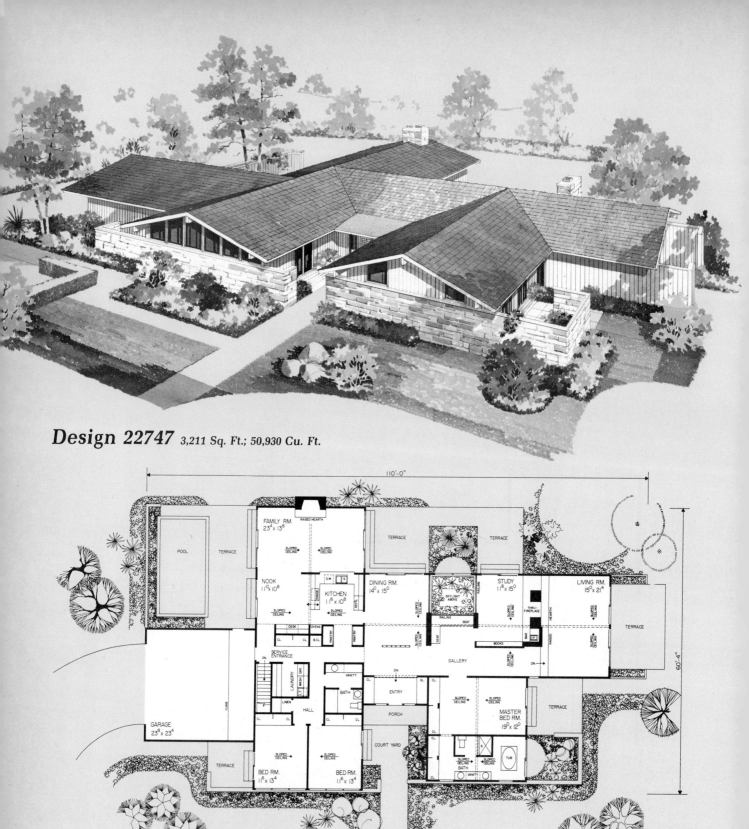

Design 22747 3,211 Sq. Ft.; 50,930 Cu. Ft.

● This home will provide its occupants with a glorious adventure in contemporary living. Its impressive exterior seems to foretell that great things are in store for even the most casual visitor. A study of the plan reveals a careful zoning for both the younger and older family members. The quiet area consists of the exceptional master bedroom suite with private terrace, the study and the isolated living room. For the younger generation, there is a zone with two bedrooms, family room and nearby pool. The kitchen is handy and serves the nook and family rooms with ease. Be sure not to miss the sloping ceilings, the dramatic planter and the functional terrace.

Design 22343 3,110 Sq. Ft.; 51,758 Cu. Ft.

● If yours is a growing active family the chances are good that they will want their new home to relate to the outdoors. This distinctive design puts a premium on private outdoor living. And you don't have to install a swimming pool to get the most enjoyment from this home. Developing this area as a garden court will provide the indoor living areas with a breathtaking awareness of nature's beauty. Notice the fine zoning of the plan and how each area has its sliding glass doors to provide an unrestricted view. Three bedrooms plus study are serviced by three baths. The family and gathering rooms provide two great living areas. The kitchen is most efficient.

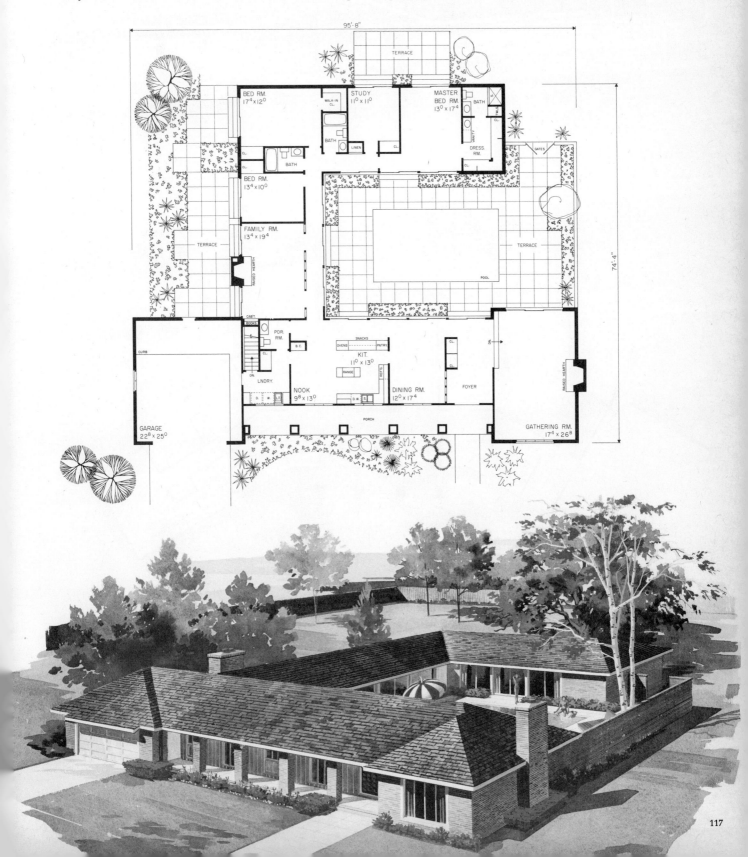

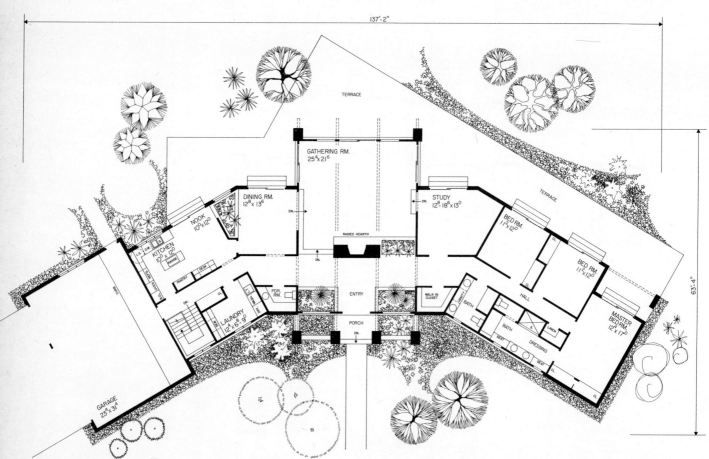

Design 22720 3,130 Sq. Ft.; 45,700 Cu. Ft.

● A raised hearth fireplace lights up the sunken gathering room which is exceptionally large and located at the very center of this home! For more living space, a well-located study and formal dining room each having a direct entrance to the gathering room. Plus a kitchen with all the right fea-

tures . . . an island range, pantry, built-in desk and separate breakfast nook. There's an extended terrace, too . . . accessible from every room! And a master suite with double closets, dressing room and private bath. Plus two family bedrooms, a first-floor laundry and lots of storage

space. A basement too, for additional space. This is a liveable home! You can entertain easily or you can hide-out with a good book. Study this plan with your family and pick out your favorite features. Don't miss the dramatic front entry planting areas, or the extra curb area in the garage.

Design 22534 3,262 Sq. Ft.; 58,640 Cu. Ft.

● The angular wings of this ranch home surely contribute to the unique character of the exterior. These wings effectively balance what is truly a dramatic and inviting front entrance. Massive masonry walls support the wide overhanging roof with its exposed wood beams. The patterned double front doors are surrounded by delightful expanses of glass. The raised planters and the masses of quarried stone (make it brick if you prefer) enhance the exterior appeal. Inside, a distinctive and practical floor plan stands ready to shape and serve the living patterns of the active family. The spacious entrance hall highlights sloped ceiling and an attractive open stairway to the lower level recreation area. An impressive fireplace and an abundance of glass are features of the big gathering room. Interestingly shaped dining room and study flank this main living area. The large kitchen offers many of the charming aspects of the family-kitchen of yesteryear. The bedroom wing has a sunken master suite.

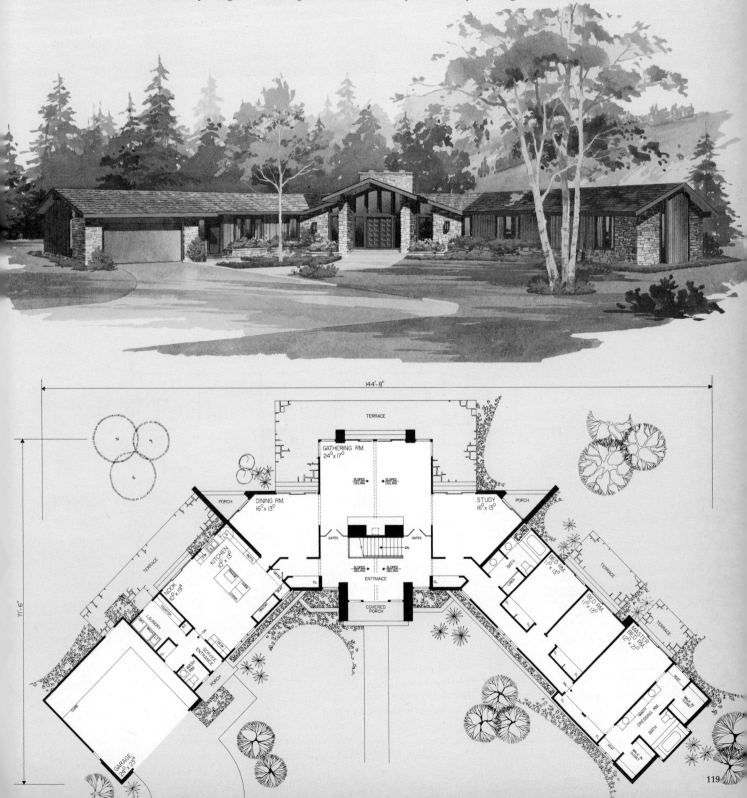

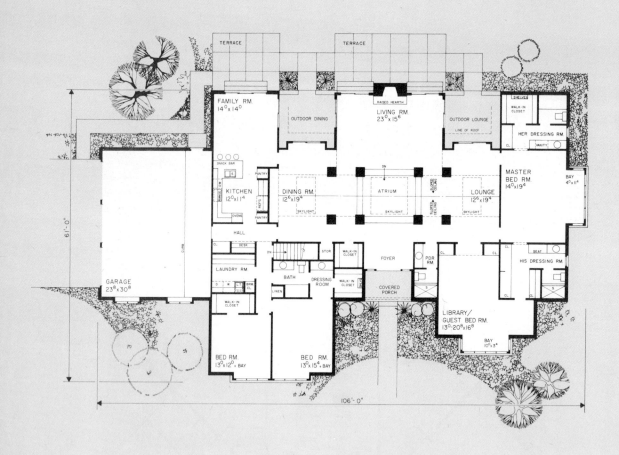

TERRACE TERRACE

RAISED HEARTH

FAMILY RM.
14⁰ x 14⁰

OUTDOOR DINING

LIVING RM.
23⁰ x 15⁶

OUTDOOR LOUNGE

LINE OF ROOF

WALK-IN CLOSET
SHELVES

HER DRESSING RM.

VANITY

SNACK BAR

PANTRY

KITCHEN
12⁰ x 11⁴

OVENS

PANTRY

DINING RM.
12⁶ x 19⁴

SKYLIGHT

ATRIUM

SKYLIGHT

LOUNGE
12⁶ x 19⁴

SKYLIGHT

MASTER BED RM.
14⁰ x 19⁴

BAY
4⁰ x 11⁴

HALL

DESK

DN

STOR

WALK-IN CLOSET

FOYER

PDR RM.

SEAT

HIS DRESSING RM.

LAUNDRY RM.

BATH

DRESSING ROOM

WALK-IN CLOSET

COVERED PORCH

GARAGE
23⁸ x 30⁸

WALK-IN CLOSET

LINEN

BED RM.
13⁰ x 12⁰ BAY

BED RM.
13⁰ x 15⁴ BAY

LIBRARY/
GUEST BED RM.
13⁰ 20⁸ x 16⁸

BAY
10⁰ x 3⁴

61'-0"

106'-0"

Design 22791 3,809 Sq. Ft.; 64,565 Cu. Ft.

● The use of vertical paned windows and the hipped roof highlight the exterior of this unique design. Upon entrance one will view a charming sunken atrium with skylight above plus a skylight in the dining room and one in the lounge. Formal living will be graciously accommodated in the living room. It features a raised hearth fireplace, two sets of sliding glass doors to the rear terrace plus two more sliding doors, one to an outdoor dining terrace and the other to an outdoor lounge. Informal living will be enjoyed in the family room with snack bar and in the large library. All will praise the fine planning of the master suite. It features a bay window, "his" and "her" dressing room with private baths and an abundance of closet space.

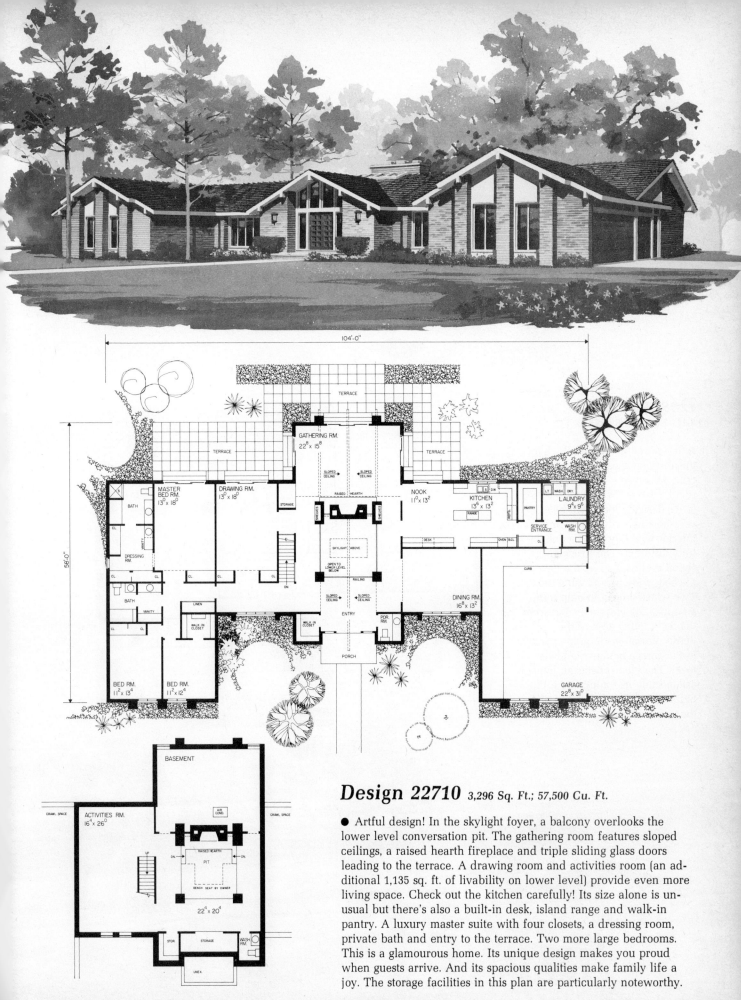

Design 22710 3,296 Sq. Ft.; 57,500 Cu. Ft.

● Artful design! In the skylight foyer, a balcony overlooks the lower level conversation pit. The gathering room features sloped ceilings, a raised hearth fireplace and triple sliding glass doors leading to the terrace. A drawing room and activities room (an additional 1,135 sq. ft. of livability on lower level) provide even more living space. Check out the kitchen carefully! Its size alone is unusual but there's also a built-in desk, island range and walk-in pantry. A luxury master suite with four closets, a dressing room, private bath and entry to the terrace. Two more large bedrooms. This is a glamourous home. Its unique design makes you proud when guests arrive. And its spacious qualities make family life a joy. The storage facilities in this plan are particularly noteworthy.

121

Design 22251

3,112 Sq. Ft.; 36,453 Cu. Ft.

● It will not matter at all where this distinctive ranch home is built. Whether located in the south, east, north or west the exterior design appeal will be breathtakingly distinctive and the interior livability will be delightfully different. The irregular shape is enhanced by the low-pitched, wide overhanging roof. Two wings project to help form an appealing entrance court from the main living area of the house. Variations in grade result in the garage being on a lower level. The plan reflects an interesting study in zoning and a fine indoor-outdoor relationship of the various areas.

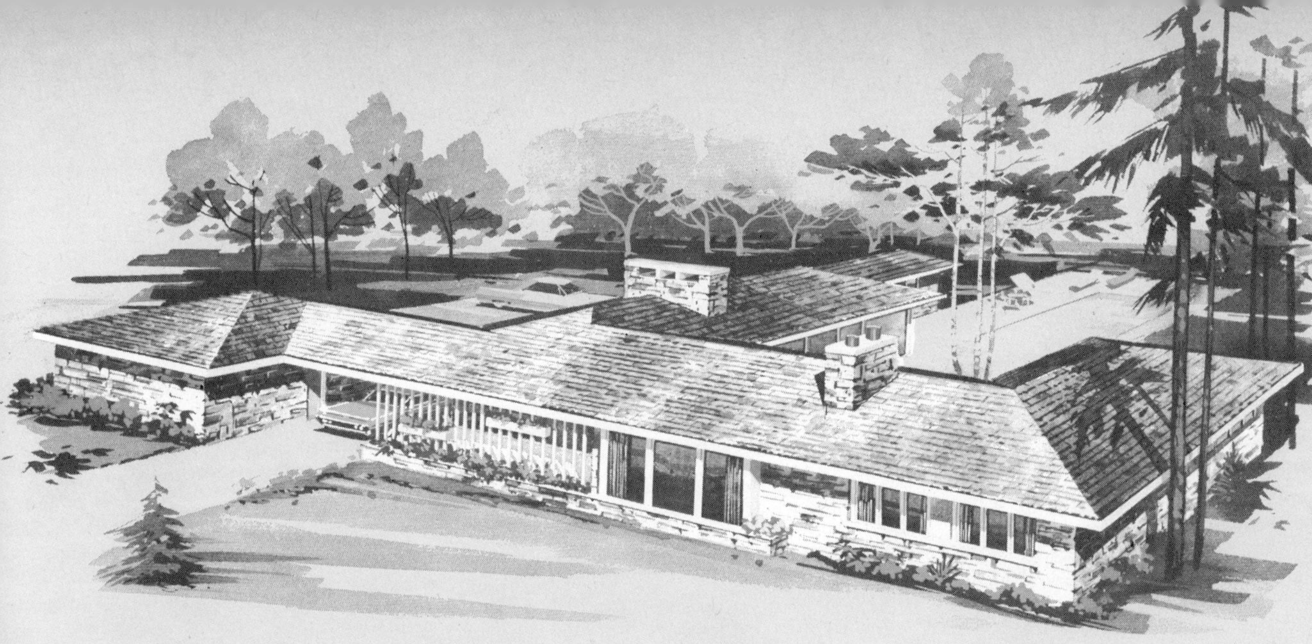

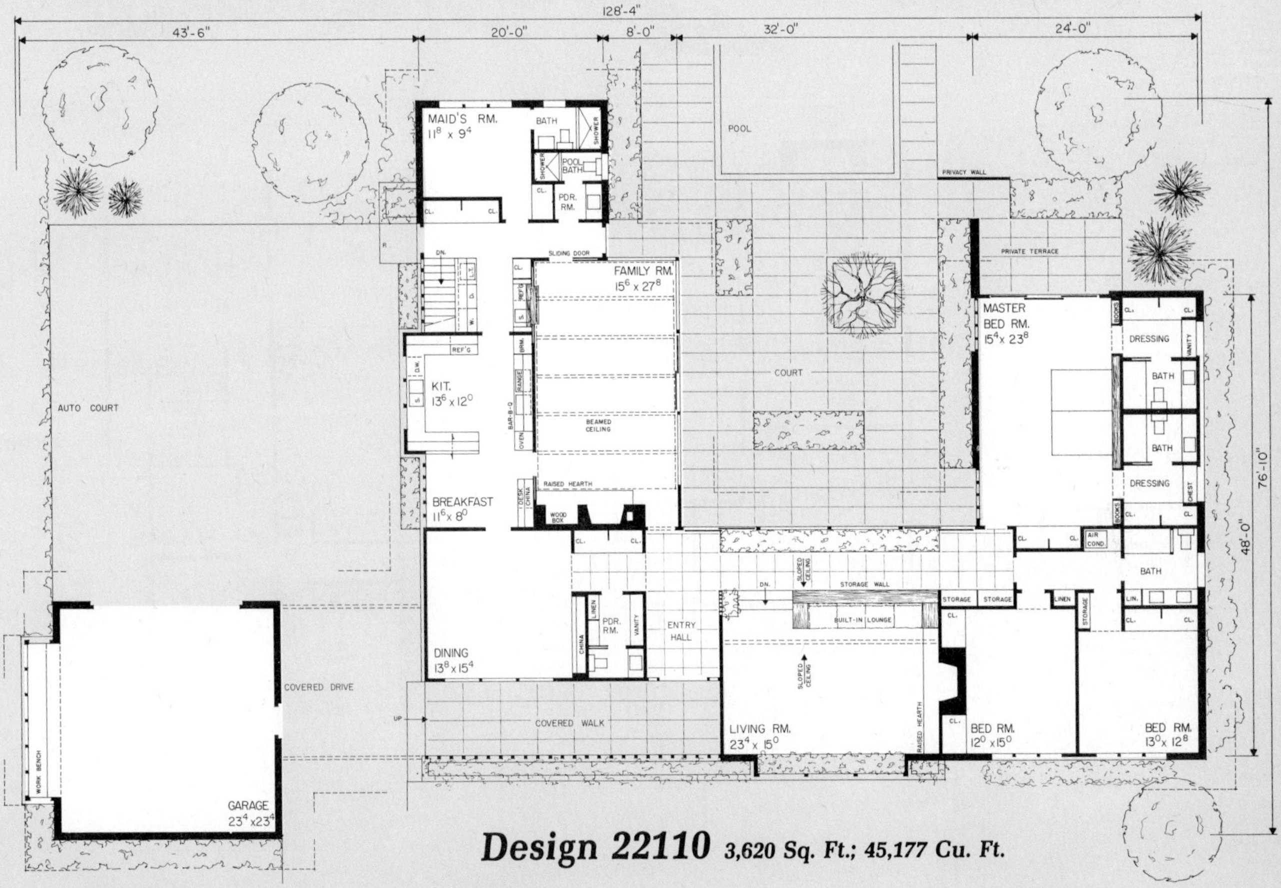

128'-4"
43'-6"
20'-0"
8'-0"
32'-0"
24'-0"
76'-10"
48'-0"
MAID'S RM. $11^{8} \times 9^{4}$
BATH
SHOWER
POOL BATH
PDR. RM.
CL.
POOL
PRIVACY WALL
PRIVATE TERRACE
DN.
SLIDING DOOR
FAMILY RM. $15^{6} \times 27^{8}$
REF'G
KIT. $13^{6} \times 12^{0}$
RANGE
OVEN
BAR-B-Q
BEAMED CEILING
RAISED HEARTH
BREAKFAST $11^{6} \times 8^{0}$
DESK
CHINA
WOOD BOX
AUTO COURT
COURT
MASTER BED RM. $15^{4} \times 23^{8}$
DRESSING
VANITY
BOOKS
CHEST
AIR COND.
STORAGE WALL
SLOPED CEILING
STORAGE
LINEN
LIN.
BUILT-IN LOUNGE
PDR. RM.
ENTRY HALL
DINING $13^{8} \times 15^{4}$
COVERED DRIVE
COVERED WALK
UP
WORK BENCH
GARAGE $23^{4} \times 23^{4}$
LIVING RM. $23^{4} \times 15^{0}$
RAISED HEARTH
BED RM. $12^{0} \times 15^{0}$
BED RM. $13^{0} \times 12^{8}$

Design 22110 3,620 Sq. Ft.; 45,177 Cu. Ft.

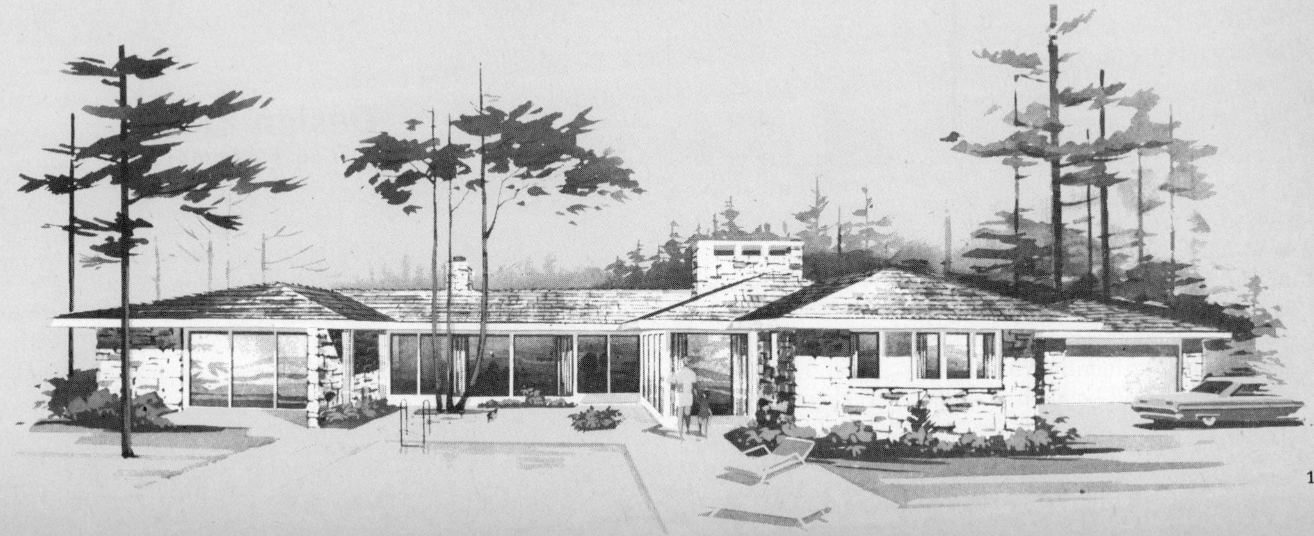

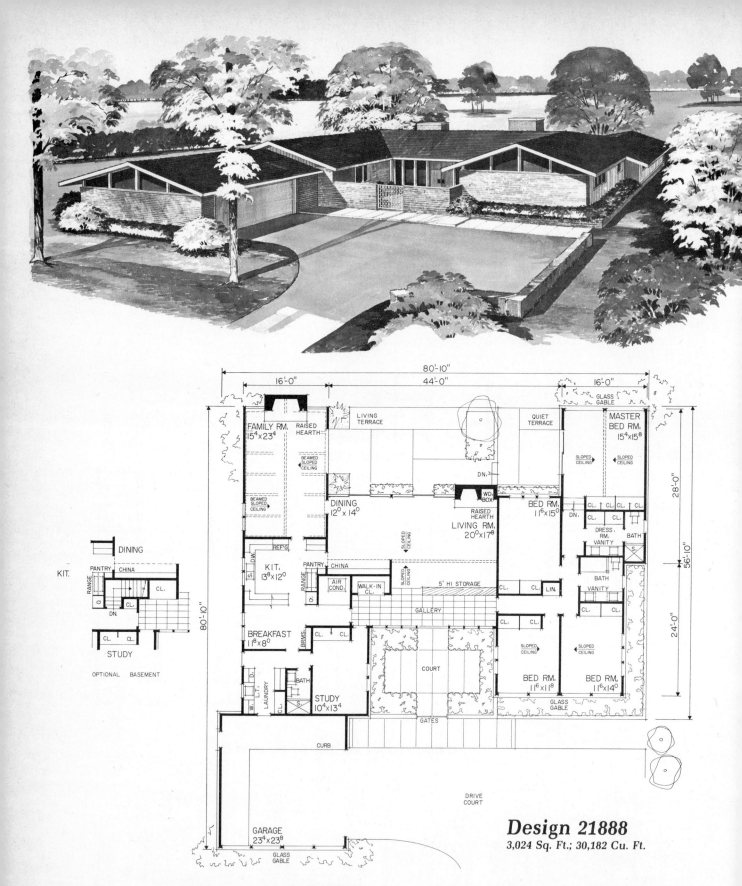

Design 21888
3,024 Sq. Ft.; 30,182 Cu. Ft.

● If you have an active family that needs plenty of well-defined space to move around, then this modified H-shaped, contemporary house may be perfect for your family. With all that space, you should be happy to know that you won't have to buy the biggest piece of property in town. The shape of the house keeps the overall dimension small enough to fit a modest sized lot. However, there is nothing modest about the inside. The list of features will be king size, indeed. Which features will be at the top of your list? The court, gallery or 32 foot living/dining area? How about the study, family room or master bedroom? Note details for an optional basement plan.

Design 21928 3,272 Sq. Ft.; 46,294 Cu. Ft.

● You'll find this contemporary home is worthy of your consideration if you're looking for a house of distinction. The dramatic exterior is a sure-fire stopper. Even the most casual passer-by will take a second look. In-teresting roof surfaces, massive brick chimney wall, recessed entrance, rais-ed planters and garden wall are among the features that spell design distinc-tion. And yet, the exterior is only part of the story this home has to tell. Its in-terior is no less unique. Consider the sunken living room, sloping, beamed ceiling of the family room, wonderful kitchen/laundry area, four-bedroom sleeping area with all those closets, bath facilities and sliding doors.

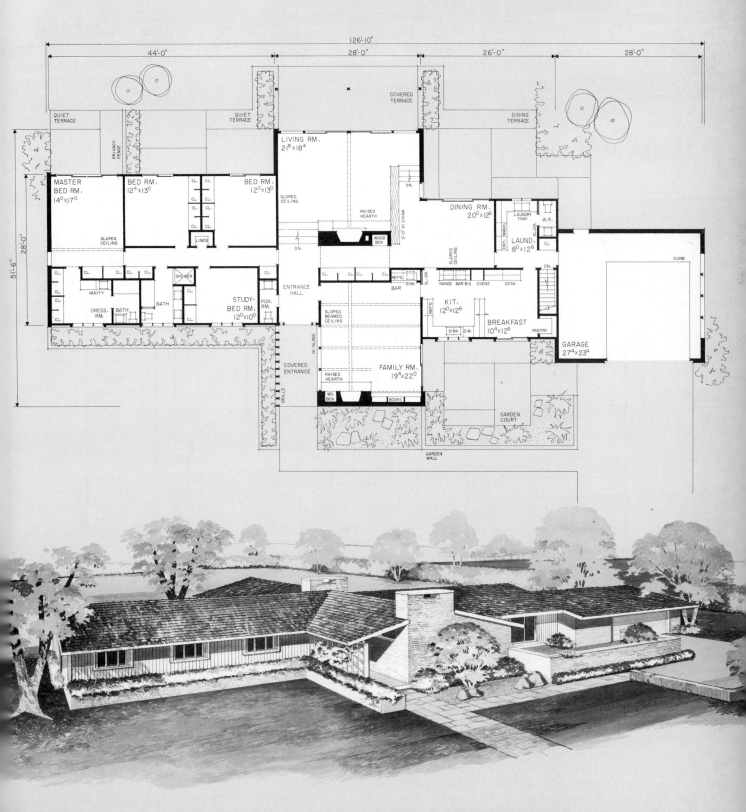

Design 22765 3,365 Sq. Ft.; 59,820 Cu. Ft.

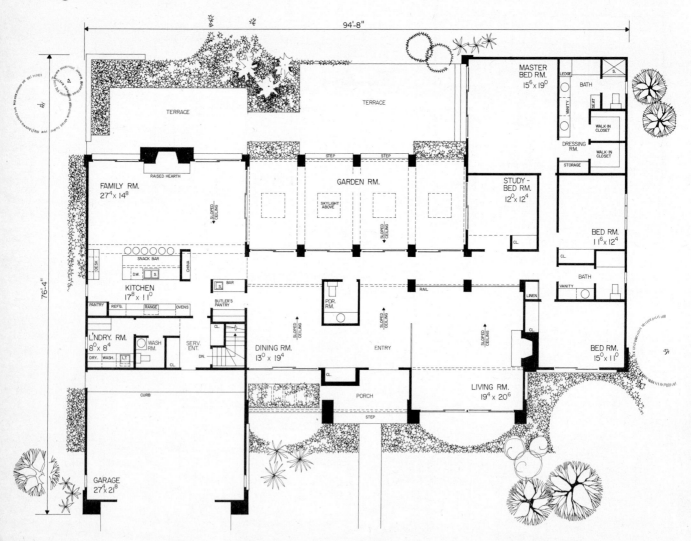

● This three (optional four) bedroom contemporary is a most appealing design. It offers living patterns that will add new dimensions to your everyday routine. The sloped ceilings in the family room, dining room and living room add much spaciousness to this home.

The efficient kitchen has many fine features including the island snack bar and work center, built-in desk, china cabinet and wet bar. Adjacent to the kitchen is a laundry room, washroom and stairs to the basement. Formal and informal living will each have its own

area. A raised hearth fireplace and sliding glass doors to the rear terrace are in the informal family room. Another fireplace is in the front formal living room. You will enjoy all that natural light in the garden room from the skylights in the sloped ceiling.

CONTEMPORARY ADAPTATIONS . . .

can offer a delightful change of pace for your new home planning program. The unique individuality of many contemporary exteriors is refreshing, indeed. The clean, simple lines of the contemporary house offer a break from the past. The lack of adornment is preferred by many. Interesting new shapes not only lead to dramatic exteriors, but to unusual floor plans which deliver exciting living patterns. Open planning, sunken living areas, open stairwells, sloping ceilings, skylights, large and prudently placed glass areas and indoor planting areas all make significant contributions to the enjoyment of contemporary living. And, of course, new materials and equipment make their contribution, too.

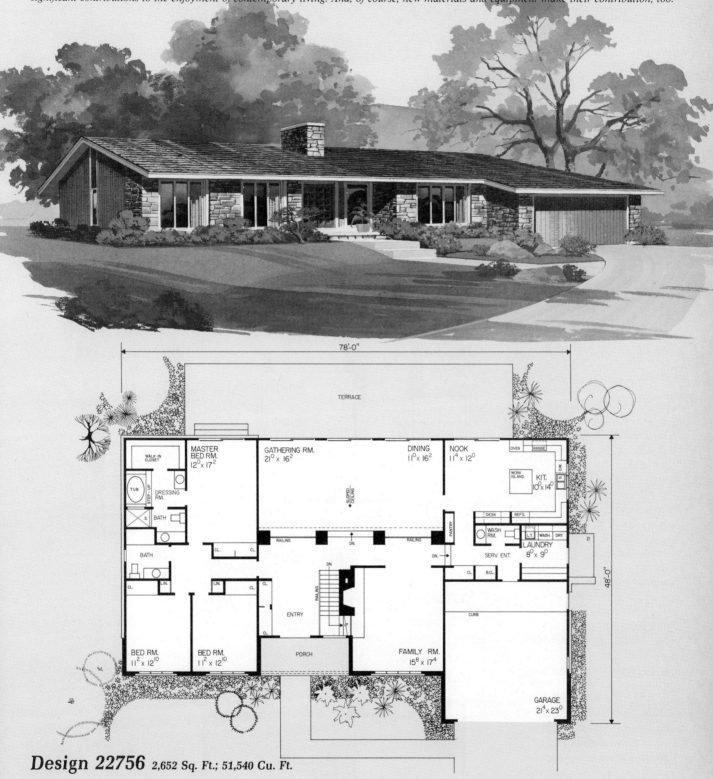

Design 22756 2,652 Sq. Ft.; 51,540 Cu. Ft.

● This one-story, contemporary design is bound to serve your family well. It will assure the best in contemporary living with its many fine features. Notice the bath with tub and stall shower, dressing room and walk-in closet featured with the master bedroom. Two more family bedrooms are adjacent. The sunken gathering room/dining room is highlighted by the sloped ceiling and sliding glass doors to the large, rear terrace. This formal area is a full 32' x 16'. Imagine the great furniture placement that can be done in this area. In addition to the gathering room, there is an informal family room with a fireplace. You will enjoy the efficient kitchen and get much use out of the work island, pantry and built-in desk. Note the service entrance with washroom and laundry.

Design 22730
2,490 Sq. Ft.; 50,340 Cu. Ft.

● Here is a basic one-story home that is really loaded with livability on the first floor and has a bonus of an extra 1,086 sq. ft. of planned livability on a lower level. What makes this so livable is that the first floor adjacent to the stairs leading below is open and forms a balcony looking down into a dramatic planting area. The first floor traffic patterns flow around this impressive and distinctive feature. In addition to the gathering room, study and family room, there is the lounge and activity room. Notice the second balcony open to the activity room below. The master bedroom is outstanding with two baths and two walk-in closets. The attached three-car garage has a bulk storage area and is accessible through the service area.

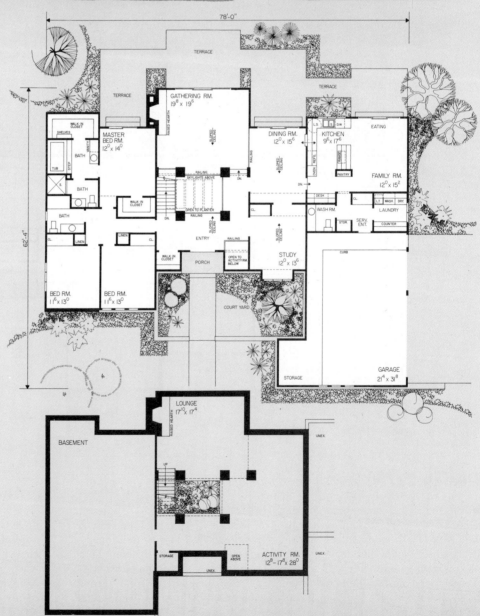

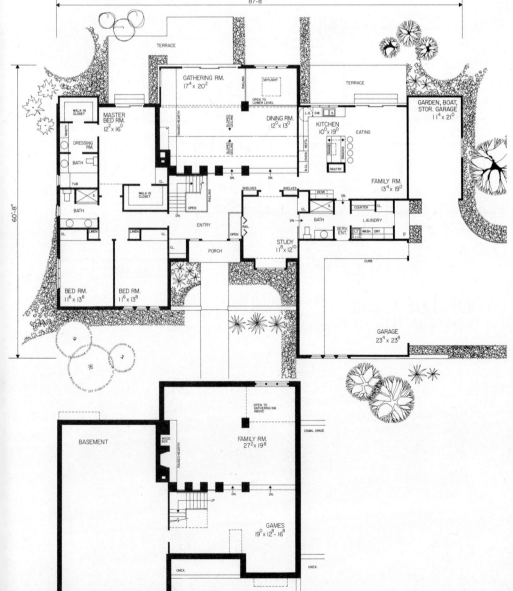

Design 22721
2,667 Sq. Ft.; 53,150 Cu. Ft.

● Visually exciting! A sunken gathering room with a sloped ceiling, raised hearth fireplace, corner balcony and skylight . . . the last two features shared by the formal dining room. There's more. Two family rooms . . . one on the lower level (1,153 sq. ft.) with a raised hearth fireplace, another adjacent to the kitchen with a snack bar! Plus a study and game room. A lavish master suite and two large bedrooms. A first floor laundry and reams of storage space, including a special garage for a boat, sports equipment, garden tools etc. There's plenty of space for family activities in this home. From chic dinner parties for friends to birthday gatherings for kids, there's always the right setting . . . and so much room that adults and children can entertain at the same time.

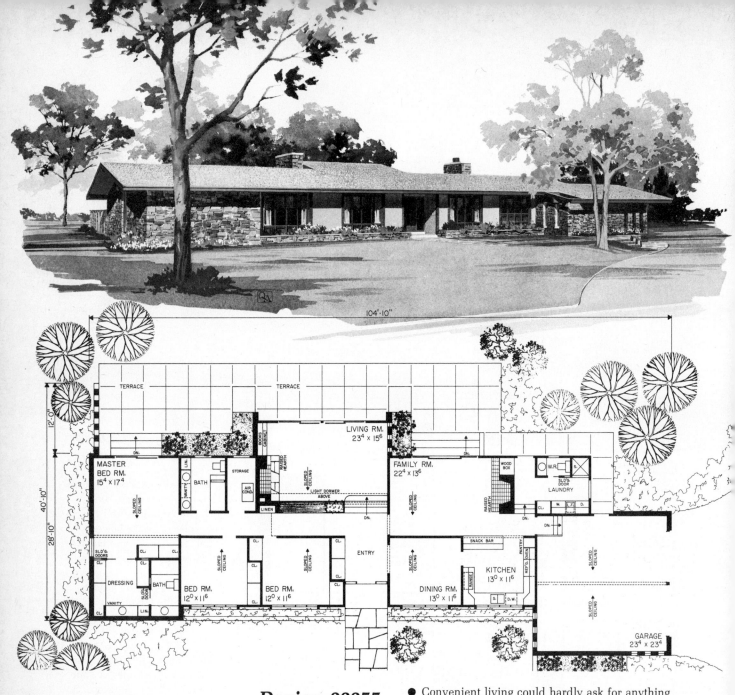

TERRACE

TERRACE

LIVING RM.
23⁴ x 15⁶

MASTER
BED RM.
15⁴ x 17⁴

BATH

STORAGE

AIR
COND.

BOOKS
CABINET

RAISED
HEARTH

SLOPED
CEILING

LIGHT DORMER
ABOVE

LINEN

FAMILY RM.
22⁴ x 13⁶

WOOD
BOX

RAISED
HEARTH

W.R.

SLD'G.
DOOR

LAUNDRY

W.   C.T.   D.

SLOPED
CEILING

SLOPED
CEILING

DRESSING

BATH

VANITY

BED RM.
12⁰ x 11⁶

SLOPED
CEILING

BED RM.
12⁰ x 11⁶

SLOPED
CEILING

ENTRY

SNACK BAR

SLOPED
CEILING

DINING RM.
13⁰ x 11⁶

KITCHEN
13⁰ x 11⁶

PANTRY

REF'G.   OVEN

RANGE

S.   D.W.

SLOPED
CEILING

GARAGE
23⁴ x 23⁴

104'-10"

12'-0"

40'-10"

28'-10"

Design 22255
2,356 Sq. Ft.; 24,145 Cu. Ft.

● Convenient living could hardly ask for anything more. Study this design inside and out. It is positively outstanding from every angle.

Design 22256 2,632 Sq. Ft.; 35,023 Cu. Ft.

● A dream home for those with young ideas. A refreshing, contemporary exterior with a unique, highly individualized interior. What are your favorite features.

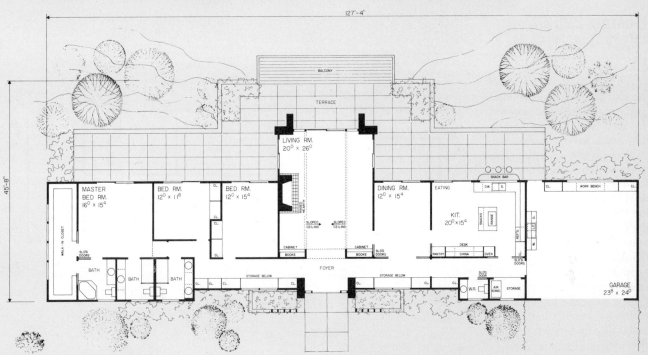

Design 22523
2,055 Sq. Ft.; 43,702 Cu. Ft.

● You'll want the investment in your new home to be one of the soundest you'll ever make. And certainly the best way to do this is to make sure your new home has unexcelled exterior appeal and outstanding interior livability. For those who like refreshing contemporary lines, this design will rate at the top. The wide overhanging roof, the brick masses, the glass areas, the raised planters, and the covered front entrance highlight the facade. As for the interior, all the elements are present to assure fine living patterns. Consider the room relationships and how they function with one another. Note how they relate to the outdoors.

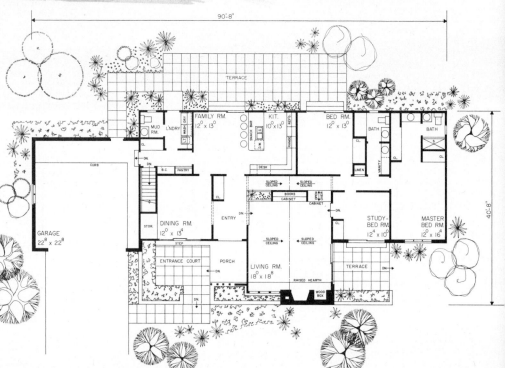

Design 21111
2,248 Sq. Ft.; 18,678 Cu. Ft.

● "Great", will be just the word to characterize the ownership of this home. The trim hip-roof with its wide overhang, the massiveness of the vertical brick piers, and the extension of the brick wall to form a front court are but a few of the features. Among the other features include the four bedrooms, two full baths and extra wash room, a spacious L-shaped living and dining area, a dramatic family room and a mud room.

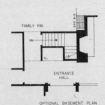

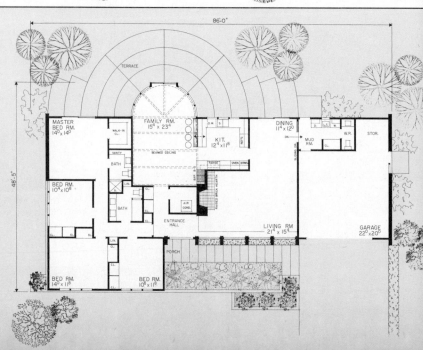

Design 22359
2,078 Sq. Ft.; 22,400 Cu. Ft.

● The low-pitched, wide-overhanging roof with its exposed beams, acts as a visor for the dramatic glass gable end of the projecting living room. This will be an exceedingly pleasant room with its sunken floor, sloped ceiling, large glass area, and raised hearth fireplace. At the rear of this living rectangle is the family room. This room also has a sloped ceiling and a glass gable end. In addition, there is the snack bar and sliding glass doors to the protected terrace. Between these two living areas is the efficient kitchen with its adjacent eating area. The utility room and its laundry equipment is nearby, as is the powder room. A separate dining room acts as the connecting link to the bedroom zone. Note the master bedroom with its dressing room, twin lavatories and two closets.

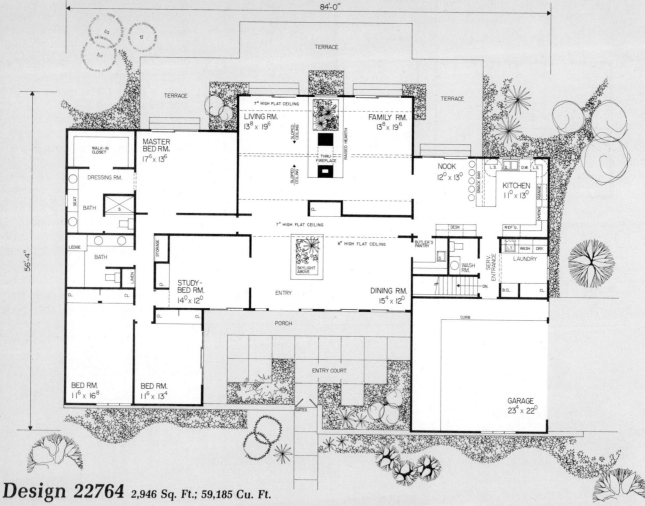

Design 22764 2,946 Sq. Ft.; 59,185 Cu. Ft.

● If uniqueness is what you're looking for in your new home then this three (optional four) bedroom design will be ideal. Notice the large gated-in entry court, vertical paned windows and contrasting exterior materials. All of these features compose an attractive design suitable for any location. Within but a second after entering this home one will be confronted with features galore. The entry/dining area has a focal point of a built-in planter with skylight above. The living room and family room both have an attractive sloped ceiling. They share a raised hearth thru-fireplace and both have access to the large wrap-around terrace. The kitchen-nook area also has access to the terrace and has the features of a snack bar, built-in desk and large butler's pantry.

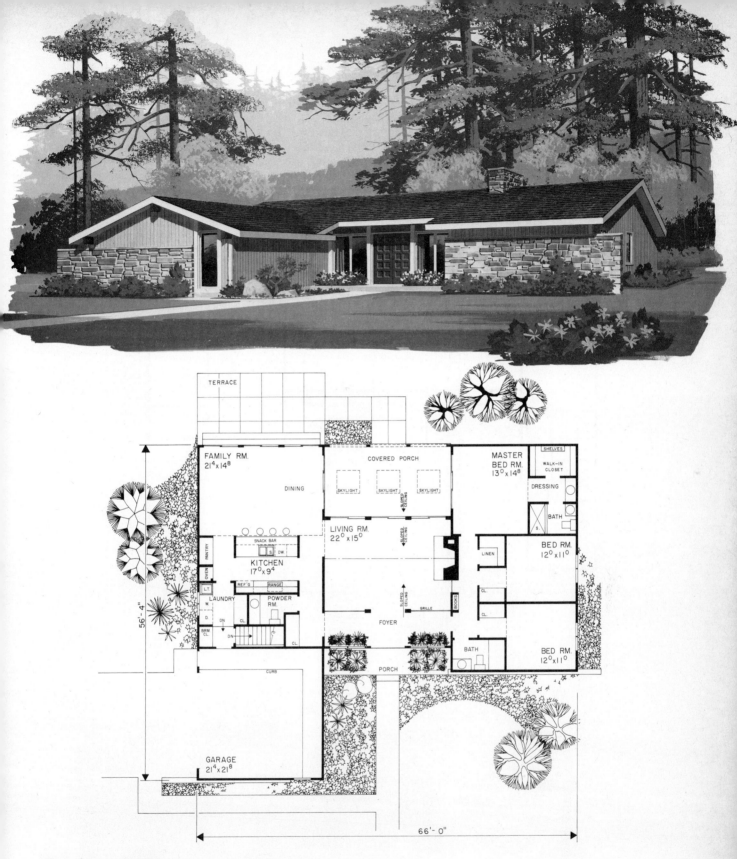

Design 22790 2,075 Sq. Ft.; 45,630 Cu. Ft.

● Enter this contemporary hip-roofed home through the double front doors and immediately view the sloped ceilinged living room with fireplace. This room will be a sheer delight when it comes to formal entertaining. It has easy access to the kitchen and also a powder room nearby. The work area will be convenient. The kitchen has an island work center with snack bar. The laundry is adjacent to the service entrance and stairs leading to the basement. This area is planned to be a real "step saver". The sleeping wing consists of two family bedrooms, bath and master bedroom suite. Maybe the most attractive feature of this design is the rear covered porch with skylights above. It is accessible by way of sliding glass doors in the family/dining area, living room and master bedroom.

Design 22866 2,371 Sq. Ft.; 50,120 Cu. Ft.

● An extra living unit has been built into the design of this home. It would make an excellent "mother-in-law" suite. Should you choose not to develop this area as indicated, maybe you might use it as two more bedrooms, a guest suite or even as hobby and game rooms. Whatever its final use, it will compliment the rest of this home. The main house also deserves mention. The focal point will be the large gathering room. Its features include a skylight, sloped ceiling, centered fireplace flanked on both sides by sliding glass doors and adjacent is a dining room on one side, study on the other. The work center is clustered together. Three bedrooms and two baths make up the private area. Note the outdoor areas: court with privacy wall, two covered porches and a large terrace.

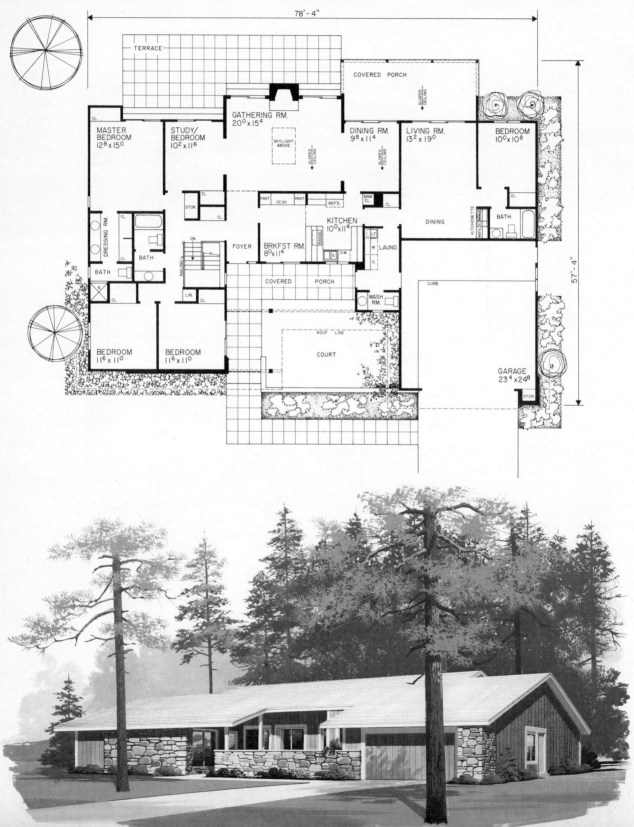

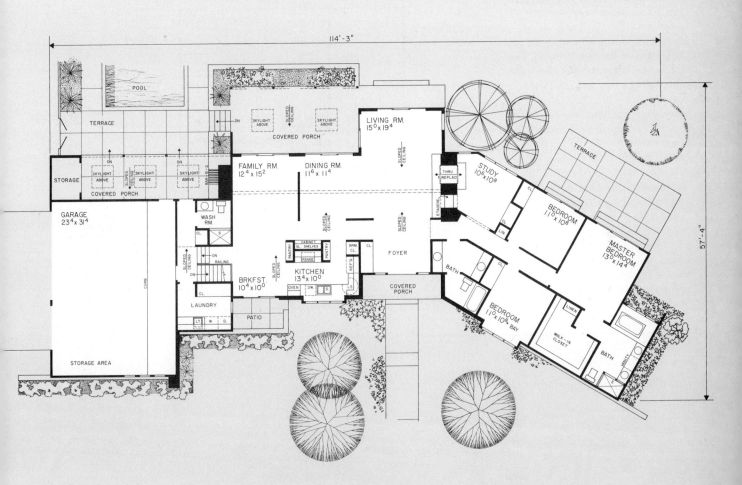

Design 22819 *2,459 Sq. Ft.; 45,380 Cu. Ft.*

● Indoor-outdoor living will be enjoyed to the fullest in this rambling one-story contemporary plan. Each of the rear rooms in this design, excluding the study, has access to a terrace or porch. Even the front breakfast room has access to a private dining patio. The covered porch off the living areas, family, dining and living rooms, has a sloped ceiling and skylights. A built-in barbecue unit and a storage room will be found on the second covered porch. Inside, the plan offers exceptional living patterns for various activities. Notice the thru-fireplace that the living room shares with the study. A built-in etagere is nearby. The three-car garage has an extra storage area.

Design 21026
2,506 Sq. Ft.; 26,313 Cu. Ft.

● When you move into this attractive home you'll find you and your family will begin to experience new dimensions in living. All areas will be forever conscious of the beauty of the out-of-doors. The front entry court provides both the quiet living room and the formal dining room with a delightful view. The functional terraces will expand the horizons of each of the other rooms. While the raised hearth fireplaces of the two living areas are major focal points, there are numerous convenient living features which will make everyday living a joy. Some of these features are the mud room, the pantry, the planning desk with china storage above, the snack bar and pass-thru. As noted in the illustration, an optional basement plan is included.

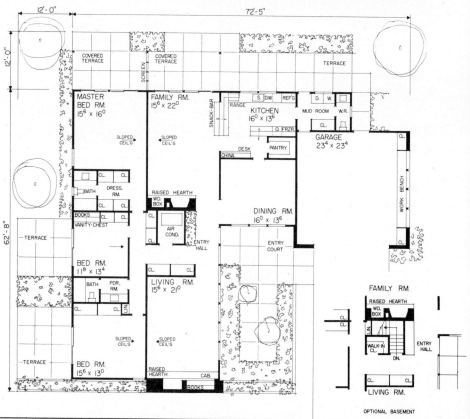

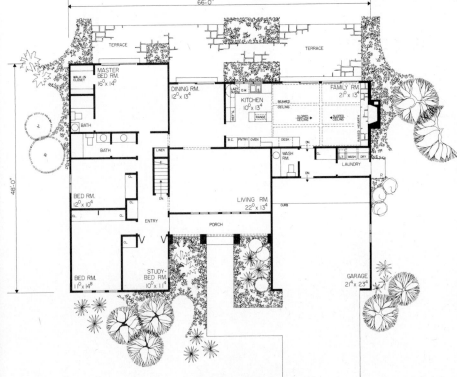

Design 22532
2,112 Sq. Ft.; 42,300 Cu. Ft.

● Here is a refreshing, modified U-shaped contemporary that is long on both looks and livability. The board and batten exterior creates simple lines which are complimented by the low-pitched roof with its wide overhang and exposed rafters. The appeal of the front court is enhanced by the massive stone columns at the edge of the covered porch. A study of the floor plan reveals interestingly different and practical living patterns. The location of the entry hall represents a fine conservation of space for the living areas. The L-shaped formal living-dining zone has access to both front and rear yards. The informal living area is a true family kitchen. Its open planning produces a spacious and cheerful area. Note sloping, beamed ceiling, raised hearth fireplace and sliding glass doors.

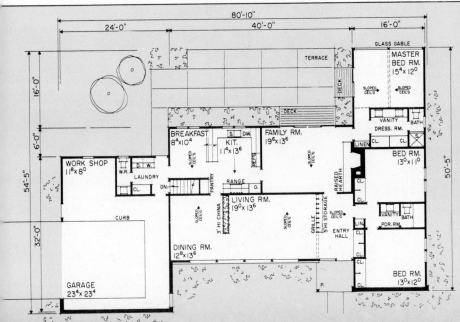

Design 21844
2,047 Sq. Ft.; 32,375 Cu. Ft.

● A sparkling contemporary with all the elements to help assure a lifetime of complete livability. This one-story home is essentially a frame dwelling with two dramatic areas of durable and colorful quarried stone. The low-pitched, wide-overhanging roof provides shelter for the front porch. In addition, it acts as a visor for the large glass areas. The plan is positively outstanding. The informal areas are to the rear of the plan and overlook the rear terrace. The formal, separate dining room and living room are strategically located to the front. The sleeping zone comprises a wing of its own with the master bedroom suite apart from the children's room. Don't miss the extra wash room, laundry and shop. Basement stairs are near this work area.

Design 22304
2,313 Sq. Ft.; 26,110 Cu. Ft.

● What an appealing home! And what a list of reasons why it is so eye-catching. First of all, there is the irregular shape and the low-pitched, wide-overhanging roof. Then, there is the interesting use of exterior materials, including vertical glass window treatment. Further, there are the raised planters flanking the proch of the recessed entrance. Inside, the traffic patterns are excellent. Among the focal points is the 33 foot, beam ceilinged living area. This will surely be fun to plan and furnish for the family's living and dining pursuits. Among other highlights is the layout of the laundry-kitchen-nook area. The extra wash room is strategically located. The sleeping wing has much to offer with its privacy, its convenient bath facilities, and its fine storage.

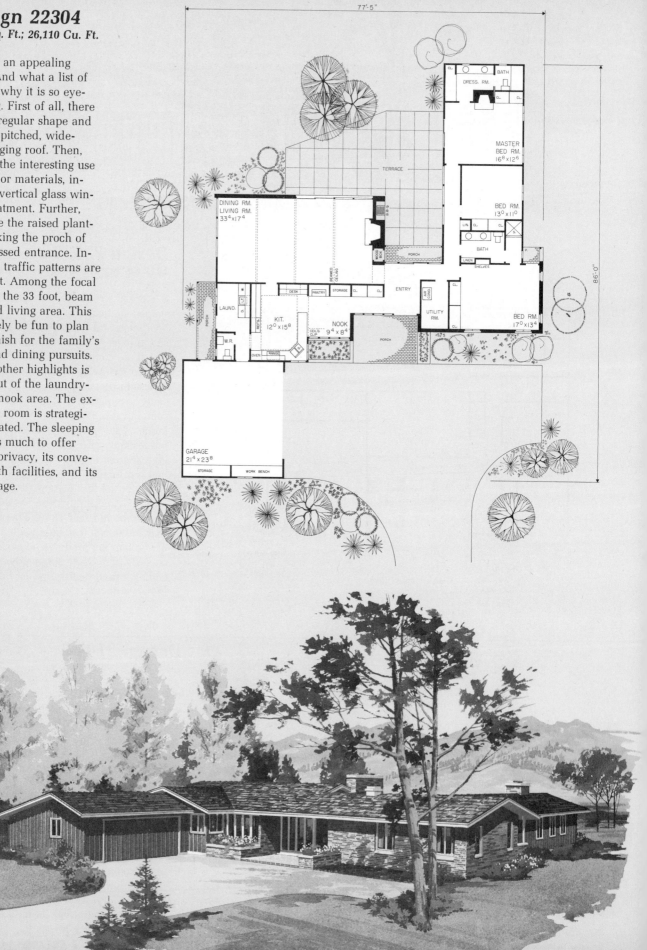

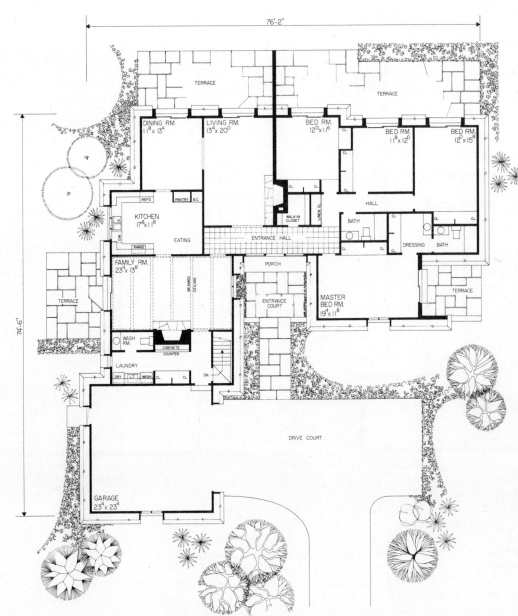

Design 22384
2,545 Sq. Ft.; 44,041 Cu. Ft.

● A dramatic Mansard roof with a contemporary adaption. The various overhanging and sloping roof planes give this L-shaped ranch home a unique appeal. Extended brick wing walls help create an entrance court leading to the attractively detailed front entry. The well-lighted entrance hall is spacious and effectively controls the traffic patterns to the major areas. Observe that each of the major rooms (kitchen excepted) enjoys direct access to outdoor living. The large master bedroom will have a full measure of privacy. On the other hand, the efficient kitchen is strategically located between dining and family rooms. A practical mud room area, adjacent to the entry from the garage, features wash room, laundry, closet and cabinet space. This home has a partial basement.

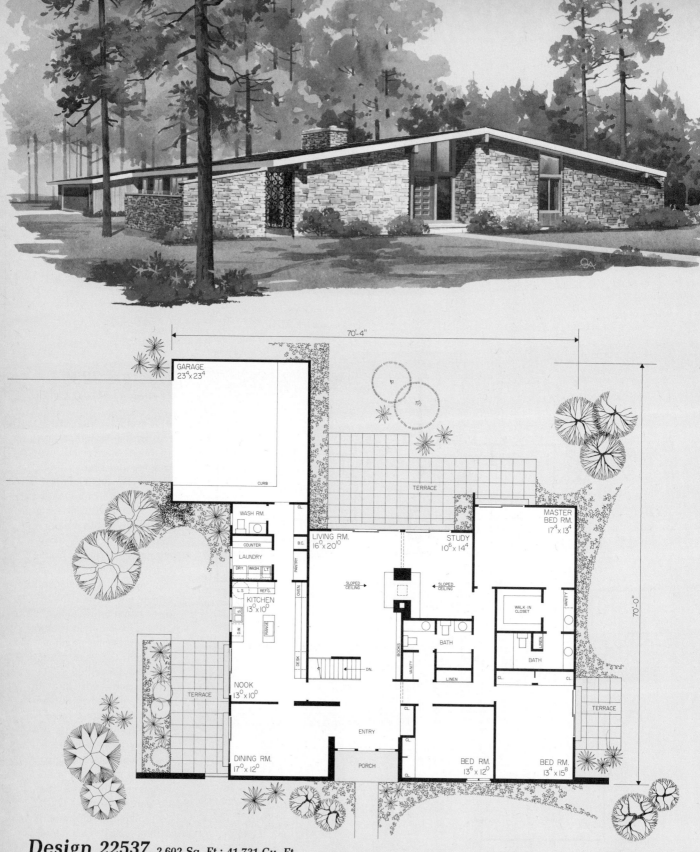

Design 22537 2,602 Sq. Ft.; 41,731 Cu. Ft.

● A low-pitched, wide overhanging roof and masses of quarried stone (make it some other material of your choice if you wish) set the character of this contemporary design. The recessed front entrance with its patterned door and glass panels is, indeed, dramatic.

An attractive wrought iron gate opens to the private, side eating terrace. Sloping ceilings and raised hearth through-fireplace highlight the living room/study area. Spaciousness is further enhanced by the open stairwell to the recreation area which may be devel-

oped below. The kitchen, with its island cooking range and plenty of counter and cupboard space will be a joy in which to function. The area between kitchen and garage is well-planned. The separate laundry has extra counter space.

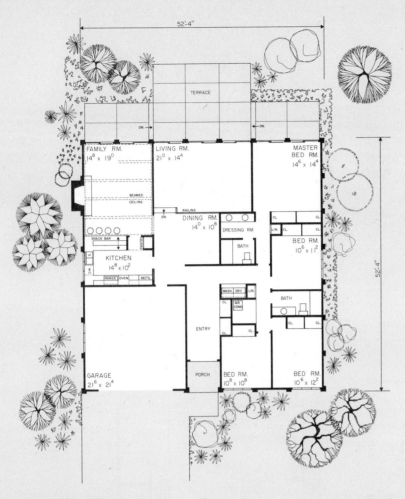

Design 22357
2,135 Sq. Ft.; 24,970 Cu. Ft.

● Palm trees on your site are not a prerequisite for the building of this distinctive home. If you and your family have a flair for things unique, the exterior, as well as the interior, of this attractive design will excite you. The low-pitched, wide overhanging hip roof has a slag surface. The equally spaced pillars and the spaces between the vertical boards are finished in stucco. This house is a perfect square measuring 52'-4''. The resulting plan is one that is practical and efficient. The kitchen will be a joy in which to work. A pass-thru provides the access to the snack bar of the beamed ceilinged family room. The formal dining area is but a couple steps away and overlooks the sunken living room. Four bedrooms and two baths make up the delightful sleeping zone.

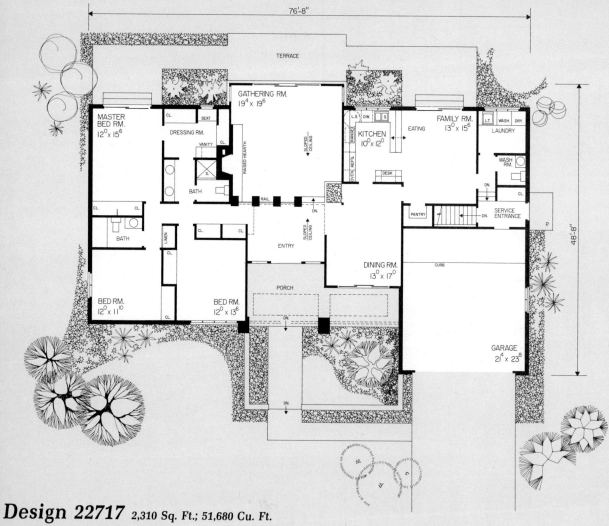

Design 22717 2,310 Sq. Ft.; 51,680 Cu. Ft.

● Great for family life! There's a spacious family room for casual activities. And a "work efficient" kitchen that features a built-in desk and appliances, a large pantry plus a pass-through to the family room for added convenience. A first floor laundry, too, with adjacent wash room and stairs to the basement. Want glamour? There's a sloped ceiling in the entry hall plus a delightful "over the railing" view of the sunken gathering room. And the gathering room itself! More than 19' by 19' . . . with a sloped ceiling, raised hearth fireplace and sliding glass doors to the rear terrace. A 13' by 17' formal dining room, too. The curb area in garage is convenient.

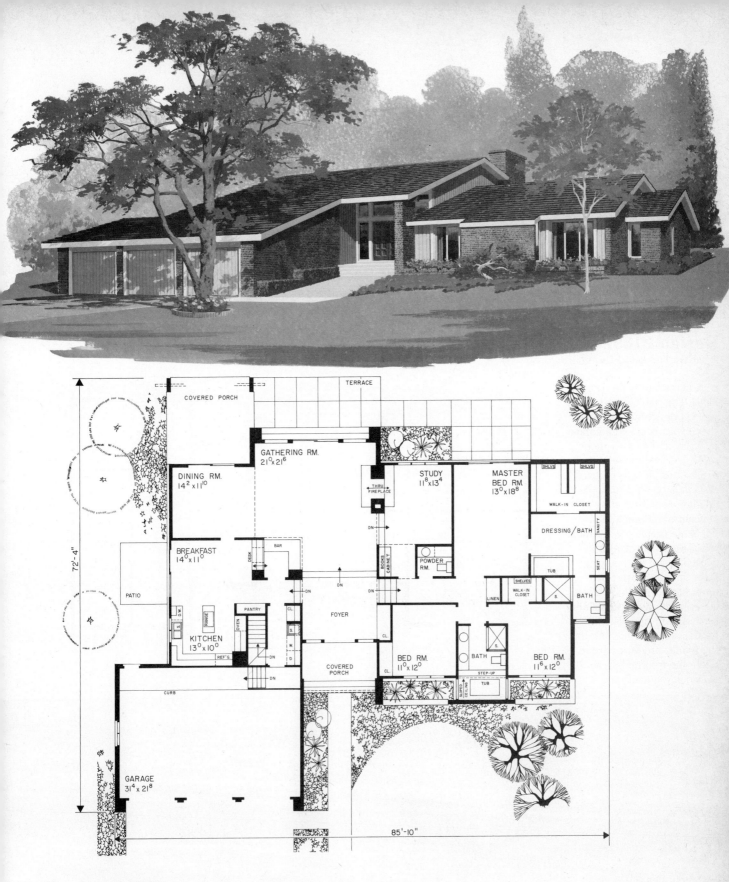

Design 22789 2,732 Sq. Ft.; 54,935 Cu. Ft.

● An attached three car garage! What a fantastic feature of this three bedroom contemporary design. And there's more. As one walks up the steps to the covered porch and through the double front doors the charm of this design will be overwhelming. Inside, a large foyer greets all visitors and leads them to each of the three areas, each down a few steps. The living area has a large gathering room with fireplace and a study adjacent on one side and the formal dining room on the other. The work center has an efficient kitchen with island range, breakfast room, laundry and built-in desk and bar. Then there is the sleeping area. Note the raised tub with sloped ceiling.

Design 21897
2,628 Sq. Ft.; 38,859 Cu. Ft.

● A home can have many faces. This refreshingly simple, yet delightfully impressive design has a contemporary flavor. The low-pitched roof has a wide overhang. Its exposed rafter tails protrude at each gable end for a distinctive look. Appealing architectural detailing highlights the projecting bedroom wing. Four bedrooms and two baths are in this wing. Note that the master bedroom has access to a private terrace. The living areas are separated in this plan. The formal areas, living and dining rooms, are in the front; while the informal areas overlook the backyard.

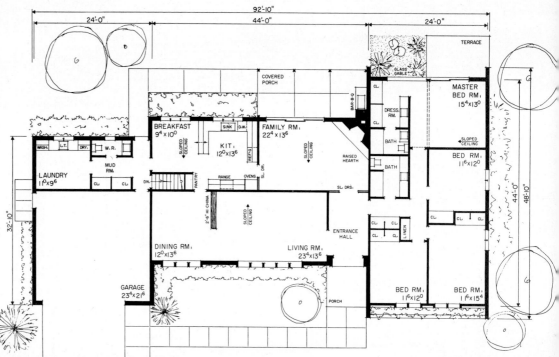

Design 22506
2,851 Sq. Ft.; 47,525 Cu. Ft.

● Here is a home that is sure to add an extra measure of fun to your family's living patterns. The exterior is extremely pleasing with the use of paned glass windows, the hipped roof and the double front doors. The initial impact of the interior begins dramatically in the large foyer. The ceiling is sloped, while straight ahead one views the sunken living room. Impressive are the masonry columns with a railing between each. The stairwell to the partial basement is open and has a view of the outdoor planter. The sleeping area consists of three bedrooms, baths and a study (or fourth bedroom if you prefer). Two raised hearth fireplaces, pantry, washroom and more. List your favorite features.

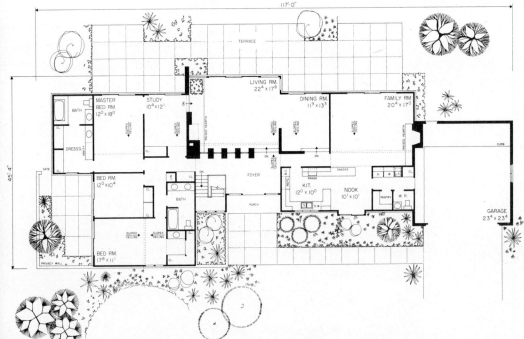

Design 21820
2,730 Sq. Ft.; 36,335 Cu. Ft.

● Whatever the location, snugly tucked in among the hills or impressively oriented on the flatlands - this trim hip-roof ranch home will be fun to own. Here is a gracious exterior whose floor plan has "everything". Traffic patterns are excellent. The zoning of the sleeping wing, as well as the formal and informal living areas, is outstanding. Indoor-outdoor living relationships are most practical and convenient.

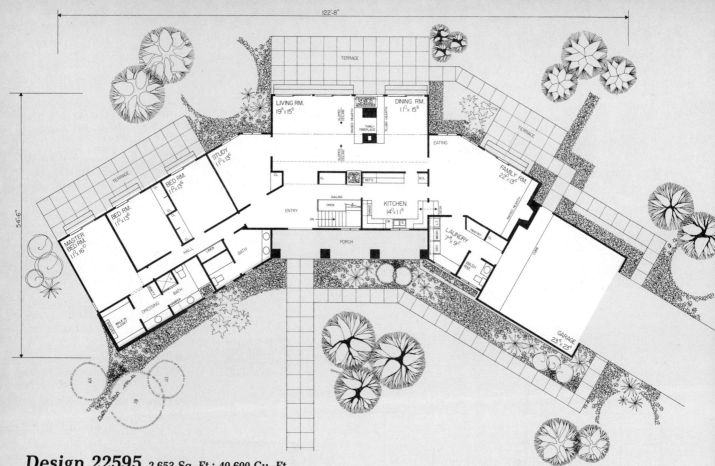

Design 22595 *2,653 Sq. Ft.; 40,600 Cu. Ft.*

● A winged design puts everything in the right place! At the center, formal living and dining rooms with sloped ceiling share one fireplace for added charm. Sliding glass doors in both rooms open onto the main terrace. In the right wing, there is a spacious family room with another raised hearth fireplace, built-in desk, dining area and adjoining smaller terrace. Also, a first floor laundry with pantry and half bath. A study, the master suite and family bedrooms (all bedrooms having access to a third terrace) plus baths are in the left wing. This home has a floor plan that helps you organize your life. Notice the open staircase leading to the basement.

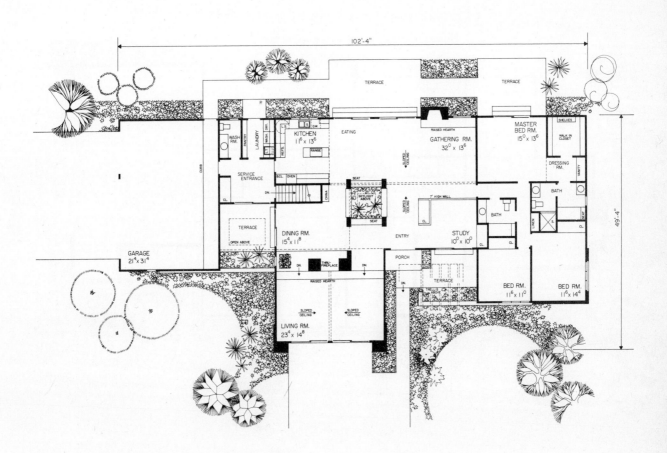

Design 22745 2,890 Sq. Ft.; 44,650 Cu. Ft.

● Just imagine the fun everyone will have living in this contemporary home with its frame exterior and accents of stone veneer (make it brick, if you prefer). The living areas revolve around the dramatic atrium-type planting area flooded with natural light from the skylight above. The formal living room is sunken and has a thru-fireplace to the dining room. Also a large gathering room with a second raised hearth fireplace, sloped ceiling, sliding glass doors to a rear terrace and informal eating area. Observe the sloping ceilings, the laundry with pantry, the wash room and the study. Master bedroom has a stall shower, a tub with seat, a vanity and two lavatories.

Design 22793 2,065 Sq. Ft.; 48,850 Cu. Ft.

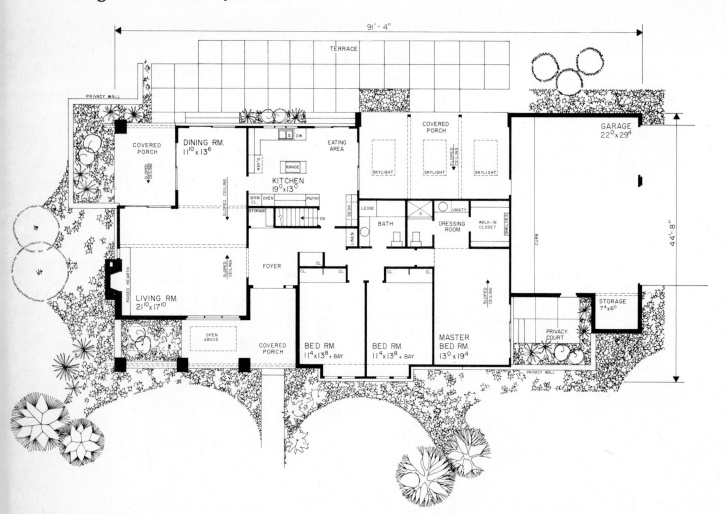

● Privacy will be enjoyed in this home both inside and out. The indoor-outdoor living relationships offered in this plan are outstanding. A covered porch at the entrance. A privacy court off the master bedroom divided from the front yard with a privacy wall. A covered porch serving both the living and dining rooms through sliding glass doors. Also utilizing a privacy wall. Another covered porch off the kitchen eating area. This one is the largest and has skylights above. Also a large rear terrace. The kitchen is efficient with eating space available, an island range and built-in desk. Storage space is abundant. Note storage area in the garage and its overall size. Three front bedrooms. Raised hearth fireplace in the living room.

Design 22303 2,330 Sq. Ft.; 26,982 Cu. Ft.

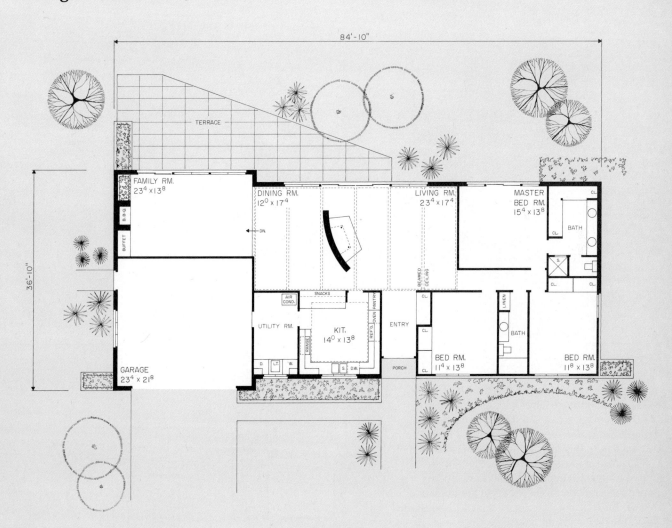

● This hip-roof ranch home has a basic floor plan that is the favorite of many. The reasons for its popularity are, of course, easy to detect. The simple rectangular shape means relatively economical construction. The living areas are large and are located to the rear to function through sliding glass doors with the terrace. The front kitchen is popular because of its view of approaching callers and its proximity to the front entry. The big utility room serves as a practical buffer between the garage and the kitchen.

Worthy of particular note is the efficiency of the kitchen, the stylish living room fireplace, the beamed ceiling, the sunken family room with its wall of built-ins (make that a music wall if you wish). Observe the snack bar and the fine master bath.

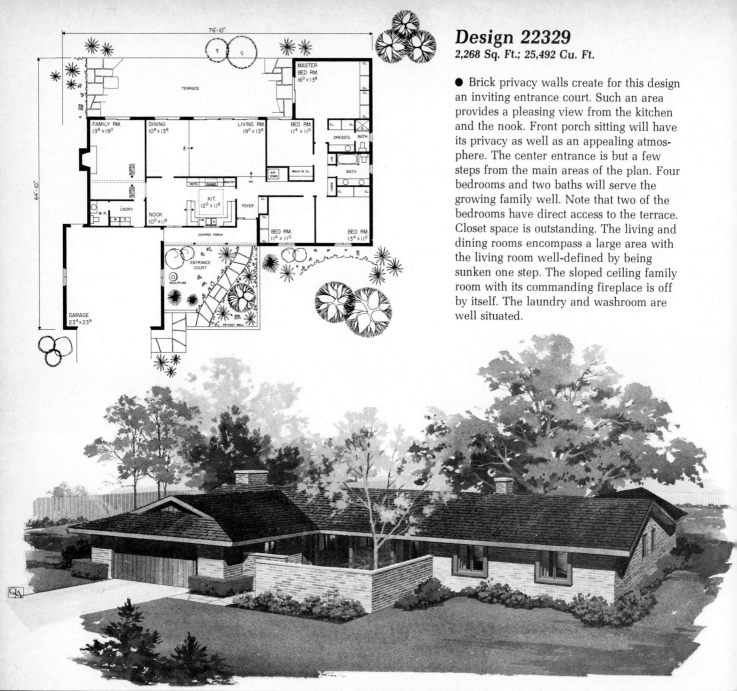

Design 22329
2,268 Sq. Ft.; 25,492 Cu. Ft.

● Brick privacy walls create for this design an inviting entrance court. Such an area provides a pleasing view from the kitchen and the nook. Front porch sitting will have its privacy as well as an appealing atmosphere. The center entrance is but a few steps from the main areas of the plan. Four bedrooms and two baths will serve the growing family well. Note that two of the bedrooms have direct access to the terrace. Closet space is outstanding. The living and dining rooms encompass a large area with the living room well-defined by being sunken one step. The sloped ceiling family room with its commanding fireplace is off by itself. The laundry and washroom are well situated.

Design 22529
2,326 Sq. Ft.; 47,012 Cu. Ft.

● The front entrance court with its plant areas and surrounding accents of colorful quarried stone (make it brick, if you prefer), provides a delightful introduction to this interesting contemporary home. The spacious entry hall leads directly to a generous L-shaped living and dining area. Sliding glass doors provide direct access to the outdoor terrace. An efficient, interior kitchen will be fun in which to work. It could hardly be more strategically located — merely a step or two from the formal dining area, the breakfast nook, and the family room. Although this home has a basement, there is a convenient first floor laundry and an extra washroom. The four bedroom sleeping wing has two full baths. Two of the rooms have access to the outdoor terraces. Notice garage storage.

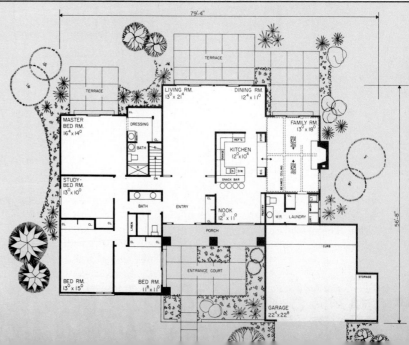

Design 22311
2,205 Sq. Ft.; 19,880 Cu. Ft.

● You could really have fun if you were to ask the various members of your family what they liked best about this contemporary design. Somebody, of course, would say the entrance court and how it functioned through sliding glass doors with the beamed ceilinged family room. Another, perhaps, would say the efficient rear kitchen flanked by the dining room and breakfast nook and overlooking the terrace. Others would chime in with the privacy of the front living room, the laundry/washroom, all those closets and the large shop room behind the garage. Naturally, sooner or later, the list of favorite features would include the raised hearth fireplace in the family room, the snack bar and pass-thru to kitchen and the isolation of the master bedroom and its private bath.

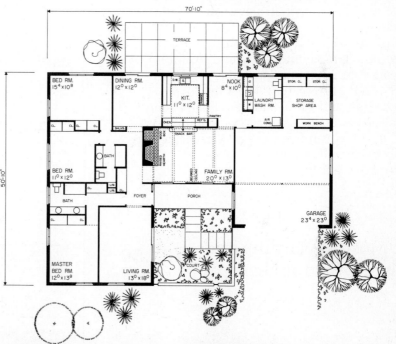

All The "TOOLS" You And Your Builder Need. . .

1. THE PLAN BOOKS

Home Planners' unique Design Category Series makes it easy to look at and study only the types of designs for which you and your family have an interest. Each of six plan books features a specific type of home, namely: Two-Story, 1½ Story, One-Story Over 2000 Sq. Ft., One-Story Under 2000 Sq. Ft., Multi-Levels and Vacation Homes. In addition to the convenient Design Category Series, there is an impressive selection of other current titles. While the home plans featured in these books are also to be found in the Design Category Series, they, too, are edited for those with special tastes and requirements. Your family will spend many enjoyable hours reviewing the delightfully designed exteriors and the practical floor plans. Surely your home or office library should include a selection of these popular plan books. Your complete satisfaction is guaranteed.

2. THE CONSTRUCTION BLUEPRINTS

There are blueprints available for each of the designs published in Home Planners' current plan books. Depending upon the size, the style and the type of home, each set of blueprints consists of from five to ten large sheets. Only by studying the blueprints is it possible to give complete and final consideration to the proper selection of a design for your next home. The blueprints provide the opportunity for all family members to familiarize themselves with the features of all exterior elevations, interior elevations and details, all dimensions, special built-in features and effects. They also provide a full understanding of the materials to be used and/or selected. The low-cost of our blueprints makes it possible and indeed, practical, to study in detail a number of different sets of blueprints before deciding upon which design to build.

3. THE MATERIALS LIST

A separate list of materials, available for a small fee, is an important part of the plan package. It comprises the last sheet of each set of blueprints and serves as a handy reference during the period of construction. Of course, at the pricing and the material ordering stages, it is indispensable.

4. THE SPECIFICATION OUTLINE

Each order for blueprints is accompanied by one Specification Outline. You and your builder will find this a time-saving tool when deciding upon your own individual specifications. An important reference document should you wish to write your own specifications.

5. THE PLUMBING & ELECTRICAL PACKAGE

The construction blueprints you order from Home Planners, Inc. include locations for all plumbing fixtures — sinks, lavatories, tubs, showers, water closets, laundry trays, hot water heaters, etc. The blueprints also show the locations of all electrical switches, plugs, and outlets. These plumbing and electrical details are sufficient to present to your local contractor for discussions about your individual specifications and subsequent installations in conformance with local codes. However, for those who wish to acquaint themselves with many of the intricacies of residential plumbing and electrical details and installations, Home Planners, Inc. has made available this package. We do not recommend that the layman attempt to do his own plumbing and electrical work. It is, nevertheless, advisable that owners be as knowledgeable as possible about each of these disciplines. The entire family will appreciate the educational value of these low-cost, easy-to-understand details.

THE DESIGN CATEGORY SERIES

210 ONE STORY HOMES OVER 2,000 SQUARE FEET
Spacious homes for gracious living. Includes all popular styles—Spanish, Western, Tudor, French, Contemporary, and others. Amenity-filled plans feature master bedroom suites, atriums, courtyards, and pools.

1. 192 pages. $4.95 ($5.95 Canada)

315 ONE STORY HOMES UNDER 2,000 SQUARE FEET
Economical homes in a variety of styles. Efficient floor plans contain plenty of attractive features—gathering rooms, formal and informal living and dining rooms, mudrooms, outdoor living spaces, and more. Many plans are expandable.

2. 192 pages. $4.95 ($5.95 Canada)

150 1½ STORY HOMES
From starter homes to country estates. Includes classic story-and-a-half styles: Contemporary, Williamsburg, Georgian, Tudor, and Cape Cod. Outstanding outdoor livability. Many expandable plans.

3. 128 pages. $3.95 ($4.95 Canada)

360 TWO STORY HOMES
Plans for all budgets and all families—in a wide range of styles: Tudors, Saltboxes, Farmhouses, Southern Colonials, Georgians, Contemporaries, and more. Many plans have extra-large kitchens, extra bedrooms, and extra baths.

4. 288 pages. $6.95 ($8.95 Canada)

215 MULTI-LEVEL HOMES
Distinctive styles for both flat and sloping sites. Tailor-made for great outdoor living. Features include exposed lower levels, upper-level lounges, balconies, decks, and terraces. Includes plans for all building budgets.

5. 192 pages. $4.95 ($5.95 Canada)

223 VACATION HOMES
Full-color volume features A-frames, chalets, lodges, hexagons, cottages, and other attractive styles in one-story, two-story, and multi-level plans ranging from 480 to 3,238 square feet. Perfect for woodland, lakeside, or seashore.

6. 176 pages. $4.95 ($5.95 Canada)

THE EXTERIOR STYLE SERIES

7.

8.

9.

10.

330 EARLY AMERICAN HOME PLANS
A heart-warming collection of the best in Early American architecture. Traces the style from colonial structures to popular Traditional versions. Includes a history of different styles.

304 pages. $9.95 ($11.95 Canada)

335 CONTEMPORARY HOME PLANS
Required reading for anyone interested in the clean-lined elegance of Contemporary design. Features plans of all sizes and types, as well as a fascinating look at the history of this style.

304 pages. $9.95 ($11.95 Canada)

135 ENGLISH TUDOR HOMES Tudor architecture may well be America's favorite style. This book is packed with Tudor and English-style homes of all types and sizes, ranging from mansions to truly affordable designs. Must reading for the Tudor lover.

104 pages. $3.95 ($4.95 Canada)

136 SPANISH & WESTERN HOME DESIGNS Includes an array of sun-filled plans that emphasize indoor-outdoor livability. Key architectural features include stucco exteriors, arches, tile roofs, terraces, patios, and more.

120 pages. $3.95 ($4.95 Canada)

PLAN PORTFOLIOS

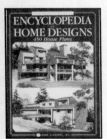

ENCYCLOPEDIA OF HOME DESIGNS (450 PLANS) The largest book of its kind—450 plans in a complete range of housing types, styles, and sizes. Includes plans for all building budgets, families, and styles of living.

11. 320 pages. $9.95 ($11.95 Canada)

MOST POPULAR HOME DESIGNS (360 PLANS) Our customers' favorite plans, including one-story, 1½-story, two-story, and multi-level homes in a variety of styles. For families large and small. Designs feature many of today's most popular amenities: lounges, clutter rooms, sunspaces, media rooms, and more.

12. 272 pages. $8.95 ($10.95 Canada)

COLOR PORTFOLIO OF HOUSES & PLANS (310 PLANS) A beautiful full-color guide to Home Planners' best plans, including Early American, Spanish, French, Tudor, Contemporary, and our own Trend Home styles. One-story, 1½-story, two-story, and multi-level designs for all budgets.

13. 288 pages. $12.95 ($14.95 Canada)

NEW FROM HOME PLANNERS

TUDOR HOUSES Here is the stuff that dream houses are made of! A superb portfolio of 80 enchanting Tudor-style homes, from cozy Cotswold cottages to impressive Baronial manors. Includes a decorating section filled with colorful photographs and illustrations showing 24 different furniture arrangements.

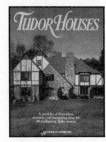

14. 208 pages. $10.95 ($12.95 Canada)

COUNTRY HOUSES Shows off 80 gorgeous country homes in three eye-catching styles: Cape Cods, Farmhouses, and Center-Hall Colonials. Each features an architect's exterior rendering, artist's depiction of a furnished interior room, large floor plans, and planning tips. Full-color section presents decorating schemes for nine different rooms.

15. 208 pages. $10.95 ($12.95 Canada)

HOME PLANS FOR OUTDOOR LIVING This book showcases more than 100 plans, each uniquely styled to bring the outdoors in. Features terraces, decks, porches, balconies, courtyards, atriums, and sunspaces, integrated into compelling home plans of all types and styles. Includes brilliant full-color photography of homes actually built and planning pointers.

16. 192 pages. $10.95 ($12.95 Canada)

HOME PLANS FOR SOLAR LIVING This beautiful book proves that passive solar design can be stylish and up-to-date as well as practical and energy efficient. Here are nearly 100 home plans chosen for their graciousness and livability, in addition to their proven solar characteristics. Each home features a detailed floor plan, artist's rendering of the front and often rear elevation, and notes on the proper siting and exposure of the design.

17. 192 pages. $10.95 ($12.95 Canada)

THE SIGNATURE SERIES PORTFOLIO A distinctive collection of thirty-five incredible home plans. Styles include Norman Country Estates, Tudor Manors, Victorians, French Chateaus, Greek Revivals, and Contemporaries. Designs feature an abundance of cherished amenities in sizes ranging from 3,200 to 7,500 square feet. Construction blueprints available. An exquisite portfolio at $15.00.

18. 35 luxury homes. $15.00 ($18.00 Canada)

**TO ORDER BOOKS BY PHONE
CALL TOLL FREE: 1-800-322-6797**

Please fill out the coupon below. We will process your order and ship it from our office within 48 hours. Send coupon and check for the total to:

 HOME PLANNERS, INC.
3275 West Ina Road, Suite 110, Dept. BK
Tucson, Arizona 85741

THE DESIGN CATEGORY SERIES - A great series of books specially edited by design type and size. Each book features interesting sections to further enhance the study of design styles, sizes and house types. A fine addition to the home or office library. Complete collection - over 1250 designs.

1. _____ 210 One Story Homes over 2,000 Square Feet @ $4.95 ($5.95 Canada) $_____
2. _____ 315 One Story Homes Under 2,000 Square Feet @ $4.95 ($5.95 Canada) $_____
3. _____ 150 1½ Story Homes @ $3.95 ($4.95 Canada) $_____
4. _____ 360 Two Story Homes @ $6.95 ($8.95 Canada) $_____
5. _____ 215 Multi-Level Homes @ $4.95 ($5.95 Canada) $_____
6. _____ 223 Vacation Homes @ $4.95 ($5.95 Canada) $_____

The interesting series of plan books listed below have been edited to appeal to various style preferences and budget considerations. The majority of the designs highlighted in these books also may be found in the Design Category Series.

THE EXTERIOR STYLE SERIES
7. _____ 330 Early American Home Plans @ $9.95 ($11.95 Canada) $_____
8. _____ 335 Contemporary Home Plans @ $9.95 ($11.95 Canada) $_____
9. _____ 135 English Tudor Homes @ $3.95 ($4.95 Canada) $_____
10._____ 136 Spanish & Western Home Designs @ $3.95 ($4.95 Canada) $_____

PLAN PORTFOLIOS
11._____ Encyclopedia of Home Designs @ $9.95 ($11.95 Canada) $_____
12._____ Most Popular Home Designs @ $8.95 ($10.95 Canada) $_____
13._____ Color Portfolio of Houses & Plans @ $12.95 ($14.95 Canada) $_____

NEW FROM HOME PLANNERS
14._____ Tudor Houses @ $10.95 ($12.95 Canada) $_____
15._____ Country Houses @ $10.95 ($12.95 Canada) $_____
16._____ Home Plans for Outdoor Living @ $10.95 ($12.95 Canada) $_____
17._____ Home Plans for Solar Living @ $10.95 ($12.95 Canada) $_____
18._____ Signature Series Portfolio @ $15.00 ($18.00 Canada) $_____

Sub total $_____
Arizona residents add 5% sales tax; Michigan residents add 4% sales tax $_____
Add postage and handling $ 2.00
TOTAL (please enclose check) $_____

Name (please print) _____

Address _____

City _____ State _____ Zip _____

CANADIAN CUSTOMERS: Please use Canadian prices noted. Remit in Canadian funds to: Home Planners, Inc., 20 Cedar St. North, Kitchener, Ontario N2H 2W8   Phone: (519) 743-4169

CV2BK

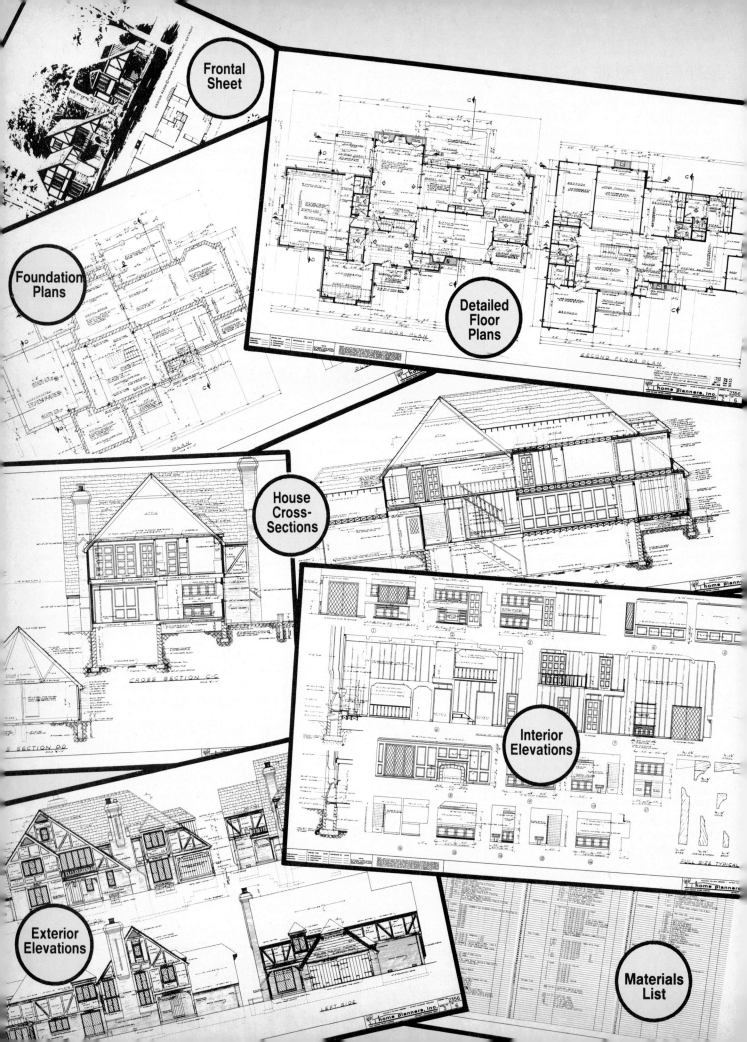

Frontal
Sheet

Detailed
Floor
Plans

Foundation
Plans

House
Cross-
Sections

Interior
Elevations

Exterior
Elevations

Materials
List

What Our Plans Include

The Blueprints

1. FRONTAL SHEET.
Artist's landscaped sketch of the exterior and ink-line floor plans are on the frontal sheet of each set of blueprints.

2. FOUNDATION PLAN.
¼" Scale basement and foundation plan. All necessary notations and dimensions. Plot plan diagram for locating house on building site.

3. DETAILED FLOOR PLAN.
¼" Scale first and second floor plans with complete dimensions. Cross-section detail keys. Diagrammatic layout of electrical outlets and switches.

4. HOUSE CROSS-SECTIONS.
Large scale sections of foundation, interior and exterior walls, floors and roof details for design and construction control.

5. INTERIOR ELEVATIONS.
Large scale interior details of the complete kitchen cabinet design, bathrooms, powder room, laundry, fireplaces, paneling, beam ceilings, built-in cabinets, etc.

6. EXTERIOR ELEVATIONS.
¼" Scale exterior elevation drawings of front, rear, and both sides of the house. All exterior materials and details are shown to indicate the complete design and proportions of the house.

7. MATERIALS LIST.
For a small additional fee, complete lists of all materials required for the construction of the house as designed are included in each set of blueprints (one charge for any size order).

THIS BLUEPRINT PACKAGE
will help you and your family take a major step forward in the final appraisal and planning of your new home. Only by spending many enjoyable and informative hours studying the numerous details included in the complete package will you feel sure of, and comfortable with, your commitment to build your new home. To assure successful and productive consultation with your builder and/or architect, reference to the various elements of the blueprint package is a must. The blueprints, materials list and specification outline will save much consultation time and expense. Don't be without them.

The Materials List

For a small extra charge, you will receive a materials list with each set of blueprints you order (one fee for any size order). Each list shows you the quantity, type and size of the non-mechanical materials required to build your home. It also tells you where these materials are used. This makes the blueprints easy to understand.

Influencing the mechanical requirements are geographical differences in availability of materials, local codes, methods of installation and individual preferences. Because of these factors, your local heating, plumbing and electrical contractors can supply you with necessary material take-offs for their particular trades.

Materials lists simplify your material ordering and enable you to get quicker price quotations from your builder and material dealer. Because the materials list is an integral part of each set of blueprints, it is not available separately.

Among the materials listed:

• Masonry, Veneer & Fireplace • Framing Lumber • Roofing & Sheet Metal • Windows & Door Frames • Exterior Trim & Insulation • Tile Work, Finish Floors • Interior Trim, Kitchen Cabinets • Rough & Finish Hardware

The Specification Outline

This fill-in type specification lists over 150 phases of home construction from excavating to painting and includes wiring, plumbing, heating and air-conditioning. It consists of 16 pages and will prove invaluable for specifying to your builder the exact materials, equipment and methods of construction you want in your new home. One Specification Outline is included free with each order for blueprints. Additional Specification Outlines are available at $5.00 each.

CONTENTS
• General Instructions, Suggestions and Information • Excavating and Grading • Masonry and Concrete Work • Sheet Metal Work • Carpentry, Millwork, Roofing, and Miscellaneous Items • Lath and Plaster or Drywall Wallboard • Schedule for Room Finishes • Painting and Finishing • Tile Work • Electrical Work • Plumbing • Heating and Air-Conditioning

More Products from Home Planners To Help You Plan Your Home

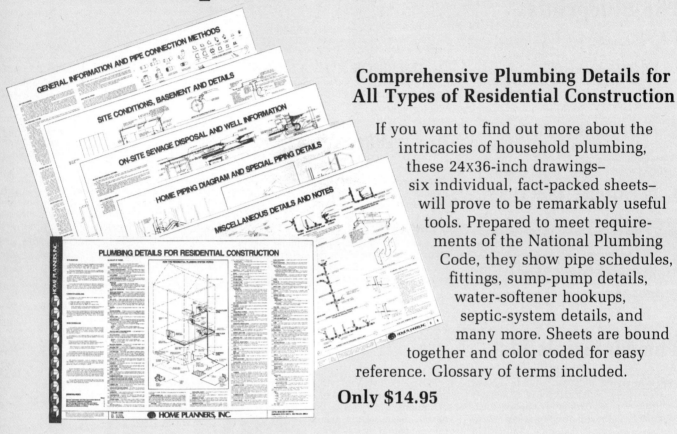

Comprehensive Plumbing Details for All Types of Residential Construction

If you want to find out more about the intricacies of household plumbing, these 24x36-inch drawings– six individual, fact-packed sheets– will prove to be remarkably useful tools. Prepared to meet requirements of the National Plumbing Code, they show pipe schedules, fittings, sump-pump details, water-softener hookups, septic-system details, and many more. Sheets are bound together and color coded for easy reference. Glossary of terms included.

Only $14.95

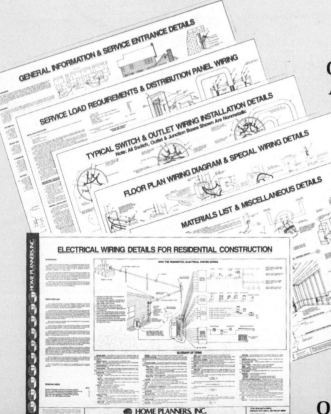

Complete Electrical Wiring Details for All Types of Residential Construction

Designed to take the mystery out of household electrical systems, these comprehensive 24x36-inch drawings come packed with details. Prepared to meet requirements of the National Electrical Code, the six fact-filled sheets cover a variety of topics, including appliance wattage, wire sizing, switch-installation schematics, cable-routing details, doorbell hookups, and many others. Sheets are bound together and color coded for easy reference. Glossary of terms included.

Only $14.95

Plan Your Home with Plan-A-Home™

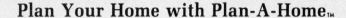

Plan-A-Home™ is a very useful tool. It's a simple product that will help you design a new home, plan a remodeling project or arrange furniture on an existing plan. Each package contains: more than 700 peel-and-stick *planning symbols* on a self-stick, vinyl sheet, including walls, windows, doors, furniture, kitchen components, bath fixtures, and many more; a reusable, transparent, ¼-inch-scale *planning grid* that can help you create houses up to 140x92 feet; *tracing paper;* and a *felt-tip pen,* with water-soluble ink that wipes away quickly. The transparent planning grid matches the scale of working blueprints, so you can lay it over existing drawings and modify them as necessary.

Only $24.95

Residential Construction Details

Home Planners' blueprint package contains everything an experienced builder needs to construct a particular plan. However, it doesn't show the thousands upon thousands of ways building materials come together to form a house. Prepared to meet requirements of the Uniform Building Code, these drawings– eight large, fact-filled sheets–depict the materials and methods used to build foundations, fireplaces, walls, floors, and roofs. What's more, where appropriate, they show acceptable alternatives. Bound together for easy reference.

Only $14.95

Get any two of Plumbing, Electrical, and Construction Details for just $22.95 (save $6.95). Get all three for only $29.95 (save $14.90).

To order, turn the page . . .

The Blueprint Price Schedule

The blueprint package you order will be an invaluable tool for the complete study of the details relating to the construction of your favorite design, as well as the master plan for building your home. Even the smallest of homes require much construction data and architectural detailing. As the house grows in size, so does the need for more data and details. Frequently, a house of only modest size can require an inordinate amount of data and detailing. This may be the result of its irregular shape and/or the complexity of its architectural features. In the pricing of its blueprints, Home Planners, Inc. has taken into account these factors. Before completing the blueprint order form on the opposite page, be sure to refer to the price schedule below for the appropriate blueprint charges for the design of your choice.

Schedule A: Single Sets, $125.00; Four Set Package, $175.00; Eight Set Package, $225.00. Additional Identical Sets in Same Order, $30.00 each.

Schedule B: Single Sets, $150.00; Four Set Package, $200.00; Eight Set Package, $250.00. Additional Identical Sets in Same Order, $30.00 each.

Schedule C: Single Sets, $175.00; Four Set Package, $225.00; Eight Set Package, $275.00. Additional Identical Sets in Same Order, $30.00 each.

Schedule D: Single Sets, $200.00; Four Set Package, $250.00; Eight Set Package, $300.00. Additional Identical Sets in Same Order, $30.00 each.

DESIGN NO.	PRICE SCHEDULE	DESIGN NO.	PRICE SCHEDULE	DESIGN NO.	PRICE SCHEDULE	DESIGN NO.	PRICE SCHEDULE	DESIGN NO.	PRICE SCHEDULE
21026	C	21888	D	22245	D	22378	C	22767	D
21054	B	21892	B	22251	D	22384	C	22768	D
21060	D	21897	C	22255	C	22385	B	22777	B
21101	D	21911	D	22256	C	22386	B	22778	C
21102	C	21916	D	22258	C	22387	C	22779	D
21111	C	21924	C	22259	B	22391	C	22783	D
21144	B	21928	D	22260	B	22506	C	22784	C
21149	B	21929	C	22264	C	22515	C	22785	C
21170	B	21931	C	22266	C	22519	C	22789	C
21174	C	21936	D	22268	B	22523	B	22790	B
21201	C	21950	B	22269	C	22527	C	22791	D
21223	C	21952	C	22270	C	22529	C	22793	B
21228	D	21989	C	22271	C	22532	B	22819	C
21238	C	21993	D	22274	C	22534	D	22820	C
21264	D	21994	D	22277	B	22537	C	22827	C
21283	C	21997	D	22278	C	22544	C	22830	C
21295	C	22109	B	22287	C	22557	B	22832	C
21345	B	22110	D	22289	C	22573	C	22833	C
21363	B	22127	B	22293	B	22590	C	22835	C
21711	D	22129	B	22294	D	22594	C	22838	C
21725	D	22133	D	22303	C	22595	C	22847	C
21754	B	22134	C	22304	C	22613	B	22851	C
21756	C	22135	C	22311	C	22615	D	22857	D
21761	C	22142	C	22316	B	22620	B	22858	C
21784	C	22144	C	22317	D	22670	D	22860	C
21786	C	22177	C	22318	B	22675	C	22861	C
21787	C	22179	C	22329	C	22678	B	22862	C
21788	C	22181	C	22335	C	22710	D	22863	C
21820	C	22183	D	22343	D	22717	C	22866	C
21825	B	22204	B	22347	C	22720	D	22867	C
21835	B	22208	C	22350	D	22721	C	22877	C
21837	C	22209	C	22352	B	22730	C	22881	C
21841	C	22212	D	22353	C	22739	D	22882	C
21844	B	22220	C	22357	B	22740	C	22883	C
21851	C	22226	D	22359	B	22745	C	22884	B
21867	B	22229	C	22360	B	22746	C	22886	B
21872	C	22231	C	22362	B	22747	D	22888	D
21874	C	22233	B	22370	C	22756	C	22900	C
21880	C	22236	C	22371	C	22764	C	22903	C
21881	C			22372	C	22765	D	22915	C
21886	C					22766	C	22920	D

Before You Order

1. STUDY THE DESIGNS . . . found in Home Planners and Heritage Homes plan books. As you review these delightful custom homes, you should keep in mind the total living requirements of your family — both indoors and outdoors. Although we do not make changes in plans, many minor changes can be made prior to construction. If major changes are involved to satisfy your personal requirements, you should consider ordering one set of sepias and having them modified. Consultation with your architect is strongly advised when contemplating major changes.

2. HOW TO ORDER BLUEPRINTS . . . After you have chosen the design that satisfies your requirements, or if you have selected one that you wish to study in more detail, simply clip the accompanying order blank and mail with your remittance. However, if it is not convenient for you to send a check or money order, you can use your credit card, or merely indicate C.O.D. shipment. Postman will collect all charges, including postage and C.O.D. fee. C.O.D. shipments are not permitted to Canada or foreign countries. Should time be of essence, as it sometimes is with many of our customers, your telephone order usually can be processed and shipped in the next day's mail. Simply call toll free 1-800-521-6797. (Arizona residents call collect 0-602-297-8200.)

3. OUR SERVICE . . . Home Planners makes every effort to process and ship each order for blueprints and books within 48 hours. Because of this, we have deemed it unnecessary to acknowledge receipt

How Many Blueprints Do You Need?

Because additional sets of the same design in each order are only $30.00 each, you save considerably by ordering your total requirements now. To help you determine the exact number of sets, please refer to the handy checklist below.

Blueprint Checklist

__OWNER'S SET(S)

__BUILDER (Usually requires at least three sets: one as legal document; one for inspection; and at least one for tradesmen — usually more.)

__BUILDING PERMIT (Sometimes two sets are required.)

__MORTGAGE SOURCE (Usually one set for a conventional mortgage; three sets for F.H.A. or V.A. type mortgages.)

__SUBDIVISION COMMITTEE (If any.)

__TOTAL NUMBER SETS REQUIRED

BLUEPRINT HOTLINE

PHONE TOLL FREE: 1-800-521-6797.
Orders received by 6 p.m. (Eastern time) will be processed the same day and shipped to you the following day. Use of this line is restricted to blueprint and book ordering only. (Arizona residents call collect 0-602-297-8200.)

KINDLY NOTE: When ordering by phone, please state Order Form Key Number located in box at lower left corner of the blueprint order form.

IN CANADA: Add 20% to prices listed on this order form and mail in Canadian funds to:
HOME PLANNERS, INC.
20 Cedar St. North
Kitchener, Ontario N2H 2W8
Phone: (519) 743-4169

---

of our customers orders. See order coupon for the postage and handling charges for surface mail, air mail or foreign mail.

4. MODIFYING OUR PLANS . . . Slight revisions are easy to do before you start building. (We don't alter plans, by the way.) If you're thinking about major changes, consider ordering a set of sepias. After changes have been made on the sepia, additional sets of plans may be reproduced from the sepia master. Should you decide to revise the plan significantly, we strongly suggest that you consult an experienced architect or designer.

5. A NOTE REGARDING REVERSE BLUE-PRINTS . . . As a special service to those wishing to build in reverse of the plan as shown, we do include

an extra set of reversed blueprints for only $30.00 additional with each order. Even though the lettering and dimensions appear backward on reversed blueprints, they make a handy reference because they show the house just as it's being built in reverse from the standard blueprints — thereby helping you visualize the home better.

6. OUR EXCHANGE POLICY . . . Since blueprints are printed in response to your order, we cannot honor requests for refunds. However, we will exchange your entire first order for an equal number of blueprints at a price of $20.00 for the first set and $10.00 for each additional set. All sets from the previous order must be returned before the exchange can take place. Please add $3.00 for postage and handling via surface mail; $4.00 via air mail.

TO: HOME PLANNERS, INC., 3275 WEST INA ROAD, SUITE 110 TUCSON, ARIZONA 85741

Please rush me the following:
___ SET(S) BLUEPRINTS FOR DESIGN NO(S). . . . . $_____
Kindly refer to Blueprint Price Schedule on opposite page.
___ SEPIA FOR DESIGN NO(S). . . . . $_____
___ MATERIALS LIST @ $25.00. . . . . $_____
___ ADDITIONAL SPECIFICATION OUTLINES @ $5.00 each . . . . $_____
___ DETAIL SETS @ $14.95 ea.; any two for $22.95; all three for $29.95 . . . . $_____
☐ PLUMBING ☐ ELECTRICAL ☐ CONSTRUCTION
___ PLAN-A-HOME™ Design Kit @ $24.95 ea. (plus $3.00 postage) . . . . $_____
Arizona Residents add 5% sales tax; Michigan residents add 4% sales tax $_____

FOR POSTAGE	☐	$4.00 Added to Order for Surface Mail (UPS) – Any Mdse.
AND HANDLING	☐	$5.00 Added for Priority Mail of One-Three Sets of Blueprints.
PLEASE CHECK	☐	$8.00 Added for Priority Mail of Four or more Sets of Blueprints.
✔ & REMIT	☐	For Canadian orders add $2.00 to above applicable rates.

$_____

☐ C.O.D. PAY POSTMAN (U.S. ONLY)   TOTAL in U.S. funds $_____

PLEASE PRINT
Name _____
Street _____
City _____ State _____ Zip _____

CREDIT CARD ORDERS ONLY: Fill in the boxes below   **Prices subject to change without notice**
Credit Card No. [ ][ ][ ][ ][ ][ ][ ][ ][ ][ ][ ][ ][ ][ ][ ][ ]   Expiration Date
Month/Year [ ][ ][ ][ ]
CHECK ONE: ☐ VISA ☐ MasterCard
Order Form Key CV2BP   Your Signature _____

BLUEPRINT ORDERS SHIPPED WITHIN 48 HOURS OF RECEIPT!

TO: HOME PLANNERS, INC., 3275 WEST INA ROAD, SUITE 110 TUCSON, ARIZONA 85741

Please rush me the following:
___ SET(S) BLUEPRINTS FOR DESIGN NO(S). . . . . $_____
Kindly refer to Blueprint Price Schedule on opposite page.
___ SEPIA FOR DESIGN NO(S). . . . . $_____
___ MATERIALS LIST @ $25.00. . . . . $_____
___ ADDITIONAL SPECIFICATION OUTLINES @ $5.00 each . . . . $_____
___ DETAIL SETS @ $14.95 ea.; any two for $22.95; all three for $29.95 . . . . $_____
☐ PLUMBING ☐ ELECTRICAL ☐ CONSTRUCTION
___ PLAN-A-HOME™ Design Kit @ $24.95 ea. (plus $3.00 postage) . . . . $_____
Arizona Residents add 5% sales tax; Michigan residents add 4% sales tax $_____

FOR POSTAGE	☐	$4.00 Added to Order for Surface Mail (UPS) – Any Mdse.
AND HANDLING	☐	$5.00 Added for Priority Mail of One-Three Sets of Blueprints.
PLEASE CHECK	☐	$8.00 Added for Priority Mail of Four or more Sets of Blueprints.
✔ & REMIT	☐	For Canadian orders add $2.00 to above applicable rates.

$_____

☐ C.O.D. PAY POSTMAN (U.S. ONLY)   TOTAL in U.S. funds $_____

PLEASE PRINT
Name _____
Street _____
City _____ State _____ Zip _____

CREDIT CARD ORDERS ONLY: Fill in the boxes below   **Prices subject to change without notice**
Credit Card No. [ ][ ][ ][ ][ ][ ][ ][ ][ ][ ][ ][ ][ ][ ][ ][ ]   Expiration Date
Month/Year [ ][ ][ ][ ]
CHECK ONE: ☐ VISA ☐ MasterCard
Order Form Key CV2BP   Your Signature _____

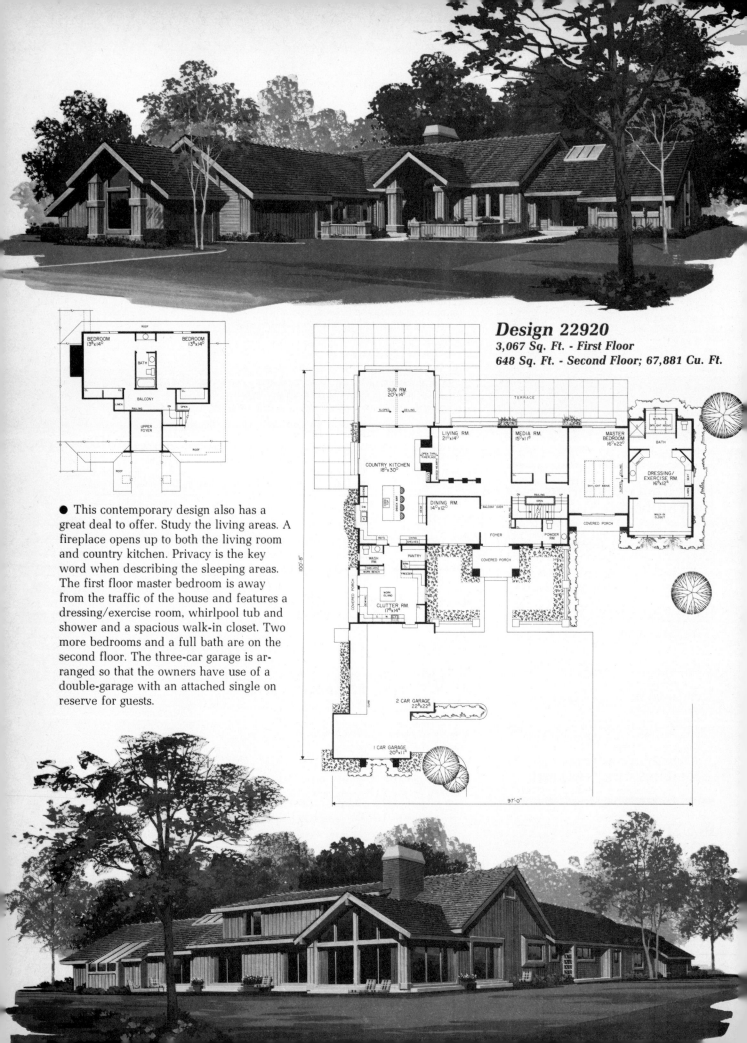

Design 22920
3,067 Sq. Ft. - First Floor
648 Sq. Ft. - Second Floor; 67,881 Cu. Ft.

Floor plan labels (second floor):
BEDROOM 13⁸x14⁰
BEDROOM 13⁸x14⁰
BATH
BALCONY
UPPER FOYER
ROOF
RAILING
LINEN
CL
DN
OPEN

Floor plan labels (first floor):
SUN RM. 20⁰x14⁰
SLOPED CEILING
TERRACE
LIVING RM. 21⁰x14⁰
MEDIA RM. 15⁰x11⁸
MASTER BEDROOM 16⁰x22⁰
COUNTRY KITCHEN 18⁰x30⁰
OPEN THRU FIREPLACE
RAISED HEARTH
WHIRLPOOL SKYLIGHT ABOVE
BATH
DRESSING/EXERCISE RM. 16⁸x12⁴
SKYLIGHT ABOVE
DINING RM. 14⁰x12⁰
BALCONY OVER
OPEN
WALK-IN CLOSET
SNACK BAR
COVERED PORCH
REF'S
CHINA SHELVES
FOYER
POWDER RM.
COVERED PORCH
WASH RM.
SHELVES WORK BENCH
PANTRY
FREEZER
COVERED PORCH
WORK ISLAND
CLUTTER RM. 17⁰x14⁴
COVERED PORCH
2 CAR GARAGE 22⁸x22⁸
I CAR GARAGE 20⁸x11⁰

100'-8"
97'-0"

● This contemporary design also has a great deal to offer. Study the living areas. A fireplace opens up to both the living room and country kitchen. Privacy is the key word when describing the sleeping areas. The first floor master bedroom is away from the traffic of the house and features a dressing/exercise room, whirlpool tub and shower and a spacious walk-in closet. Two more bedrooms and a full bath are on the second floor. The three-car garage is arranged so that the owners have use of a double-garage with an attached single on reserve for guests.

SOLAR ORIENTED DESIGNS . . .

exist in almost limitless sizes, shapes and types. Most houses can be made more, or less, solar oriented by proper planning of room locations in relation to the siting of the structure on a piece of property. Selection of a floor plan with an array of windows that will face the north in the winter can hardly be recommended. Better to choose either a different plan or site. However, the designs in this section offer a study of the many alternatives to planning a more solar oriented house. Note the atriums, greenhouses, sunspaces, garden rooms, underground and berm houses and even the solar panels that are presented for your consideration.

Design 22832

2,805 Sq. Ft. - Excluding Atrium; 52,235 Cu. Ft.

● The advantage of passive solar heating is a significant highlight of this contemporary design. The huge skylight over the atrium provides shelter during inclement weather, while permitting the enjoyment of plenty of natural light to the atrium below and surrounding areas. Whether open to the sky, or sheltered by a glass or translucent covering, the atrium becomes a cheerful spot and provides an abundance of natural light to its adjacent rooms. The stone floor will absorb an abundance of heat from the sun during the day and permit circulation of warm air to other areas at night. During the summer, shades afford protection from the sun without sacrificing the abundance of natural light and the feeling of spaciousness. Sloping ceilings highlight each of the major rooms, three bedrooms, formal living and dining and study. The conversation area between the two formal areas will really be something to talk about. The broad expanses of roof can accommodate solar panels should an active system be desired to supplement the passive features of this design.

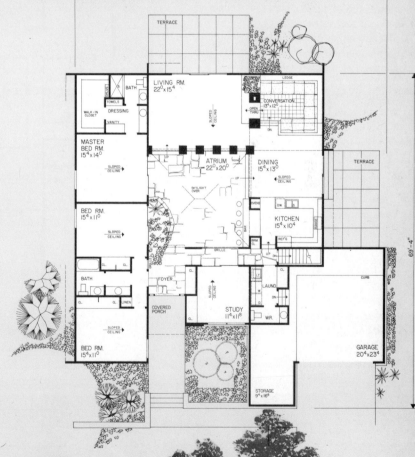

Design 22857
2,982 Sq. Ft.; 60,930 Cu. Ft.

● Imagine yourself occupying this home! Study the outstanding master bedroom. You will be forever pleased by its many features. It has "his" and "her" baths each with a large walk-in closet, sliding glass doors to a private, side terrace (a great place to enjoy a morning cup of coffee) and an adjacent study. Notice that the two family bedrooms are separated from the master bedroom. This allows for total privacy both for the parents and the children. Continue to observe this plan. You will have no problem at all entertaining in the gathering room. Your party can flow to the adjacent balcony on a warm summer evening. The work center has been designed in an orderly fashion. The U-shaped kitchen utilizes the triangular work pattern, said to be the most efficient. Only a few steps away, you will be in the breakfast room, formal dining room, laundry or washroom. Take your time and study every last detail in this home plan.

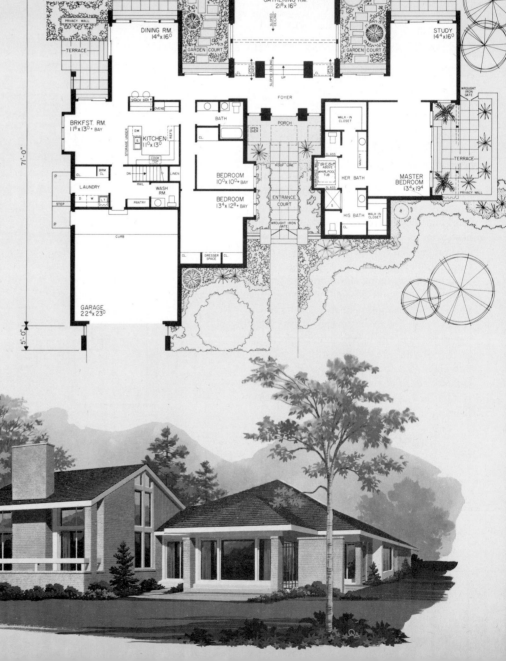

Design 22886
1,733 Sq. Ft.; 34,986 Cu. Ft.

● This one-story house is attractive with its contemporary exterior. It has many excellent features to keep you and your family happy for many years. For example, notice the spacious gathering room with sliding glass doors that allow easy access to the greenhouse. Another exciting feature of this room is that you will receive an abundance of sunshine through the clerestory windows. Also, this plan offers you two nice-sized bedrooms. The master suite is not only roomy but also unique because through both the bedroom and the bath you can enter a greenhouse with a hot tub. The hot tub will be greatly appreciated after a long, hard day at work. Don't forget to note the breakfast room with access to the terrace. You will enjoy the efficient kitchen that will make preparing meals a breeze. A greenhouse window here is charming. An appealing, open staircase leads to the basement. The square and cubic footages of the greenhouses are 394 and 4,070 respectively and are not included in the above figures.

Design 22882
2,832 Sq. Ft.; 59,635 Cu. Ft.

● This contemporary, one-story design should be oriented on a west-facing site if it is built in the northern regions of the country. The result will be minimal exposure to the cold northern winds during the winter. Study the north side of this plan. There is only one small window and it will be protected by the privacy wall. This means that the rooms on the opposite side of the house will have the desirable southern exposure. A westerly exposure for the living room will be most beneficial in many areas of the country. This plan reflects interesting living patterns and excellent indoor/outdoor relationships. Wide overhanging roofs, skylights, glass gables, vented walkways, wind-buffering privacy fences and 2x6 construction are among this design's energy oriented features.

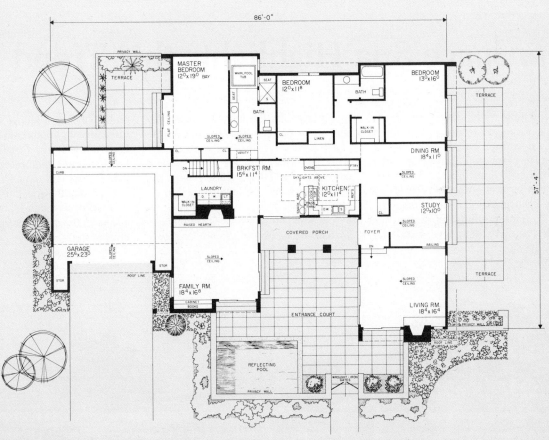

Design 22881 2,770 Sq. Ft.; 60,315 Cu. Ft.

● Energy-efficiency will be obtained in this unique, contemporary design. This plan has been designed for a south facing lot in the temperate zones. There is minimal window exposure on the north side of the house so the interior will be protected. The eastern side of the plan, on the other hand, will allow the morning sunlight to enter. As the sun travels from east to west, the various rooms will have light through windows, sliding glass doors or skylights. The garage acts as a buffer against the hot afternoon sun. The living areas are oriented to the front of the plan. They will benefit from the southern exposure during the cooler months. During the summer months, this area will be shielded from the high, hot summer sun by the overhanging roof. If you plan to build in the south, this house would be ideal for a north facing site. This results in a minimum amount of hot sun for the living areas and a maximum amount of protection from the sun on the rear, southern side of the house.

A Sunspace Spa Highlights this Trend House

● Contemporary in exterior styling, this house is energy oriented. It calls for 2 x 6 exterior wall construction with placement on a north facing lot. Traffic flows through the interior of this plan by way of the foyer. Not only is the foyer useful, but it is dramatic with its sloped ceiling and second floor balcony and skylight above. Excellent living areas are throughout. A spacious, sunken living room is to the left of the foyer. It shares a thru-fireplace, faced with fieldstone, with the study. Sloped ceilings are in both of these rooms. Informal activities can take place in the family room. It, too, has a fireplace and is adjacent to the work center. Two of the bedrooms are on the second floor with a lounge overlooking the gathering room below. The master bedroom is on the first floor. A generous amount of closet space with mirrored doors will enhance its appearance. Study the spacious master bath with all of its many features. Its direct access to the sunspace spa. will be appreciated.

Design 22900 2,332 Sq. Ft. - First Floor; 953 Sq. Ft. - Second Floor; 46,677 Cu. Ft.

● Passive solar benefits will be acquired from the spa. It transmits light and heat to the other parts of the house. Heat stored during the day, by the stone floor, will be circulated at night by mechanical means. Shades may be used to control the amount of heat gain. This spa provides a large area where various activities can be done at the same time. Note the bar, whirlpool and exercise area. It will be a cheerful and spacious family recreation area. There are 551 square feet and 9,200 cubic feet in the sunspace spa which are not included in the above totals.

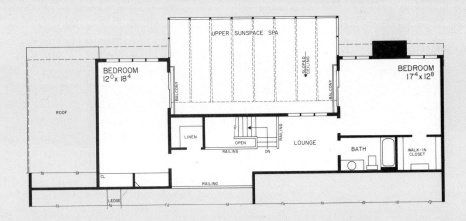

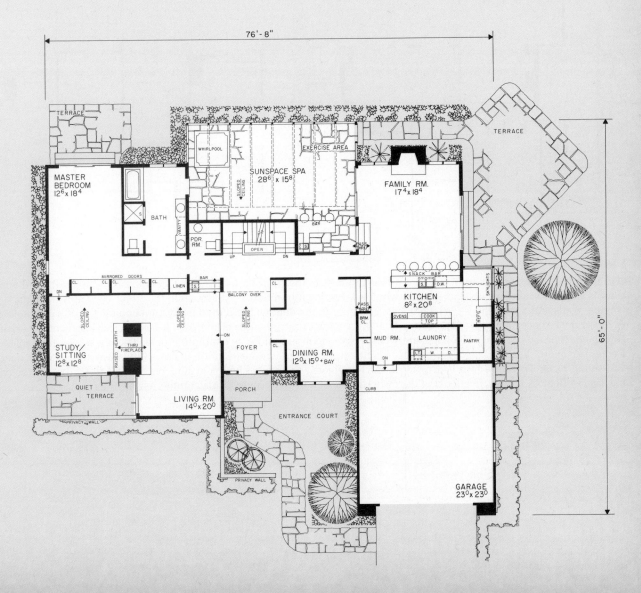

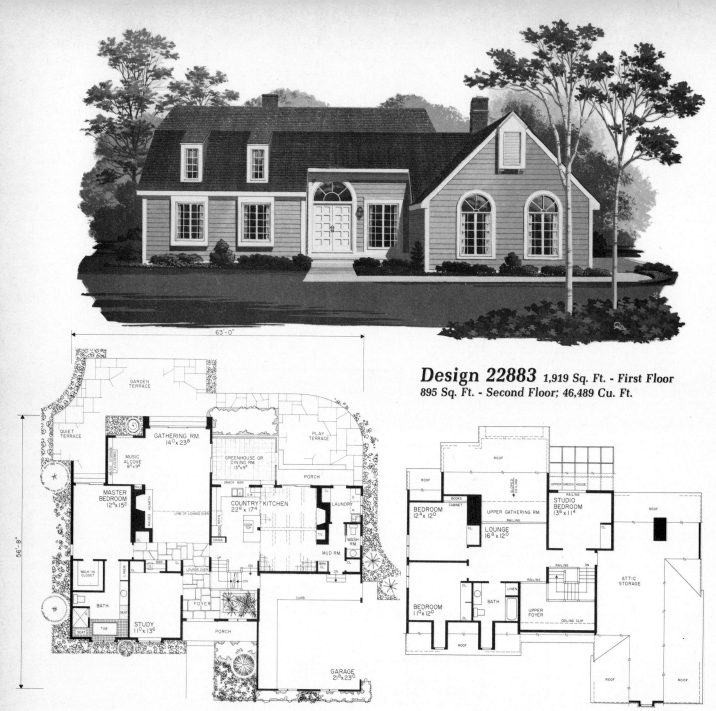

Design 22883 1,919 Sq. Ft. - First Floor
895 Sq. Ft. - Second Floor; 46,489 Cu. Ft.

● A country-style home is part of America's fascination with the rural past. This home's emphasis of the traditional home is in its gambrel roof, dormers and fanlight windows. Having a traditional exterior from the street view, this home has window walls and a greenhouse, which opens the house to the outdoors in a thoroughly contemporary manner. The interior meets the requirements of today's active family. Like the country houses of the past, it has a gathering room for family get-togethers or entertaining. The adjacent two-story greenhouse doubles as the dining room. There is a pass-thru snack bar to the country kitchen here. This country kitchen just might be the heart of the house with its two areas - work zone and sitting room. There are four bedrooms on the two floors - the master bedroom suite on the first floor; three more on the second floor. A lounge, overlooking the gathering room and front foyer, is also on the second floor.

Design 22863 2,955 Sq. Ft.; 30,387 Cu. Ft.

● Livability is outstanding in this earth-shelter design. Each of the three bedrooms has access to the terrace, along with the gathering and dining rooms. All of the sliding glass doors, along with the atrium, will brighten the interior nicely. The atrium will be enjoyed from the lounge, kitchen and gathering/dining rooms. Efficient work space will be found in the kitchen. It has easy access to the atrium and dining room.

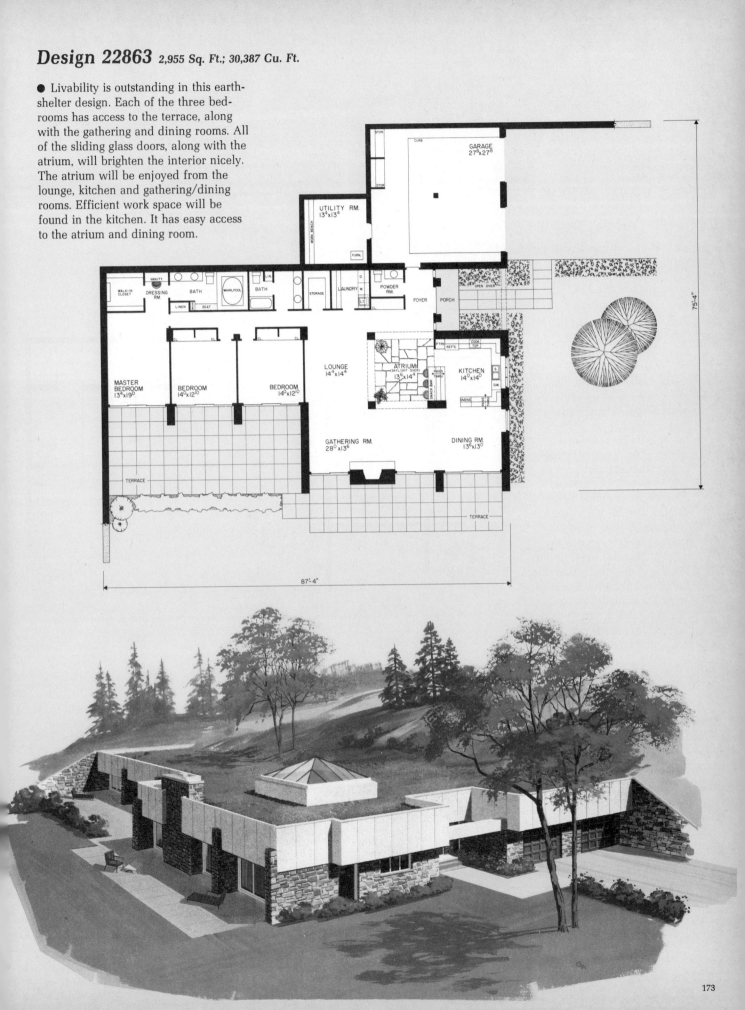

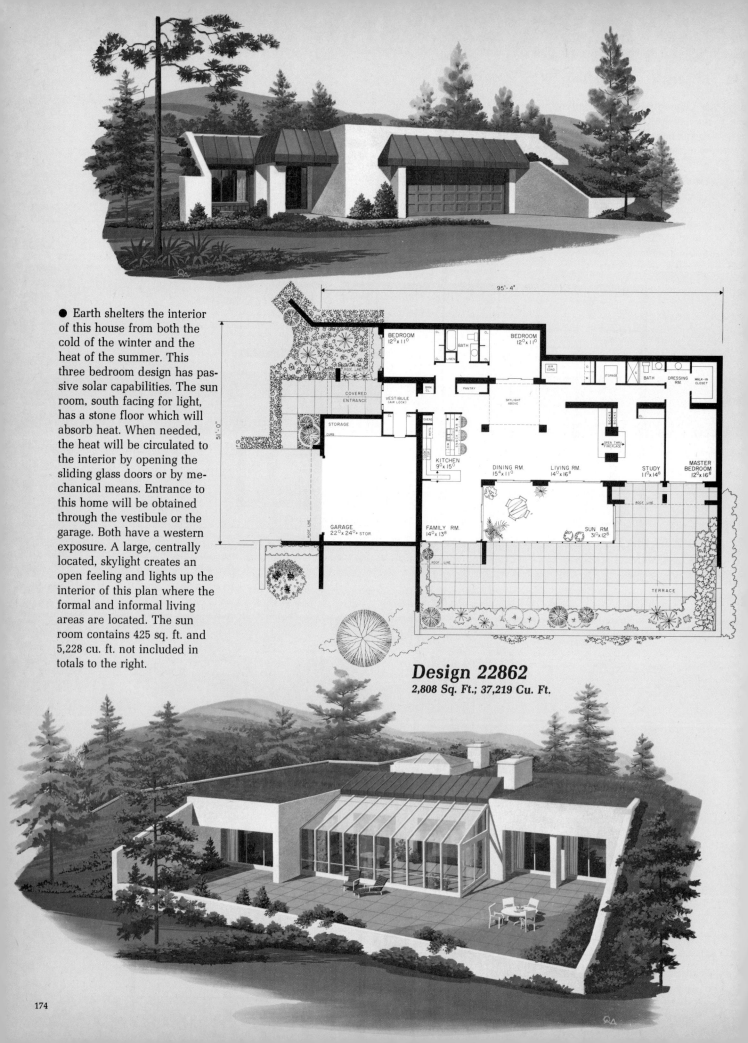

● Earth shelters the interior of this house from both the cold of the winter and the heat of the summer. This three bedroom design has passive solar capabilities. The sun room, south facing for light, has a stone floor which will absorb heat. When needed, the heat will be circulated to the interior by opening the sliding glass doors or by mechanical means. Entrance to this home will be obtained through the vestibule or the garage. Both have a western exposure. A large, centrally located, skylight creates an open feeling and lights up the interior of this plan where the formal and informal living areas are located. The sun room contains 425 sq. ft. and 5,228 cu. ft. not included in totals to the right.

Design 22862
2,808 Sq. Ft.; 37,219 Cu. Ft.

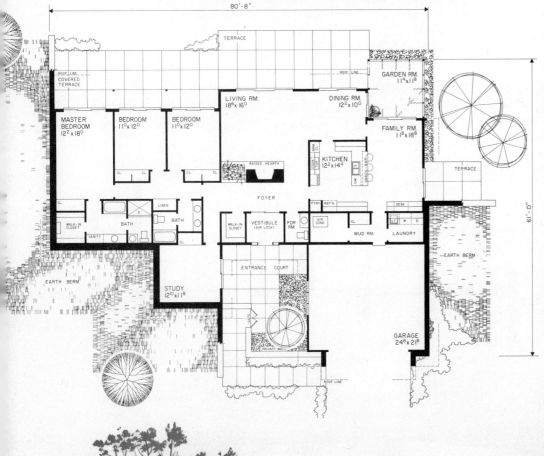

Design 22903
2,555 Sq. Ft.; 32,044 Cu. Ft.

● Earth berms on the sides of this house help it achieve energy-efficiency. The maximum amount of light enters this home by way of the many glass areas on the southern exposure. Every room in this plan, except the study, has the benefit of the southern sun. A garden room, tucked between the family and dining rooms, can be used for passive solar capabilities. A front privacy wall and the entrance court will shield the interior from the harsh northern winds. The air-locked vestibule also will be an energy saver. Summer heat gain will be reduced by the wide overhanging roof. The occupants of this home will appreciate the excellent interior planning. Garden room contains 144 sq. ft. and 1,195 cu. ft. not included in above totals.

Design 22860

2,240 Sq. Ft.; 27,685 Cu. Ft.

● Here is truly a unique home to satisfy your family's desires for something appealing and refreshing. This three bedroom home is also, the very embodiment of what's new and efficient in planning and technology. This is an excellent example of outstanding coordination of house structure, site, interior livability and the sun. Orienting this earth sheltered house toward the south assures a warm, bright and cheerful interior. Major contributions to energy-efficiency result from the earth covered roof, the absence of northern wall exposure and the lack of windows on either end of the house. This means a retention of heat in the winter and cool air in the summer. An effective use of skylights provide the important extra measure of natural light to the interior. Sliding glass doors in the living and dining rooms also help bring the light to the indoors. This earth sheltered house makes no sacrifice of good planning and excellent, all 'round livability. The section is cut through the living room and the skylit hall looking toward the bedrooms.

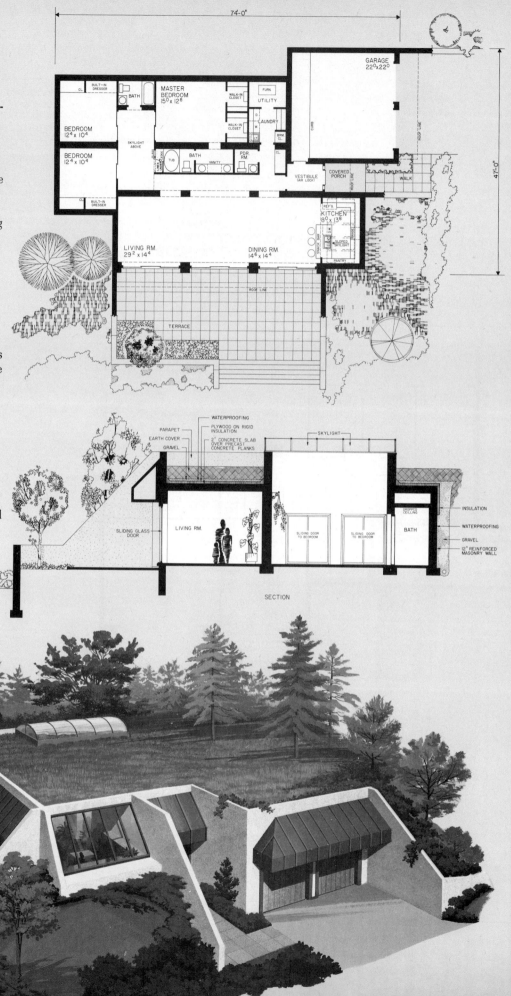

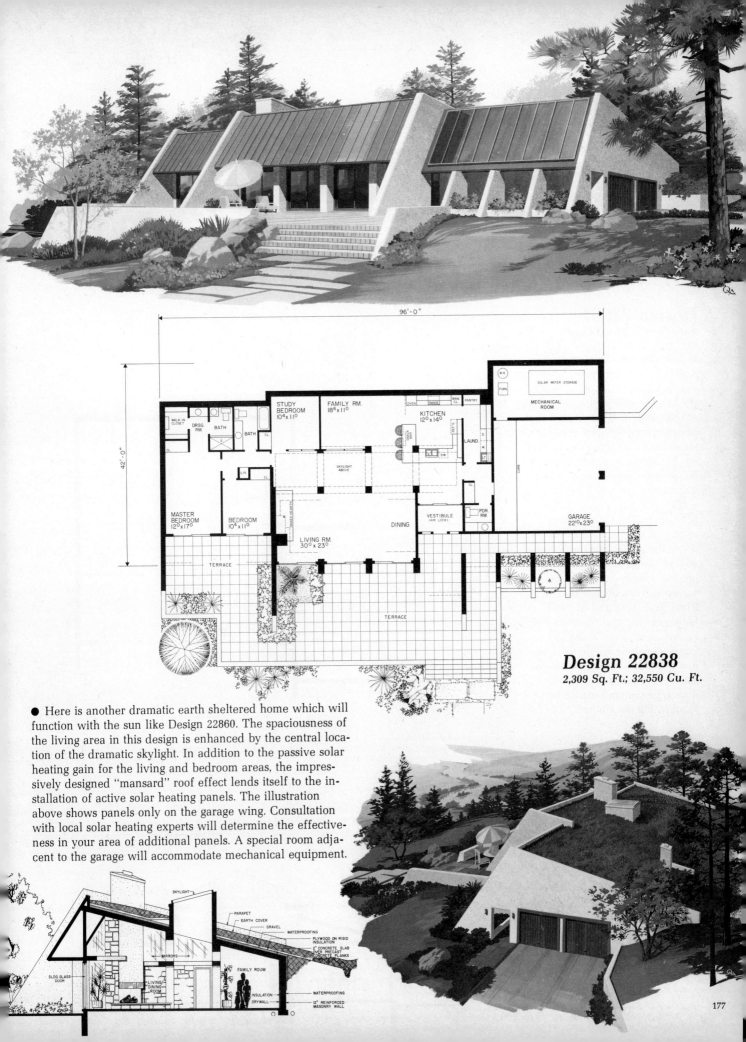

Design 22838

2,309 Sq. Ft.; 32,550 Cu. Ft.

● Here is another dramatic earth sheltered home which will function with the sun like Design 22860. The spaciousness of the living area in this design is enhanced by the central location of the dramatic skylight. In addition to the passive solar heating gain for the living and bedroom areas, the impressively designed "mansard" roof effect lends itself to the installation of active solar heating panels. The illustration above shows panels only on the garage wing. Consultation with local solar heating experts will determine the effectiveness in your area of additional panels. A special room adjacent to the garage will accommodate mechanical equipment.

Design 22861
2,499 Sq. Ft.; 29,100 Cu. Ft.

● Berming the earth against the walls of a structure prove to be very energy efficient. The earth protects the interior from the cold of the winter and the heat of the summer. Interior lighting will come from the large skylight over the garden room. Every room will benefit from this exposed area. The garden room will function as a multi-purpose area for the entire family. The living/dining room will receive light from two areas, the garden room and the wall of sliding glass doors to the outside. Family living will be served by the efficient floor plan. Three bedrooms and two full baths are clustered together. The kitchen is adjacent to the air-locked vestibule where the laundry and utility rooms are housed. The section is cut through the dining, garden and master bedroom facing the kitchen.

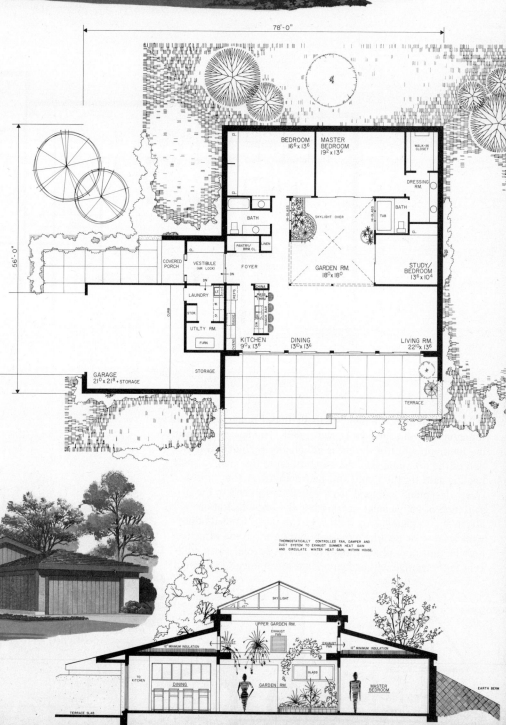

● Earth berms are banked against all four exterior walls of this design to effectively reduce heating and cooling demands. The berming is cost-efficient during both hot and cold seasons. In the winter, berming reduces heat loss through the exterior walls and shields the structure from cold winds. It helps keep warm air out during the summer. The two most dramatic interior highlights are the atrium and thru-fireplace. Topped with a large skylight, the atrium floods the interior with natural light. Shades are used to cover the atrium in the summer to prevent solar heat gain. Three bedrooms are featured in this plan and they each open via sliding glass doors to the atrium. This would eliminate any feeling of being closed in. An island with range and oven is featured in the kitchen. Informal dining will be enjoyed at the snack bar. The family/dining room can house those more formal dining occasions. The section at the right is cut through the study, atrium and rear bedroom looking toward master bedroom.

SECTION

Design 22833
2,386 Sq. Ft.; 27,735 Cu. Ft.

Design 22830 1,795 Sq. Ft. - Main Level; 1,546 Sq. Ft. - Lower Level; 49,900 Cu. Ft.

● Outstanding contemporary design! This home has been created with the advantages of passive solar heating in mind. For optimum energy savings, this delightful design combines passive solar devices, the solarium, with optional active collectors. Included with the purchase of this design are four plot plans to assure that the solar collectors will face the south. The garage in each plan acts as a buffer against cold northern winds. Schematic details for solar application also are included. Along with being energy-efficient, this design has excellent living patterns. Three bedrooms, the master bedroom on the main level and two others on the lower level at each side of the solarium. The living area of the main level will be able to enjoy the delightful view of the solarium and sunken garden.

Design 22884 1,855 Sq. Ft. - First Floor
837 Sq. Ft. - Second Floor; 50,137 Cu. Ft.

● The greenhouse in this design enhances its energy-efficiency and allows for spacious and interesting living patterns. Being a one-and-a-half story design, the second floor could be developed at a later date when the space is needed. The greenhouses add an additional 418 sq. ft. and 8,793 cu. ft. to the above quoted figures.

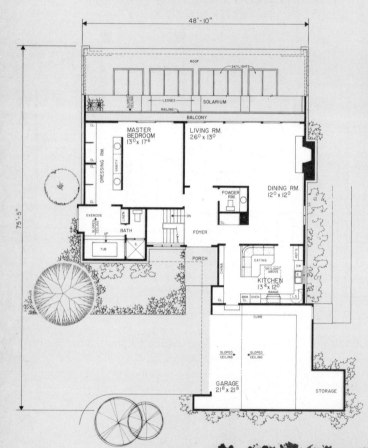

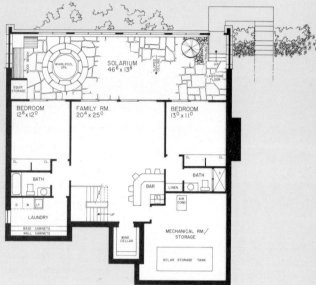

MASTER BEDROOM 13⁰ x 17⁶
LIVING RM. 26⁰ x 13⁰
DINING RM. 12⁰ x 12⁰
KITCHEN 13⁴ x 12⁰
GARAGE 21⁸ x 21⁸

SOLARIUM 46⁶ x 13⁸
BEDROOM 12⁸ x 12⁰
FAMILY RM. 20⁴ x 25⁰
BEDROOM 13⁰ x 11⁰
MECHANICAL RM./ STORAGE

Design 22835 *1,626 Sq. Ft. - Main Level*
2,038 Sq. Ft. - Lower Level; 50,926 Cu. Ft.

● Passive solar techniques with the help of an active solar component - they can work together or the active solar component can act as a back-up system - heat and cool this striking contemporary design. The lower level solarium is the primary passive element. It admits sunlight during the day for direct-gain heating. The warmth, which was absorbed into the thermal floor, is then radiated into the structure at night. The earth berms on the three sides of the lower level help keep out the winter cold and summer heat. The active system uses collector panels to gather the sun's heat. The heat is transferred via a water pipe system to the lower level storage tank where it is circulated throughout the house by a heat exchanger. Note that where active solar collectors are a design OPTION, which they are in all of our active/passive designs, they must be contracted locally. The collector area must be tailored to the climate and sun angles that characterize your building location.

Design 22827 1,618 Sq. Ft. - Upper Level
1,458 Sq. Ft. - Lower Level; 41,370 Cu. Ft.

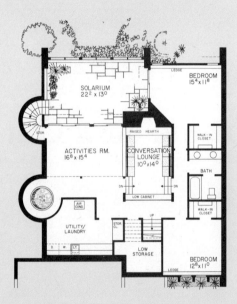

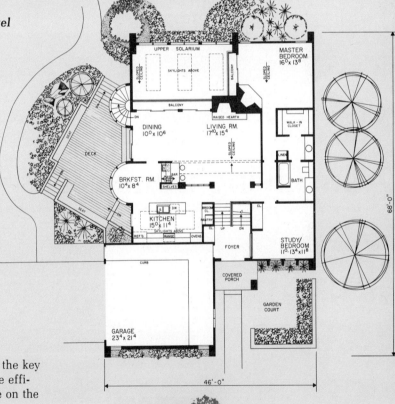

● The two-story solarium with skylights above is the key to energy savings to this bi-level design. Study the efficiency of this floor plan. The conversation lounge on the lower level is a unique focal point.

New Living Dimensions - Inside And Out

● Here is an impressive application of the Mansard type roof. Its wide overhang effectively compliments the simplicity of the brick masses. The curving driveway court strikes an appealing note. The entrance, flanked by planting areas, highlights double front doors. To each side, is an attractive glass panel. The breadth of the house is increased by the extension of the front wall. This, in turn, provides privacy for the side living terrace. To the rear, free standing brick walls provide further privacy as well as decorative appeal. The gently sloping roof has plastic domes which permit the interior to enjoy an added measure of natural light. Notice the indoor-outdoor living relationships available from every room in this design. For the active, growing family they are truly outstanding.

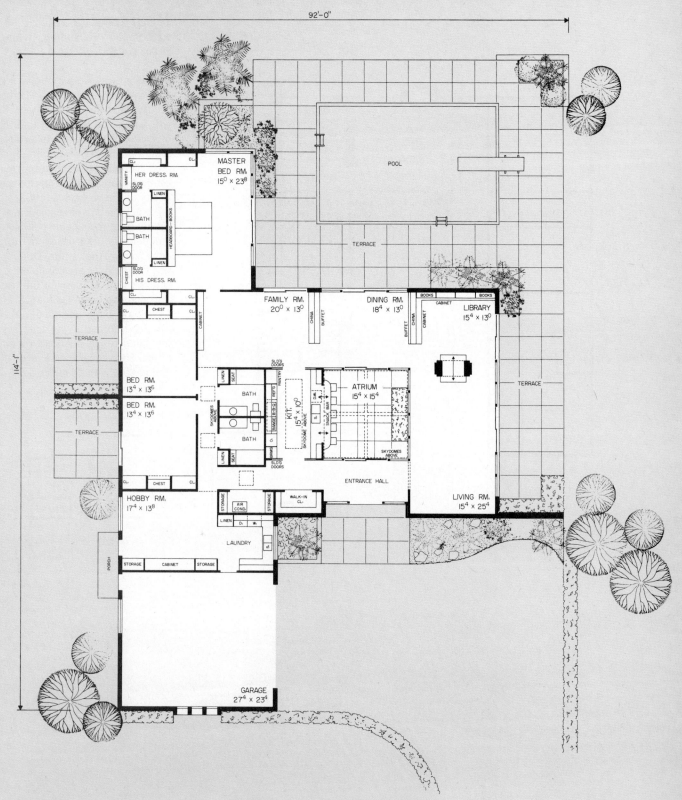

92'-0"

114'-1"

CL. HER DRESS. RM. CL.

MASTER BED RM.
15⁰ x 23⁸

POOL

VANITY

SLD'G DOOR

LINEN

BATH

HEADBOARD - BOOKS

BATH

LINEN

CHEST

SLD'G DOOR

HIS DRESS. RM.

TERRACE

CL. CL.

CHEST

CABINET

FAMILY RM.
20⁰ x 13⁰

CHINA

BUFFET

DINING RM.
18⁴ x 13⁰

BOOKS

BUFFET

CHINA

CABINET

BOOKS

CABINET

LIBRARY
15⁴ x 13⁰

TERRACE

TERRACE

BED RM.
13⁴ x 13⁶

LINEN

SEAT

BATH

SKYDOMES ABOVE

REFG.

RANGE B-B-Q

PANTRY

SLD'G DOORS

DW

SNACK BAR

ATRIUM
15⁴ x 15⁴

BED RM.
13⁴ x 13⁶

KIT.
15⁴ x 10⁰

SKYDOME ABOVE

SKYDOMES ABOVE

TERRACE

BATH

LINEN

SEAT

SLD'G DOORS

CL.

CHEST

CL.

ENTRANCE HALL

HOBBY RM.
17⁴ x 13⁸

STORAGE

AIR COND.

STORAGE

WALK-IN CL.

LIVING RM.
15⁴ x 25⁴

LINEN

D.

W.

LAUNDRY

PORCH

STORAGE

CABINET

STORAGE

GARAGE
27⁴ x 23⁴

Design 22226 3,340 Sq. Ft. — Excluding Atrium; 41,290 Cu. Ft.

● If anything has been left out of this home it would certainly be difficult to determine just what it is that is missing. Containing over 3,300 square feet, space for living is abundant, indeed. Each of the various rooms is large. Further, each major room has access to the outdoors. The efficient inside kitchen is strategically located in relation to the family and dining rooms. Observe how it functions with the enclosed atrium to provide a snack bar. Functional room dividers separate various areas. Study closely the living area. A two-way fireplace divides the spacious living room and the cozy library highlighted by built-in cabinets and bookshelves. A hobby room with laundry adjacent will be a favorite family activities spot. This home surely has numerous, impressive qualities to recommend it.

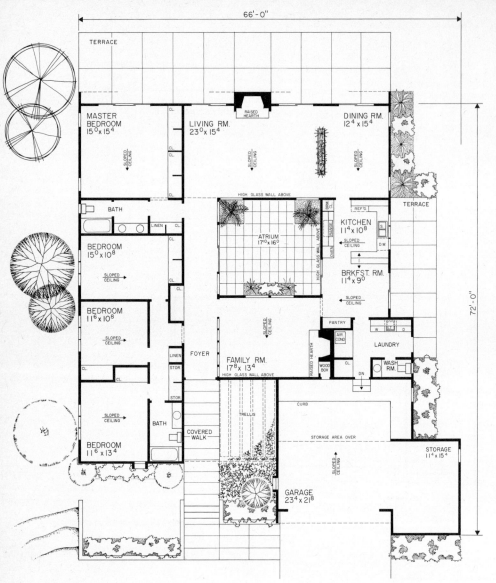

66'-0"

TERRACE

MASTER BEDROOM 15⁰ x 15⁴
SLOPED CEILING

LIVING RM. 23⁰ x 15⁴
SLOPED CEILING

RAISED HEARTH

DINING RM. 12⁴ x 15⁴
SLOPED CEILING

TERRACE

BATH
LINEN CL.

BEDROOM 15⁰ x 10⁸
SLOPED CEILING

HIGH GLASS WALL ABOVE

ATRIUM 17¹⁰ x 16⁰
SLOPED CEILING

BRM. CL.
REF'G
KITCHEN 11⁴ x 10⁸
S.
OVEN
D.W.
SLOPED CEILING

BRKFST. RM. 11⁴ x 9⁰
SLOPED CEILING

BEDROOM 11⁶ x 10⁸
SLOPED CEILING

PANTRY

SLOPED CEILING

W LT D

FOYER
LINEN
STOR
STOR

FAMILY RM. 17⁸ x 13⁴
HIGH GLASS WALL ABOVE

AIR COND
WOOD BOX
CL.

LAUNDRY

WASH RM.
DN

CL.
CL.

BATH

BEDROOM 11⁶ x 13⁴
SLOPED CEILING

COVERED WALK

TRELLIS

CURB

STORAGE AREA OVER
SLOPED CEILING

STORAGE 11⁴ x 15⁴

72'-0"

GARAGE 23⁴ x 21⁸

Design 22135
2,495 Sq. Ft. - Excluding Atrium
28,928 Cu. Ft.

● For those seeking a new experience in home ownership. The proud occupants of the contemporary home will forever be thrilled at their choice of such a distinguished exterior and such a practical and exciting floor plan. The variety of shed roof planes contrast dramatically with the simplicity of the vertical siding. Inside there is a feeling of spaciousness resulting from the sloping ceilings. The uniqueness of this design is further enhanced by the atrium. Open to the sky, this outdoor area, indoors, can be enjoyed from all parts of the house. The sleeping zone has four bedrooms, two baths and plenty of closets. The informal living zone has a fine kitchen and breakfast room. The formal zone consists of a large living-dining area with fireplace.

FAM. RM.
BRKFST. RM.
PANTRY
W LT D
LAUNDRY
WOOD BOX
DN DN
W.R.
GARAGE
CURB

OPTIONAL PARTIAL BASEMENT

Design 21283 *1,904 Sq. Ft. - Excluding Atrium; 18,659 Cu. Ft.*

● Here is a unique home whose livable area is basically a perfect square. Completely adaptable to a narrow building site, the presence of the interior atrium permits the enjoyment of private outdoor living "indoors". Glass sliding doors open onto this delightful area with its attractive planting areas. In colder climates the atrium may be adapted to function as the formal living room, thus permitting the present living room to function as a study/guest room. In addition to the formal dining room, there is the informal snack bar in the family room accessible from the kitchen via the pass-thru. Three bedrooms, two baths, a fireplace and excellent storage facilities also are highlights of this plan. Don't miss the planting areas.

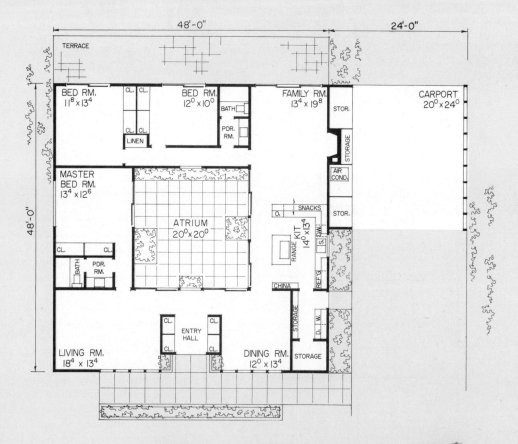

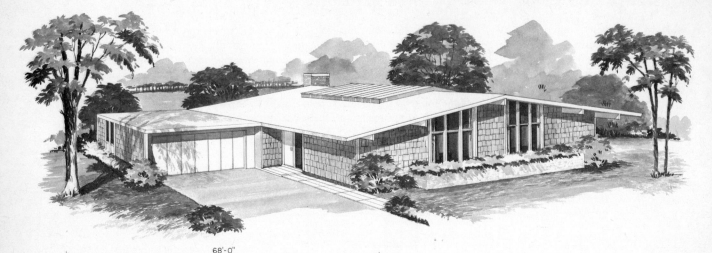

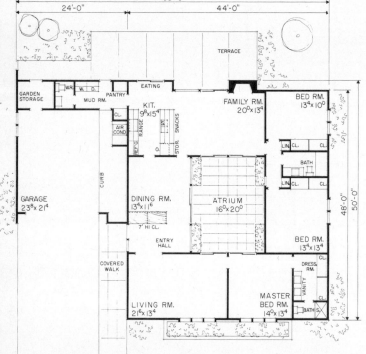

Design 21841
1,920 Sq. Ft. - Excluding Atrium
19,806 Cu. Ft.

● Atrium living is wonderfully illustrated by this attractive design. You forever will be aware of its delightful presence and it will offer pleasingly different patterns of living to your family. It may be in constant use since the skylight provides protection during inclement weather. Clever planning results in excellent zoning of the basic area of the plan. The formal living room and master bedroom are located to the front and enjoy plenty of peace and quiet. The children's rooms are by themselves and are but a few steps from the informal family room. The efficient kitchen has eating space and functions ideally with the dining and family rooms. A mud room is accessible from the garage and the rear terrace.

Design 21837 *2,016 Sq. Ft. - Excluding Atrium; 27,280 Cu. Ft.*

Design 21867

1,692 Sq. Ft. - Excluding Atrium
21,383 Cu. Ft.

● Looking for a new house involves a number of varied considerations. One that is most basic involves what you would like your family's living patterns to be. If you would like to introduce your family to something that is different and is sure to be fun for all, consider this dramatic atrium house. Parents and children alike will be thrilled by the experience and the environment engendered by this outdoor living area indoors. A skylight provides for the protection during inclement weather without restricting the flood of natural light. Notice how this atrium functions with the various areas. Observe relationships between children's rooms and family room between master bedroom and the quiet living room.

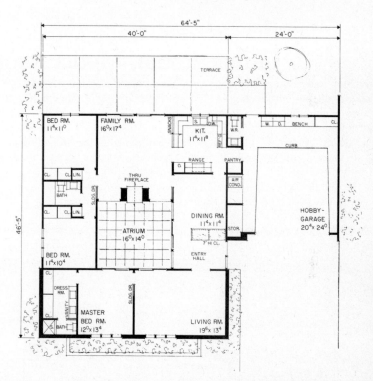

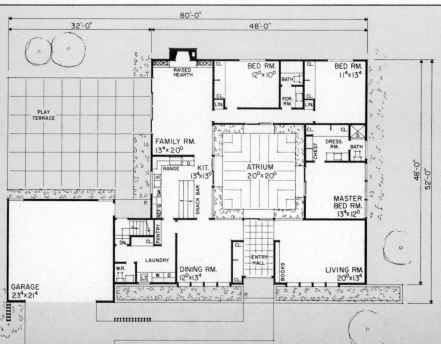

● Picture yourself and your family enjoying this new home. Sheltered from the weather, whatever the season, the atrium will be favorite spot for eating, reading, playing games or just plain sitting. Amidst all that natural light and those attractive planting areas, you'll enjoy the informality of outdoor living under controlled conditions. Four pairs of sliding glass doors make the atrium accessible from all areas of the house. Observe how the formal living room is located from the informal family room. Note kitchen snack bar and the separate dining room. Don't miss the laundry, pantry and extra wash room. The family room will also be a favorite spot. Its focal point is the raised hearth fireplace.

Clutter Room, Media Room To The Fore

● Something new? Something new, indeed!! Here is the introduction of two rooms which will make a wonderful contribution to family living. The clutter room is strategically placed between the kitchen and garage. It is the nerve center of the work area. It houses the laundry, provides space for sewing, has a large sorting table, and even plenty of space for the family's tool bench. A handy potting area is next to the laundry tray. Adjacent to

the clutter room, and a significant part of the planning of this whole zone, are the pantry and freezer with their nearby counter space. These facilities surely will expedite the unloading of groceries from the car and their convenient storing. Wardrobe and broom closets, plus washroom complete the outstanding utility of this area. The location of the clutter room with all its fine cabinet and counter space means that the often numerous family projects

can be on-going. This room is ideally isolated from the family's daily living patterns. The media room may be thought of as the family's entertainment center. While this is the room for the large or small TV, the home movies, the stereo and VCR equipment, it will serve as the library or study. It would be ideal as the family's home office with its computer equipment. Your family will decide just how it will utilize this outstanding area.

Design 22915 2,758 Sq. Ft.; 60,850 Cu Ft.

● The features of this appealing contemporary design go far beyond the clutter and media rooms. The country kitchen is spacious and caters to the family's informal living and dining activities. While it overlooks the rear yard it is just a step from the delightful greenhouse. Many happy hours will be spent here enjoying to the fullest the outdoors from within. The size of the greenhouse is 8'x18' and contains 149 sq. ft. not included in the square footage quoted above. The formal living and dining areas feature spacious open planning. Sloping ceiling in the living room, plus the sliding glass doors to the outdoor terrace enhance the cheerfulness of this area. The foyer is large and routes traffic efficiently to all areas. Guest coat closets and a powder room are handy. The sleeping zone is well-planned. Two children's bedrooms have fine wall space, good wardrobe facilities and a full bath.

The master bedroom is exceptional. It is large enough to accommodate a sitting area and has access to the terrace. Two walk-in closets, a vanity area with lavatory and a compartmented bath are noteworthy features. Observe the stall shower in addition to the dramatic whirlpool installation. The floor plan below is identical with that on the opposite page and shows one of many possible ways to arrange furniture.

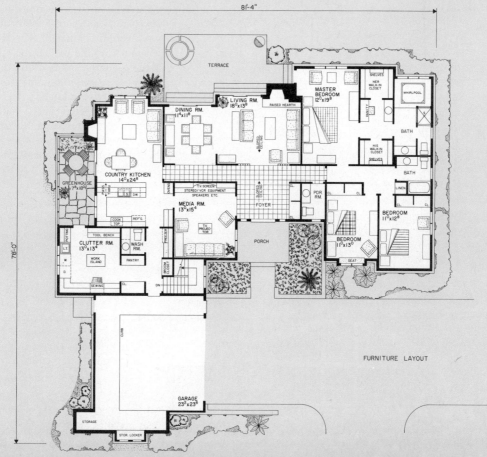

FURNITURE LAYOUT

Design 22858
2,231 Sq. Ft.; 28,150 Cu. Ft.

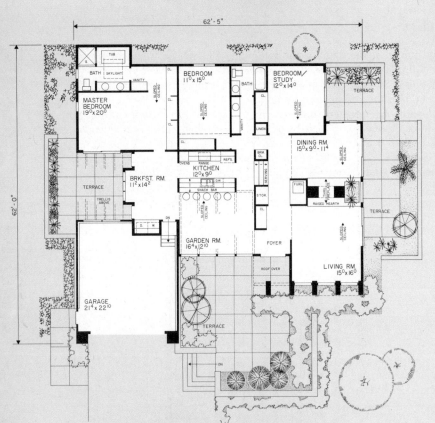

● This sun oriented design was created to face the south. By doing so, it has minimal northern exposure. It has been designed primarily for the more temperate U.S. latitudes using 2 x 6 wall construction. The morning sun will brighten the living and dining rooms, along with the adjacent terrace. Sun enters the garden room by way of the glass roof and walls. In the winter, the solar heat gain from the garden room should provide relief from high energy bills. Solar shades allow you to adjust the amount of light that you want to enter in the warmer months. Interior planning deserves mention, too. The work center is efficient. The kitchen has a snack bar on the garden room side and a serving counter to the dining room. The breakfast room with laundry area is also convenient to the kitchen. Three bedrooms are on the northern wall. The master bedroom has a large tub and a separate shower with a four foot square skylight above. When this design is oriented toward the sun, it should prove to be energy efficient and a joy to live in.